D1553162

Aesthetics
of Care

BLOOMSBURY AESTHETICS

Series Editor: Derek Matravers

The Bloomsbury Aesthetics series looks at the aesthetic questions and issues raised by all major art forms. Stimulating, engaging and accessible, the series offers food for thought not only for students of aesthetics, but also for anyone with an interest in philosophy and the arts.

Titles published in the series:

Aesthetics and Literature, by David Davies
Aesthetics and Architecture, by Edward Winters
Aesthetics and Music, by Andy Hamilton
Aesthetics and Nature, by Glenn Parsons
Aesthetics and Film, by Katherine Thomson-Jones
Aesthetics and Painting, by Jason Gaiger
Aesthetics and Morality, by Elisabeth Schellekens Dammann
Aesthetics of Care, by Yuriko Saito

Aesthetics
of Care

Practice in Everyday Life

YURIKO SAITO

BLOOMSBURY ACADEMIC
LONDON • NEW YORK • OXFORD • NEW DELHI • SYDNEY

BLOOMSBURY ACADEMIC
Bloomsbury Publishing Plc
50 Bedford Square, London, WC1B 3DP, UK
1385 Broadway, New York, NY 10018, USA
29 Earlsfort Terrace, Dublin 2, Ireland

BLOOMSBURY, BLOOMSBURY ACADEMIC and the Diana logo are trademarks
of Bloomsbury Publishing Plc

First published in Great Britain 2022

Copyright © Yuriko Saito, 2022

Yuriko Saito has asserted her right under the Copyright, Designs and Patents Act,
1988, to be identified as Author of this work.

For legal purposes the Acknowledgments on p. vii constitute an extension of this
copyright page.

Cover design by Louise Dugdale
Cover image: riya-takahashi / iStock

All rights reserved. No part of this publication may be reproduced or transmitted
in any form or by any means, electronic or mechanical, including photocopying,
recording, or any information storage or retrieval system, without prior
permission in writing from the publishers.

Bloomsbury Publishing Plc does not have any control over, or responsibility for,
any third-party websites referred to or in this book. All internet addresses given
in this book were correct at the time of going to press. The author and publisher
regret any inconvenience caused if addresses have changed or sites have ceased
to exist, but can accept no responsibility for any such changes.

A catalogue record for this book is available from the British Library.

A catalog record for this book is available from the Library of Congress.

ISBN: HB: 978-1-3501-3419-5
PB: 978-1-3501-3420-1
ePDF: 978-1-3501-3421-8
eBook: 978-1-3501-3418-8

Series: Bloomsbury Aesthetics

Typeset by Deanta Global Publishing Services, Chennai, India
Printed and bound in Great Britain

To find out more about our authors and books visit www.bloomsbury.com and
sign up for our newsletters.

Contents

Figures

Acknowledgments

One of the themes of this book is that whatever one accomplishes is made possible by a team of supporters. If it takes a village to raise a child, as the saying goes, it took a community of caring individuals for me to complete this book project. My family and friends lent hands as unofficial librarians, tech assistants, copy editors, as well as cheerleaders throughout this process. I owe Gerry Glaser, Sarah Glaser, Adam Glaser, Kristie Serota, E. J. Koh, and Don Keefer a deep gratitude.

For the past few years, I have been thinking about our care relationship with the material world and its aesthetic implications by exploring the notion of imperfection in objects, such as damage and defects, and their repair. These issues form a significant part of the discussion in this book. I am grateful for the opportunity to have presented ideas regarding them at various venues: University of Tokyo, Dōshisha University, Tsukuba University, Kansai University, all in Japan; Amsterdam; York University, UK; Uppsala University; Bard Graduate Center, University of Illinois at Chicago, Emerson College, Rhode Island School of Design; the American Society for Aesthetics Rocky Mountain Division meeting in Santa Fe; and the annual meeting of the British Society for Aesthetics. The feedback and comments I received at these meetings were invaluable, and many of them were folded into my discussion in this book, some explicitly but many implicitly. I thank the participants at these meetings for their insights and suggestions.

I was also able to develop my thinking related to this book through contributing chapters and articles in anthologies and journals. I want to express my specific appreciation to some of the editors: Ellen Rutten, Peter Cheney, Ivan Gaskell, Anne Eaton, Markus Berger, Max Ryynänen, Zoltán Somhegyi, Endre Szécsényi, A. Minh Nguyen, Jeanette Bicknell, Jennifer Judkins, Carolyn Korsmeyer, Sandra Shapshay, and Levi Tenen. All of them gave me opportunities to freely explore the issues that interested me, which together formed the materials for this book.

As it is clear from the entire book and particularly the Introduction, Arnold Berleant's work on aesthetic engagement and social aesthetics has provided both the foundation and the direction of my inquiry. The inspiration I continue to derive from his work is immeasurable. In addition, I have been a lucky recipient of his unfailing mentorship and friendship, for which I am deeply indebted.

Without Derek Matravers's encouragement, support, and patience throughout this project, including many twists and turns on my part, this book would not have existed. He read the first draft and helped me improve its content and writing. It has been a most rewarding journey and I sincerely hope that the end result reciprocates the trust he placed in me and in this project.

Finally, I thank Colleen Coalter of Bloomsbury and an anonymous reviewer for helping me with this project. I may not have succeeded in meeting all the criticisms, but I am much happier with the revised manuscript which incorporates many points raised by the reviewer.

As with my work on everyday aesthetics, I hope that this book, too, opens a rich reservoir of aesthetic potential, and I look forward for a lively debate to ensue.

November 2021

Introduction

The notion of "care" has gained a particular urgency today, with the pandemic sweeping the entire globe. The importance of medical care and professional caregivers to treat patients is garnering well-deserved attention. In today's dire situation, the care given by medical personnel extends beyond treatment to include dispensing emotional and psychological care to patients, as they are the only ones allowed to directly interact with those who are gravely ill. We have almost become numbed by the heartbreaking ways in which only the medical personnel share the patients' last moments.

Although these examples of needed care under the pandemic situation shed a harsh light on what is involved in this activity, the notion of care appears frequently, though less dramatically, in today's popular discourse. It often conjures up the image of vulnerable population, primarily the young, the old, and the sick who need care. We think of various care facilities, such as hospitals, nursing homes, childcare centers, and the like. In addition, care is today often associated with body care, such as skin care and hair care, as well as spa treatment and various diets, no doubt promoted by beauty industries. Then there are various objects of daily use, such as clothes, furniture, houses, cars, and yards, that need constant care.

The subject of this book, care as an ethical and aesthetic practice, is not unrelated to these popular sites of manifestation, and the discussion will make some reference to them. However, the exploration here is directed toward the conceptual dimensions of care that inform various specific care activities and practices. While the relevance of ethical considerations may be apparent in care for the elderly, childcare, and medical care, the aesthetic relevance of care may not be as obvious. Conversely, the aesthetic concerns may be clear in caring for various objects and our appearance, but the ethical commitment of care underlying aesthetic experiences and practices in general is often unnoticed. It is my contention that "care" offers a site where the ethical and the aesthetic are integrated and deeply entrenched in the management of our daily life. It defines the way in which we relate to the other, whether other humans, nonhuman nature, or the artifactual world, situate ourselves in the world, and cultivate a virtuous way of living and, in short, a good life. The care relationship determines the ethical and aesthetic mode of being in the world.

The relationship between the aesthetic and the ethical is a lively debated issue in aesthetics. The discussion primarily surrounds the aesthetic relevance, if at all, of ethical considerations when judging the aesthetic or artistic value of an object, such as the moral content of a work of art, the moral character of the artist or performer, and the moral (dis)value of the process of making an object. The relationship between the aesthetic and the ethical that interests me, however, is rather directed toward a larger issue of the ethical grounding of our aesthetic life and the role aesthetics plays in our ethical life. I gained guidance from the writings of a number of thinkers who also pursued the intimate relationship, or even inseparability, between the aesthetic and the ethical in this regard. Their views together inspired me and provided me with a sense of assurance (as well as hope!) that my exploration of their relationship through the notion of care is on the right track. Let me cite those thinkers whose views helped me in my exploration.

Perhaps one of the most passionate advocates of the interrelationship between the ethical and the aesthetic is Iris Murdoch. She stresses the critical importance of developing "the patient eye of love" and "the attention" to the world with which we interact so that we do not subjugate it to our self and fantasy. Attending to a blade of grass or another person "purely, without self, brings with it an increasing awareness of the unity and interdependence of the moral world."[1] Successful art, which she claims is rather rare, shares the artist's vision of reality who has "to silence and expel self, to contemplate and delineate nature with a clear eye," which "demands a moral discipline."[2] The spectator's appreciation also demands "an analogous task . . . to be disciplined enough to see as much reality in the work as the artist has succeeded in putting into it, and not to 'use it as magic'" for her to derive consolation that simply reinforces the familiar world and fantasy.[3] Thus, for both the artist and the spectator, "unsentimental, detached, unselfish, objective attention" is required and "in moral situations a similar exactness is called for."[4] In short, for Murdoch, "aesthetic situations are not so much analogies of morals as cases of morals."[5]

Ronald Hepburn, who early in his career engaged in a discussion of vision and choice in morality with Iris Murdoch, characterizes aesthetic experience as an educational journey.[6] He makes clear that cultivating a rewarding aesthetic experience is not just a matter of enriching one's aesthetic life but also edifying one's world. For example, developing an aesthetic appreciation of nature beyond sentimentalizing or anthropomorphizing requires extending ourselves beyond our comfort zone and "such exercises of reason—attentive, flexible, empathizing—are of course equally necessary to the moral context of our understanding of self and others."[7] Although Hepburn cautions against putting the aesthetic and the ethical too close, his *oeuvre* makes clear that an aesthetic experience is ultimately a moral practice of cultivating one's self in its interaction with the world.

As my subsequent discussion with reference to his works makes clear, Arnold Berleant's view on aesthetics is also inseparable from ethical considerations. We humans are aesthetic creatures insofar as we negotiate and interact with this world through sensory perception and sensibility. As such, the quality of life and the society is largely affected, indeed sometimes determined, by the quality of the aesthetic experience we gain in our everyday life and from our society. For example, when we suffer from aesthetic deficit, deprivation, pain, and harm, the quality of our life is damaged. Such negative aesthetic experiences "can produce not only aesthetic pain but moral suffering, both of which are, at times, inseparable," indicating that "aesthetic theory and experience are intimately bound up with the moral, negatively as well as positively."[8] Hence, "this merging of the aesthetic with the activities and objects of human life must be acknowledged in aesthetic theory as well as recognized in human practice."[9]

No doubt inspired by Buddhism and the Japanese aesthetic tradition, among others, David E. Cooper argues for a virtue-based aesthetics that conceives of beauty as a manifestation of moral virtues, whether in a person or in an object. He speculates that like-minded thinkers "are likely to welcome an emphasis . . . on an overall, integrated human good which only later, and with some artificiality, got carved up into discrete components—the moral, the aesthetic, the prudential, and the like."[10] He illustrates the merging and integration of these arenas by the aesthetics of making and appreciating a Zen garden. Instead of a unidirectional interpretation of the aesthetic experience leading to enlightenment or vice versa, he advocates a view in which "the components we tend to allocate to the respective realms of the moral and aesthetic intimately, indeed inseparably, combine."[11]

Josephine Donovan whose work on the aesthetics of care is primarily directed toward the treatment of animals is critical of the dualistic legacy of Enlightenment with its further development that created the division between mind and body, self and other, and subject and object. She declares that "the most grievous of these divisions . . . is the divorce between the ethical and the aesthetic."[12] Instead, she holds that "an aesthetics of care . . . *enables* ethical concern for the subject matter, which is seen not as dead material available for aesthetic manipulation and framing, but as a living presence, one located in a particular, knowable environment, who has a history and is capable of dialogical communication."[13] Although her primary concern is nonhuman animals, her argument, in her own account, applies not only to the natural world in general but "even to physical matter itself."

Finally, as the title of her seminal work, *Merit: Aesthetic and Ethical*, indicates, Marcia Eaton suggests the possibility and even a requirement of "the integration of aesthetics and ethics" and argues against a clear separation between the ethical and the aesthetic.[14] While not denying the possibility of such a separation, she points out that "our experiences, our encounters with and in the world, and the decisions we make as a result do not typically come in separate packets, with the moral, aesthetic, economic, religious, political, scientific, and so on serving as viewing stands distanced from one another so that we look at the world first from one and then from another standpoint."[15] She instead advocates "the conceptual interdependence and mutual nurturing" of the aesthetic and the ethical, the thesis I shall develop in this book by promoting the cross-pollination of the two through exploring the role of care.

The subsequent discussion develops as follows. Chapter 1 begins by situating the main thesis of this book, the interdependent relationship between the aesthetic and the ethical, within the landscape of contemporary Western aesthetics. I pay particular attention to the virtue theory of aesthetics for its focus on the experiencing agent's activities, whether creating or appreciating aesthetic objects, in comparison to the central place given to the aesthetic judgments made of the objects themselves that otherwise dominates aesthetics discourse. I conclude that, while I share with the virtue theory the aesthetic relevance of the agents' ethical life, their interest is ultimately justifying an aesthetic judgment of the object of appreciation. Although the aesthetics of care that I will develop is not anathema to making an aesthetic judgment of an object, my interest remains the ethical and aesthetic life of the experiencing agents.

When exploring what is involved in having an aesthetic experience and engaging in a care relationship, I find some remarkable structural similarities, and I devote Chapter 1 to drawing this parallel. The same mode of interacting with the world, whether regarding other people, natural world, or built environments and artifacts within, underlies the care relationship and aesthetic experience. Specifically, both require attention to the particularity of the other, open-minded responsiveness, and imaginative engagement. These shared requirements suggest mutual enhancement. That is, although care as an ethical commitment and care as a condition for aesthetic experience are not identical, we imagine a person with rich caring relationships with others to also enjoy a rich and satisfying aesthetic life, as both modes of relating and experiencing other-than-self encourage appreciating it on its own terms. At the same time, cultivating an aesthetic sensibility to appreciate the object of experience in its singularity and wholeness nurtures the ethical attention and respect for the person being cared for.

What becomes clear from exploring the commonality between care ethics and aesthetic experience is the fundamental relationality of our self and the world, as well as the interdependent nature of our existence. Chapter 2 develops the ethical and aesthetic implications of relationality between humans and the world, particularly in light of the increasing attention being given to this concept in medicine, design, and art. Several considerations are necessary for developing and sustaining successful relationality: the worthiness of the object of care, whether a person or an object; a relationship based upon equality rather than exploitation or contractual obligation; and practical wisdom to avoid indiscriminate and universal caring. Equally important is self-care. Contrary to the all-too-common image of self-indulgence and absorption, self-care has been promoted in various religious and philosophical traditions for providing a foundation for a virtuous self and good life, and the effective means of practicing self-care is identified by many thinkers to be aesthetics. Relationality cannot be successfully upheld without one's work on shaping oneself to be a certain kind of person.

Chapter 3 delves into the mutual enhancement of the ethical and aesthetic practices of the care relationship in interpersonal interactions. Whether regarding conversations between two people or social gatherings, satisfying interactions are generated by the participants' caring attitude toward each other to create a convivial atmosphere that has distinct aesthetic features, such as a certain rhythm, collaborative creation, equality of participation, and spontaneity, regardless of what topic gets discussed or whether any kind of consensus is reached. The social interactions are also by necessity mediated by body aesthetics which often determines their character. While we can remain as a spectator making a judgment on the ethical and aesthetic significance of others' social interactions, more often than not we are participants in such interactions. Particularly with the efficacy of practicing body aesthetics, both care ethics and aesthetics benefit from the first-person account, that is, the perspective of a person engaged in practicing the care relationship.

At the same time, what is often neglected in both ethical and aesthetic discourses is how objects can serve as a vehicle for expressing care. While objects do not have the same agency as humans do, they often shape human actions, for better or worse. Depending upon how they shape our actions, we attribute characteristics such as generosity, kindness, humility, and courtesy, or callousness, hostility, pretentiousness, or impudence. These are aesthetic judgments insofar as they refer to the perceptual experience of the objects, but at the same time they are ethically grounded insofar as they are concerned with whether or not and how the objects contribute to the quality of life. When our environment and objects within exude care given for our experience, we are apt to spread the caring attitude toward others, either directly or through the creation or maintenance of the environment. Care begets care.

While the experience of the material world in Chapter 3 is more from the perspective of a spectator being affected by its characteristics, our first-person account of engaging with it needs exploration. How do we characterize our interactions with the material world guided by care? Does it even make sense to think of our interactions with it as an ethical relationship? I argue in Chapter 4 that we should discuss our ethical relationship with the material world as cultivating and practicing a way of living in this world, rather than as a response to the possible moral status of the material world. Although some objects are not worthy of our care, as argued in Chapter 2, the default mode of relating to the material world should be one of care, and it is expressed not only by handling an object carefully and refraining from damaging it but also by proactively taking measures to maintain it in good stead. While maintenance and repair work often concern keeping the functionality of the object, such as a computer or an elevator, at other times the work is performed to keep its *appearance* free of signs of wear and tear, its own aging process, and accidental damage. Repair work accordingly is commonly understood as restoring the object to its original, perfect condition. However, I question this common assumption that the appearance of a material object should be frozen in its tracks, so to speak, and when that is not possible, it is not worth keeping. This easy disposability of material objects, which is exacerbated today by rampant consumerism, compromises the relationality and interdependence between us and the material world by diminishing the opportunity to live with it through various stages of vicissitude together. Caring for material objects should include accepting and working with such vicissitudes. We live and grow (old) with the objects. We cherish them for what they are, with warts and all, just as care ethics guides us to accept, respect, and appreciate the other person for who she is and work with her to promote her well-being through acts of care.

These four chapters together show that the cultivation of a virtuous self needs practice. It cannot happen by simply following a rule, developing an abstract understanding of virtues, or forming judgments. We have to walk the walk and we have to live it. Aesthetics here offers a potent and effective tool for this practice. It encompasses various dimensions, ranging from sharpening one's attentive perception, opening oneself to the other, exercising imagination, and collaboratively working with the other for a common goal. At the same time, a satisfying and fulfilling aesthetic life is not possible without the attitude of care regarding the world.

Let me conclude this Introduction by explaining my methodology. My discussion presents the notion of care as a site of entanglement and border-crossing. First, as it should be clear from the previously cited writers whose views inspired me, the ethical and aesthetic dimensions associated with care are closely intertwined and I prefer to explore them in their intertwined state rather than disentangling them. I believe that by discussing care as an integration of the ethical and the aesthetic we capture our lived experience more accurately. That is, ethical care acts require sensibility and imagination that are most effectively nurtured through aesthetic means. They also need to be manifested through aesthetic expressions. At the same time, cultivating an aesthetic sensibility requires ethically grounded engagement with the world, and the satisfaction and fulfillment offered by the resultant aesthetic experience nourishes both the aesthetic and the ethical dimensions of our lives. Although the discussion presupposes a generally accepted distinction between the aesthetic and the ethical and proceeds accordingly, the ultimate outcome is the melding of the two spheres.

Similarly, care offers a space where investigation invites different approaches and perspectives from various disciplines, some theoretical and others practical. Although the overall framework is philosophical, I find writings and reports from practitioners engaged in activities related to care, such as education, medicine, and design, to be particularly helpful and illuminating. In addition, the theoretical disciplinary distinctions get blurred between and among philosophy, psychology, sociology, art history, art criticism, and anthropology. As such, my discussion keeps crisscrossing these disciplines, as well as the theoretical and the practical. I don't think philosophical thinking is the exclusive domain of philosophers, and I will be teasing out what I think to be philosophically fertile ideas from different sources. In a similar fashion, some parts of my discussion are illustrated by specific examples from daily life, as I firmly believe that the theoretical discussion can only gain from how it is reflected in real-life examples. Many examples are utterly mundane, not typical examples found in a book dealing with aesthetics. However, I hope that my exploration of these examples will make clear their significance.

This amalgamation of many sources makes my discussion decidedly more exploratory and heuristic than argumentative. I consider my project here to be weaving a tapestry with various strands of care ethics and aesthetics that have been already provided by many thinkers and practitioners. I am well aware that the exact content and nature of care ethics, as well as its place in the ethical discourse, remains hotly debated.[16] For example, care ethics often generates questions about its compatibility with matters concerning justice, such as whether sometimes concerns for impartiality and equality trump one's personal care relationship, or how one should go about adjudicating a conflict caused by the need for care by different persons. It remains debatable whether one's ethical life can be completely fulfilled by addressing concerns for care alone. Similarly, various issues in aesthetics that I address in this book continue to generate controversies, ranging from aesthetic experience and body aesthetics to the aesthetics of functional objects and the nature of expressive qualities. While each of these issues deserves a thorough examination, doing so will make the overall discussion too unwieldy and obscures the main thesis I want to present, namely the interdependence and mutual enhancement of care ethics and aesthetics. I expect that many aspects of my discussion deserve critical examinations and will invite objections. However, in the interest of keeping my overall aim to construct a general framework for the aesthetics of care, my brushstroke is going to be bold rather than fine-tuned and detail-oriented.

In my previous work, I defined everyday aesthetics as something distinct from art-centered aesthetics, primarily to overcome what I considered to be an unduly limited scope of aesthetics. However, particularly with the recent developments in philosophical aesthetics to broaden its reach, I am reconsidering my previous position that minimized the continuity of art and everyday life. I have come to realize that it is more helpful and productive to explore the cross-pollination between art and everyday life rather than giving them a separate treatment. Accordingly, I changed my initial plan of devoting one chapter to art dealing with the theme of care. Instead, I am weaving discussion of various art projects on the theme of care into the overall discussion whenever relevant, thereby avoiding making a clear boundary between art and everyday life. I find that many examples from art help us to attend to the often-invisible care acts in our daily life, to reflect upon the nature of our care relationship with the world around us, and to sometimes actually participate in care activities outside of our daily chore.

Another border-crossing my discussion presents regards cultural traditions. I often incorporate materials from the Japanese cultural tradition and aesthetics. While it is valuable in itself to introduce this cultural tradition, some aspects of which may not be well known beyond its cultural border, that is not my main purpose. I found in this tradition, which also happens to be my own upbringing and background, rich materials for exploring the relationship between the ethical and the aesthetic via the notion of care. This is most likely due to the long-held legacy of the Shintoist and the Buddhist thought that permeated people's lives and aesthetic tradition there. No doubt there are many other cultural traditions that offer equally rich resources for the integration of care ethics and aesthetics. However, since my interest is in how this integration gets manifested in people's everyday lives, I want to rely on my firsthand experience of this specific cultural milieu. At the same time, my frequent reference to Japanese examples is meant to illustrate general points regarding the aesthetics and ethics of care, rather than presenting them as culturally bound issues. Hence, it is my hope that the meta-level issues suggested by these specific references will be clear and offer a focal point.

By frequently referencing the Japanese cultural tradition and practice in my discussion, I am by no means suggesting their superiority or idealization. In fact, various criticisms have been raised about this aesthetic tradition. For example, the court culture during the Heian era (794–1185), sometimes dubbed as the cult of beauty, based the moral evaluation of a person exclusively on his aesthetic sensibility without considering other factors such as courage and righteousness.[17] Or, the time-honored aesthetic appreciation of the ephemeral beauty of falling cherry blossoms provided a potent justification for the suicide mission of Kamikaze pilots.[18] Finally, the tradition of promoting artistic activities primarily as a self-cultivation and -discipline fails to address wider social and political implications.[19] I believe that some of these criticisms are still valid in contemporary Japan. At the same time, particularly after Westernization began in late nineteenth century, Japan has come to be known as a nation of aesthetics, for better or worse, and part of this characterization comes from its long-held integration of the aesthetic and ethical, which is still prevalent in today's environment, as some of my examples show. I do believe, and the subsequent discussion will show, that the aesthetic expression of care contributes to making a society humane and social interactions fulfilling. However, it does not provide a sufficient condition for a good society and a good life. Other equally important considerations, such as justice and equality, must complement aesthetics and ethics of care, and Japan is no exception.

If I started my investigation from a standpoint that does not adhere to a distinction between self and others or the aesthetic and the ethic, the trajectory of the discussion would have been very different. I can be accused of starting my exploration with these distinctions that dominated much of Western philosophical tradition, although my aim is to overcome them. However, I would like to think that this way of proceeding creates an opportunity of a genuine dialogue between different cultural traditions and disciplinary discourses.

1

Care Ethics and Aesthetic Experience

Shared Commonality

This chapter lays the groundwork for the rest of the book by delineating the parallel between care ethics and aesthetic experience. I first discuss contemporary aesthetic discussion on the relationship between the aesthetic and the ethic, with a particular attention paid to the virtue theory of aesthetics, to provide a context in which to situate my aesthetics of care. Developing my discussion on the parallel between care ethics and aesthetic experience in comparison with the same parallel drawn by the virtue theory of aesthetics helps illuminate my overall interest in the interdependence of the aesthetic and the ethical. Specifically, my focus is on the cultivation of an ethically grounded aesthetics and aesthetically guided ethics, rather than making an aesthetic judgment of an object, which I argue is the case with the virtue theory of aesthetics.

The comparison between care ethics and aesthetics begins with the salient features of care ethics that emerged as an alternative to justice-centric ethics which emphasizes impartiality, detachment, and generality. They include attention to the particularity of the other, open-minded attempt for understanding and appreciating the other, and active engagement with the other expressed through an appropriate care action. These constituents of care ethics correspond to the way in which aesthetic experience unfolds. Characterized as a collaborative venture, aesthetic experience is developed through attention to the specifics of the object in its entirety without imposing preconceived ideas or judgments, while activating imagination and actively engaging with the object of appreciation. These parallels suggest that the fundamental attitude encouraged by care ethics also underlies aesthetic experience. At the same time, aesthetic sensibility nurtured by aesthetic experience makes realization of care ethics possible. Ultimately, both practices concern the mode of being in the world through interacting with others, whether people or objects.

1 Virtue Theory of Aesthetics

The main goal of this book is to demonstrate the intimate connection and interdependence between the aesthetic and ethical dimensions of our lives, with the notion of care as the central site. The relationship between the aesthetic and the ethical is not a new subject; it has been a perennial issue in aesthetics. In this section, I situate my subsequent discussion within the contemporary Western aesthetic landscape. I pay particular attention to the so-called virtue theory of aesthetics that has been proposed in the last two decades. This theory resonates with my view because of the central place assigned to the consideration of virtues in aesthetics. However, despite this shared focus, there is a significant difference in the overall goal of referencing virtues in aesthetics. The virtue theory's primary interest is in justifying the aesthetic judgment of a creative act, an object, or an appreciative activity. My primary interest in involving virtues, such as care and respect for the other, in aesthetics is rather directed toward giving a first-person account of our lived experience and how cultivating and practicing the aesthetics of care enriches one's life and leads to a good life.

Before discussing the virtue theory of aesthetics, let me first give the contemporary aesthetics' lay of the land regarding the relationship between the aesthetic and the ethical, in order to contextualize the virtue theory of aesthetics and my proposed aesthetics of care. The debate over the aesthetic and the ethical that has dominated contemporary Western aesthetic discourse revolves around the relevance of the ethical considerations when making an aesthetic judgment of a work of art. Sometimes the content of or the vision expressed in a work of art, usually through representation or narrative, is deemed morally problematic. Other times, the process of creating art harms humans' or animals' well-being or environments. Yet other times, the concern is over the morally repugnant character of the artist or the performer. Wherever the negative moral value is located, the main point of the debate is whether such negative moral considerations adversely affect the aesthetic value of art.

While matters related to art dominate the debate, with the establishment of environmental aesthetics and everyday aesthetics, similar issues came to be raised about objects outside the realm of art. There are basically two concerns, paralleling the first two issues regarding art mentioned earlier. The first concerns whether the morally problematic function of an artifact, such as a torture device or a lethal weapon, compromises its aesthetic value.[1] The other question has to do with whether the harm to humans, nature, or environment caused by the creation, transport, maintenance, or disposal of an object negatively affects its aesthetic value. For example, many of today's consumer products are produced in dismal working conditions in the developing nations where environments are destroyed, while a perfectly manicured green lawn is maintained by the inordinate amount of water and toxic chemicals.

In response to these thorny cases, various positions have been proposed. On the one end is the so-called radical autonomism or separatism that insists on the strict separation between the aesthetic and the ethical. On the other end is ethicism or moralism that views the ethical considerations to be determinant when making an aesthetic judgment. Various versions of moderate views are located somewhere between these two polar positions.[2]

This all-too-brief sketch does not do justice to the rich array of finely nuanced views, but what I want to emphasize is that, in general, whatever particular position is taken, the main focus is on the aesthetic judgment of an object formed by a spectator. The ethical considerations in this debate are, if thought to be aesthetically relevant, one among many features associated with the object that affect its aesthetic value. As such, it does not concern the spectator's ethical life when making a judgment on the aesthetic value of an object.

The preponderance of this judgmental and object-centered approach in Western aesthetics deserves to be highlighted by comparing it with an aesthetic discourse from a different cultural tradition. Case in point is the Japanese aesthetic tradition which is mostly concerned with aesthetic practices as a means of self-cultivation and self-discipline. What may first appear to be training manuals for artistic practices, hence can be considered as offering the criteria of aesthetic judgment, are primarily treatises on what constitutes a good life and how to live such a life. As such, one commentator of Japanese aesthetics observes, "Japanese aestheticians . . . have generally very little to say about the relationship between the work and the audience, or about the nature of literary and art criticism."[3] The point is not to claim one approach is better than the other, but rather to indicate that the judgment- and object-oriented aesthetic approach does not exhaust the arena of aesthetics.

In this regard, the recently proposed so-called virtue theory of aesthetics (or art) appears to stand out. It defines aesthetics by focusing on the inner life of the experiencing agent, as a creator, a critic, or an appreciator, when engaging in the aesthetically related act of creating or appreciating, in addition to the objects or their qualities. Its primary interest is the relationship between the experiencing agent, when appreciating or creating, and the object. It is characterized as paralleling the virtue theory of ethics. Both are concerned with the moral character of the motivation and attitude behind a certain act. It is not enough that the resultant product or act exhibits certain features. Tom Roberts characterizes this theory as encouraging "a redirection of philosophical attention, such that the primary objects of aesthetic enquiry and evaluation are taken to include not only art objects, but also artistic activities of creation, performance, and appreciation," specifically, "the qualities of the person performing such activities, including her individual virtues and vices."[4]

Peter Goldie also argues that prioritizing the object in this endeavor "runs the risk of our being concerned only incidentally and instrumentally with the various activities, intentions, dispositions, feelings, and so on, that are involved in the whole practice of the production and appreciation . . . of artworks."[5] It is more important to grasp the aesthetic practice "from the inside," that is, "from within the practices of production and of appreciation, where the importance and point of the practices can be given due weight to those who engage in them."[6] In short, as pointed out by David Woodruff, one of the initial proponents of this theory, it emphasizes "the relational features" of the products and the agent of actions.[7]

Despite some differences, the advocates of the virtue theory of aesthetics generally agree that the aesthetic judgment of an object must stem from the right motivation, attitude, and appropriate skills, all of which are shared by virtue ethics. They include, according to Goldie, following a list suggested by Woodruff, "imagination, insight, sensibility, vision, creativity, wit, authenticity, integrity, intelligence, persistence, open-mindedness, and courage" and "when they are expressed in artistic activity, that activity is chosen for its own sake, 'under the concept of art.'"[8] Regardless of the resultant product, the fact that the artist or the critic just went through the motion without passion or commitment, for example not caring about what they are producing, compromises the aesthetic value of the result. The concern with the creative agent's moral character here seems to differ from the more common consideration, such as the artist being a misogynist, a white supremacist, or a sadist. While such a consideration is not irrelevant, the virtues or vices the virtue theory of aesthetics invokes pertain specifically to the act of producing an art object.

The same consideration applies to aesthetic appreciation, according to Matthew Kieran. Even if an appropriate judgment based upon the right kind of reasons is made, the appreciator's motivation must be for the sake of appreciating the object, rather than, for example, gaining social standing by giving the impression that she belongs to an elite group of those who display fine aesthetic sensibility, what he calls "snobbery."[9]

My view developed in this book regarding the relationship between the ethical and the aesthetic around the notion of care shares with the virtue theory of aesthetics the centrality of the activity or process of aesthetic experience. I also draw a parallel between the ethical practice of engaging in care activities and what is involved in an aesthetic experience by pointing out that they share the same attitudes and skills such as attentiveness, open-mindedness, receptivity, respect, collaborative spirit, and activation of imagination, and this list is similar to the virtues listed by the virtue theory of aesthetics.

Where my aesthetics of care diverges from the current virtue theory of aesthetics outlined earlier is that I emphasize the interaction and interdependence of aesthetic and ethical virtues. Although I begin by drawing a parallel between the aesthetic and the ethical, it is in preparation for arguing for their ultimate interdependence. In order to engage in an ethically virtuous act, we need a refined aesthetic sensibility and an aesthetically modulated expression. In addition, a successful aesthetic experience depends upon an ethically grounded relationship with the other. This cross-pollination between the aesthetic and the ethical does not seem to garner attention in the virtue theory of aesthetics. For example, Goldie points out that "in ethics we are right to think less of the person who does what he ought to do begrudgingly, resentfully or with an air of indifference— such a person would be less than fully virtuous."[10] While he offers this observation as an *ethical* failure, I view that this failure is caused by an *aesthetic* failure. One's bodily expression, such as a sigh, the sharp tone of voice, or a rough manner of rendering physical assistance, betrays either one's begrudging or indifferent attitude or lack of sensitivity or practice in carrying out an act appropriately. Goldie also refers to the importance of delicacy of discrimination as an ethical virtue by observing that "it is an integral part of the virtue of kindness or of generosity—the ability to see what is the kind thing to do to help an independently-minded person, or to see what is the right sort of generosity to the friend who has little money of her own."[11] He suggests that this sensibility "has a home in art production and art appreciation." I agree that figuring out what form of generosity the other party wishes my act to take requires my imaginative engagement, which is most effectively cultivated by our experience of art. I would also add that, if my interaction with the other person is direct, face to face, I need to attend to the subtlety of her bodily expression and demeanor and respond appropriately, which requires perceptual acuity and sensitivity. These are all aesthetic skills. In these cases, the practice and execution of virtuous acts require aesthetics, and I wonder how clearly we can separate the aesthetic and the ethical. In our lived experience, it is not as if we put on an ethical hat to decide I ought to help my friend, then switch to an aesthetic hat to read her demeanor, and then determine and carry out the most appropriate act. I believe we experience these concerns as being fully integrated.

At the same time, virtue theorists' characterization of various aesthetic virtues, without which aesthetic activity will not be successful, *are* moral virtues, insofar as they are exercised as part of a respectful relationship with the other. As mentioned before, according to the virtue theory of aesthetics, the seemingly successful product of an artistic activity done without any passion on the part of the artist is really not successful and does not enhance the artist's life. Similarly, the aesthetic experience I develop with an object does not help enrich my life or contribute to my well-being if I approach it, for example, simply for gaining pleasure from my predetermined expectation without allowing the object to invite me to *its* world. As I explain in Section 4, Iris Murdoch insists that the attitude of unselfing, which underlies our ethical mode of being in the world, is necessary for our aesthetic experience. According to the view of other thinkers, whom I will also cite together, facilitating a successful aesthetic experience *is* an ethical act in the sense of our respectful engagement with the other.

In discussing how aesthetic virtues contribute to the good life and well-being of humans, Goldie seems to make them distinct from ethical and intellectual virtues. Engaging in artistic activities in a noninstrumental way, according to him, "along with ethical and contemplative activity, is what is constitutive of well-being or the good life for us humans, as creatures with reason and language— and . . . with imagination."[12] However, as the previous discussion of deciding on the best course of action to help a friend, I find it often difficult to separate the ethical and the aesthetic dimension of our lived experiences. Keeping the distinction between the aesthetic and the ethical may reflect a deeply entrenched assumption in Western philosophy that the realm of aesthetics always presupposes objects while the realm of ethics does not. This results in a belief that our relationship and interaction with objects, unlike social interactions, are not subject to ethical judgment (except when they affect other beings, primarily human), a view I will argue against in Chapter 4.

Despite its purported emphasis on the activity and the account from the inside, the virtue theory of aesthetics is ultimately concerned with the judgment and evaluation of art or the appreciative judgment. That is, the presence or absence of virtuous motives is taken to affect the aesthetic value of art, and the same determines the status of the aesthetic appreciation. Virtues and vices are attributes of the creator or the appreciator whose product is being judged by us as spectators. Though it is possible to interpret this theory as a recommendation for us to cultivate virtues, the emphasis is clearly on the judgment-making task. For example, Tom Roberts claims that "how the work was executed matters to our *evaluation*" by referring to whether it can be considered the artist's achievement.[13] Similarly, "*an artwork can gain value* through its relation to the qualities of its creator's character" by referring to whether it was produced with the right motivation.[14] In short, what was involved in the artist's creative act should figure into our "*evaluative* practises," and "when a virtue is manifested in a work . . . it is appropriate to *evaluate it* on this basis, as an object that is the product not only of an individual's skilled agency, but as something shaped and crafted according to what she cares about."[15] Hence, despite his pronouncement about the virtue theory that it shifts focus from the object to the aesthetically related activities, the ultimate focus is still the evaluation of the aesthetic value of the art object.

Matthew Kieran's focus in the virtue theory of aesthetics is on the value of the appreciator's evaluation of art, specifically whether her motivation in making the evaluation is for a snobbish reason. Essentially, the virtue theory makes a judgment on the nature of the judgment made by the appreciator: "a snob's judgement may be justified, but the problematic motivation *infects* aesthetic appreciation," that is, "snobs *fail* to appreciate a work *qua* aesthetic object properly because they are badly motivated and evaluate works according to incorrect criteria bound up with social esteem."[16] The focus on the motivation driving the appreciator's appreciative act is a means to making a judgment on her judgment, the product of the appreciative act.

My aesthetics of care rather focuses on the first-person practice of cultivating the virtuous mode of relating to the other in our aesthetic experience through care. Making a judgment on an object or an appreciative judgment is not incompatible with the aesthetics of care I will develop, and from time to time I discuss such judgments. However, unlike the virtue theorists whose ultimate goal seems to be judgment-making on the product of aesthetic activities, my focus is on how care is an aesthetic and ethical practice that we ourselves can engage in, which contributes to a good life. Virtue theory of aesthetics certainly claims its stake in the notion of good life, and Goldie in particular makes this dimension of virtue theory explicit: "Virtues . . . are dispositions which are valued as necessary for virtuous activity, and virtuous activity is what well-being consists of."[17] He specifically develops his version of virtue theory of aesthetics by arguing that "having the concept of art, understanding it from the inside, enables one to have the right artistic intentions, feelings, and dispositions; having these dispositions—virtues—enables one to engage in artistic activity; and artistic activity, of production or appreciation, is one of the kinds of activity— of virtuous activity—that is constitutive of well-being."[18] Furthermore, Goldie claims that art enables emotional sharing with others, whether the artists or fellow appreciators, as we direct our attention to the same object and experience it for its own sake. Such possibility of intersubjectivity enhances one's well-being.

However, unlike most proponents of virtue theory, I hold that the aesthetics' contribution to a good life and well-being is not limited to art. Even when it is presented as the virtue theory of aesthetics, the discussion is almost exclusively on art. Given the twentieth-century history of Western aesthetics that is often identified as the philosophy of art and dominated by issues regarding art, their primary interest in art is understandable. Woodruff is one of the few who holds that this theory is not limited to art. By taking a chess match as an example, he argues that insofar as the appreciation of the match is concerned with "the way the victory came about and not so much with the victory itself, or some practical issue such as the implication for ranking," one's appreciation is aesthetic.[19] One can play a chess game for its own sake, not merely concerned with winning but also appreciating the ingenious moves and daring strategies that led to a victory. Hence, Woodruff continues, "this appreciation of the embodiment of the victory or we might say the appreciation of the way the victory was achieved seems to me to be an aesthetic appreciation, and furthermore it seems quite reasonable to generalize this to a huge array of similar cases." However, how far can we extend this observation to cover "a huge array of similar cases"?

When it comes to nonart artifacts, whether in their creation or appreciation, two questions may be raised about the applicability of the virtue theory. First, most artifacts are primarily utilitarian objects, so in both their creation/design and their appreciation, their functionality and easy-useability cannot but be included in our experience and evaluation. Then, doesn't my motivation as a designer to make the most smooth-operating and user-friendly can opener, or my evaluation as a user based upon the object's functional efficiency and effectiveness, compromise the virtuous attitude free of ulterior motives called for in the virtue theory of aesthetics? That is, I am concerned with how well the object serves my needs. So, the objection goes, the virtue theory of aesthetics cannot apply to utilitarian artifacts.

In response, I suggest that we can consider the function of an object to be one of the factors that direct its creation or appreciation and determine its parameter. The function can be compared to a specific type of an art object for creation or appreciation: a sonata, a sonnet, a religious painting in honor of a saint, and so forth. These specific kinds of art impose certain restrictions or expectations that determine what the artist can or cannot do, even while allowing her to exercise her freedom, imagination, and creativity. Similarly, the function intended for a can opener limits what the designer can do, and the creative act and appreciation of the object need to occur within that framework. It will be unreasonable for me to criticize the can opener for not being able to cut paper or for the designer to create an object that does not fulfill its can-opening function. So, even in the case of a utilitarian object with a predetermined function, one can still consider virtues, such as imagination, creativity, persistence, and courage, to be exercised within the framework of the said utilitarian purpose. The designer's motivation in creating the most smooth-operating and user-friendly kind of can opener and my appreciation accordingly can be considered virtue-guided and can be distinguished from the extraneous motivations, such as the designer wanting to make a lot of money from her design or my using the can opener to show off to my friends that I have acquired the state-of-the art object designed by a famous designer. Thus, although seldom explored, the virtue theory of aesthetics seems to be applicable to nonart artifacts.

Another question may be raised about the applicability of the virtue theory to artifacts: generally speaking, we know who created a work of art but not artifacts. Except for those objects designed by famous designers, most artifacts do not come with the designers' signatures, so to speak. There is no way for us, therefore, to know the designer's motivation, attitude, and so forth that is critical in the virtue theory.

Despite this commonly regarded difference between most art and artifacts, it does not make a significant difference in this context, because we as the appreciator, or sometimes even as artists, rarely know the attitude and motivation with which the art object was created, either. The best we can do is to settle for an approximation based upon what we can gather about the agent's general personality, practices, and behavior. So, even with art, the facts we need in order to put the virtue theory into practice remain elusive, so the fact that we don't know who the designer is, nor his motivation and attitude, does not seem to pose a unique problem of applying the virtue theory to artifacts. If it is the case that the object's features reflect or embody the agent's motivation, then we are making a judgment of the object first and foremost, depriving the theory of the force of putting the premium on the agent's activity and the motives behind it.

Thus, the two worries about applying the virtue theory of aesthetics to nonart artifacts can be resolved, supporting a wider scope of the virtue theory. This leads me to formulate my principal question as "why aesthetics matters," instead of the prevailing question for the virtue theory of aesthetics, "why art matters."[20] Our aesthetic life includes daily interactions with objects and environments around us and our social interactions with other people, in addition to the experience of art. The latter perhaps provides the most concentrated and intense aesthetic experience dedicated to enriching our lives, but even without noticing, our daily management of life always has an aesthetic dimension, although its palette is wide and diverse, and not always offering pleasure or excitement. Aesthetics matters not only because, as the virtue theory suggests, engaging in creative or aesthetically judgmental acts with virtuous motivations and attitudes contributes to a good life and well-being, but also because it is intimately connected with the ethical mode of living in this world where we constantly interact with others, whether humans, nature, or artifacts. Just as ethics requires aesthetic sensibility and practice, aesthetics also requires an ethically grounded relationship with the world. A successful aesthetic experience is premised upon our care-filled and -guided interaction with the world, and it gives rise to enjoyment and delight. But equally important is when the relationship is not successful. Such occasions should spur us to correct our own course of action, or sometimes lead us to determine that the change needs to be made by, or brought onto, the other party.

In comparison with more object-oriented discussion regarding the aesthetic and the ethical with which I began this section, virtue theory of aesthetics resonates with me most in terms of shifting the focus from objects to activities involved in aesthetic creation and appreciation. However, despite its pronounced aim to redirect the aesthetic discussion from objects to activities, the ultimate goal of the virtue theory turns out to be the evaluation of the resultant objects, whether they be the products of creation or appreciation. The presence or absence of a virtuous motivation becomes a means to evaluating the aesthetic value of the object or appreciation. While I share aligning the virtues involved in aesthetic experience and the ethical way of living, my interest is rather in exploring the way in which the aesthetic virtues and ethical virtues are interdependent. In what follows, I will explore the interdependent relationship between the aesthetic and the ethical and promote the care relationship with others as a foundation for an ethically and aesthetically fulfilling life.

2 Care Ethics

In Western philosophy, the primary concern for ethics had long been dominated by rule-governed objectivity, rationality, fairness, impartiality, and universality. Concepts such as justice, equality, and rights have received most attention and weight in the ethical discourse. The well-known figure of the Lady Justice is blindfolded while weighing a scale. The blindfold is regarded as ensuring impartiality and fairness so as not to be affected by the specifics of the case, such as a particular circumstance, the identity of the person involved being judged, the judging person's personal relationship with the judged, and the like. Typical court proceedings are supposed to exemplify this impartial judgment-making. The particulars of the individuals and situations are considered theoretically irrelevant; so are the personal investments and motivations guiding one's engagement with others.[21]

Feminist ethics emerged as a challenge to this justice-centric ethics, which was considered to neglect an important dimension of our moral life. Advocates of feminist ethics maintain that our everyday moral concerns tend to be dominated by concrete relationships and interactions with specific individuals, often involving emotional investment. Objectivity, rationality, and impartiality that are paramount in justice-centric ethics are considered unsuitable when negotiating the moral terrain of our everyday life. Carol Gilligan's seminal work, *In a Different Voice* (1982), on the gender difference among children's moral deliberations established the so-called feminine-oriented care ethics in contrast to the so-called male-oriented justice ethics. Care ethics thus identified by Gilligan was further developed by Nel Noddings in *Caring: A Feminine Approach to Ethics and Moral Education* (1984).[22] These works, now considered to be classics of care ethics, have given rise to considerable debate, criticisms, and refinements.[23] For my purpose, however, I will rely on their formulation of the notion of care and address some of the critiques only in the context of shedding light on its comparison to aesthetics.

Gilligan bases her argument for care ethics on the discovery that boys and girls go about solving moral problems in different ways. Boys tend to follow justice-centric ethics by appealing to rules and generality of the situation, while girls tend to invoke considerations derived from sympathetic relationship and emotional involvement. Against Lawrence Kohlberg's theory that associates the former with moral maturity, Gilligan argues in support of the way in which a moral problem can be addressed by sympathetically attending to, instead of ignoring, the particularity of the individuals involved and the specific context and circumstance that comprise the morally charged situation. She questions the wisdom of favoring disinterested ethical deliberations that seek universal applicability by eliminating adventitious and accidental over context-relative deliberations associated with what is characterized as the feminine mode of thinking.

Noddings similarly observes that many people do not approach moral problems formally by applying a fixed rule. Instead, in our lived experience, we grapple with moral matters in their concrete specificities. She further observes that "women, in particular, seem to approach moral problems by placing themselves as nearly as possible in concrete situations and assuming personal responsibility for the choices to be made" and "this position or attitude of caring activates a complex structure of memories, feelings, and capacities."[24] According to her, the model of care ethics is found in a mother's intimate relationship with her child, as well as a teacher's relationship with her student.

Care ethics in general is concerned with both the process and the result, the attitude and the action, or the disposition and the practice. On the one hand, one cannot claim to care about somebody if it is not translated into some kind of action, at least sometimes. As Noddings reminds us, "to care . . . requires some action in behalf of the cared-for."[25] My insistence that I care about my friend rings hollow if I never lift a finger to do anything for her when she needs help, particularly if I am in the position to be able to help her. Similarly, I cannot claim to care about my mother if I never visit her, phone her, or write to her, when doing at least one of those things is possible. Such a case invites a proverbial comment, "talk is cheap."

This necessity of some actions, however, does not imply that care is incompatible with intentionally withholding a certain action. For example, my parental care for my child may sometimes include letting her fail because I believe that it is in her best interest to learn a life's lesson rather than being always protected from failure and disappointment. That the expression of care should vary according to situations is most clear in how the pandemic of Covid-19 that raged when this book was being written upended many ordinary actions that have always been practiced. For example, my care for my loved ones which used to be expressed by hugging and kissing was expressed by refraining from such close physical contact during the pandemic.

This situation-dependent expression of care extends to care of objects. For example, in her discussion of care regarding built structures, Caitlin DeSilvey states that "sometimes practical taking care may involve acts of repair and maintenance that secure the material fabric of the thing; at other times, taking care may involve withholding repair and letting the thing carry on with its changes."[26] Similarly, Christopher Groves points out that "people need responsiveness but also time to themselves and independence; places need tending, reconstructing or letting alone so that natural forms grow wild."[27] In short, there is no "one-size-fits-all" mode of expressing care.

At the same time, engaging in some action that care requires is not sufficient for the action to count as an action of care, either. An action can be performed for a number of reasons. I may do something that care ethics requires because I am contractually obligated to do so, or I may be just following what I understand to be a moral rule. Noddings thus claims that "we do not say with any conviction that a person cares if that person acts routinely according to some fixed rule."[28] In addition, I may be forced to act because the object of my care has power over me; I may be expecting a reward for my action; or I don't want to appear as an uncaring person. All these reasons may lead me to perform "the same" action that coincides with what care ethics expects, say, taking a friend to her doctor. Although care ethics diverges from Kantian ethics that locates the moral worth of an action in the sense of duty, they share the view that the moral worth of an action needs to refer to the motivation guiding one's action. Noddings thus points out that "we all know of cases in which persons assigned to provide care have performed the tasks of caregiving without conveying care."[29] Hence, "when we consider the action component of caring in depth, we shall have to look beyond observable action to acts of commitment, those acts that are seen only by the individual subject performing them."[30] For Noddings, therefore, the ethics of care requires a certain mode of commitment to the other's well-being that gets expressed in actions. In other words, the process of deciding on a certain course of action regarding the other is as important as, or perhaps more important than, what the action accomplishes.

Furthermore, care ethics is also concerned with the manner in which one carries out an action. Noddings points out, and I believe we can readily agree, that "I cannot claim to care for my relative if my caretaking is perfunctory or grudging."[31] Similarly, Daniel Engster states that "caring means not only achieving certain aims but also doing so in a caring manner," specifically "*in an attentive, responsive and respectful manner.*"[32] Even if the goal is accomplished by taking my friend to a doctor, if I do so in a mechanical, indifferent, or spiteful manner, the action can hardly be characterized as an act of caring, although I may insist that it is better than refusing to drive her.

Care ethics' focus is on our relationship with and action on other human beings, and today it often extends to nonhuman creatures. There is also an increasing attention to our care relationship with our environment and objects within. As I shall argue in Chapter 4, our care relationship with the inanimate world needs to be illuminated and cultivated particularly today. As noted by Iris Murdoch when referring to Simone Weil, "moral change comes from an *attention* to the world . . . through an increased sense of the reality of . . . other people, but also other things."[33] Echoing Murdoch, Josephine Donovan argues that the aesthetics of care applies not only to human beings and natural world in general but "even to physical matter itself."[34]

The care relationship with the material world is a function of various forms of attachment, whether the object be a treasured personal possession, a home, or a place of special significance. Our caring attitude and action regarding these objects are reciprocated by their gift of what Groves calls "ontological security" that affords us stability and security to let us develop our freedom and autonomy.[35] As Groves states, "subject and object are interdependent: the subject is 'held together' by the object; the subject tends to and protects— cares for—the object."

Thus, care ethics expands from an interpersonal relationship to our interdependent relationship to the material world. This expansion from persons to objects has a reverse formulation: from "objects into persons," to use Arnold Berleant's formulation.[36] The subject matter of aesthetics has been dominated by objects for a long time, most notably works of art, then nature, environment, and functional objects. However, Berleant's notion of the aesthetic field expands the object-centered domain of aesthetics to include the environment and interpersonal relationships. I will reserve the discussion of social aesthetics to Chapter 3, but I want to point out here that, just as both care ethics and aesthetic experience emphasize the reciprocal interrelationship between the subject and the object, my overarching thesis is that there is also a reciprocal relationship between care ethics and aesthetics, at times blurring the distinction between the two.

3 Attentiveness to the Particularity of the Other

As previously stated, care ethics requires attending to the particularities of the other person and the situation and tailoring our response accordingly. Marilyn Friedman defines care ethics as primarily committed to "other persons in their wholeness and their particularity," while the justice perspective requires commitment to "general and abstract rules, values, or principles."[37] Similarly, Lawrence Blum emphasizes, "care morality is about the particular agent's caring for and about the particular moral patient. Morality is not (only) about how the impersonal 'one' is meant to act toward the impersonal 'other.'"[38] Care ethics generally rejects rule-governed moral deliberation or a "one-size-fits-all" solution that is expected to be applicable to all similar cases. Many of us know from our experiences of parenting and teaching, often regarded as the quintessential cases of care, that the most effective and appropriate strategy for nurturing their growth varies from child to child, student to student. In short, as Noddings claims: "to act as one-caring . . . is to act with special regard for the particular person in a concrete situation."[39] Phronesis, practical wisdom, requires sensitive grasp of the individual in a specific predicament which informs and guides our ethical response. As pointed out by Andrew Sayer, this is why Aristotle claims that experience and maturity are needed for practical wisdom, while young people may excel in things like mathematics that deals with abstract generality and universality.[40]

Grasping the particularity of a person requires a direct encounter that enables me to experience her holistically. An individual person's specific personhood cannot be adequately captured by her age, gender, sexual orientation, race, religion, marital status, ethnicity, political affiliation, and occupation. While these categories are relevant, she is not merely their sum total. Understanding and appreciating her for who she is and gaining a holistic grasp of her requires a firsthand experience of interacting with her, observing how she conducts herself, as well as having some understanding of her life story. As pointed out by Daniel Putman, "caring is an intentional act that makes the person completely present to whomever or whatever is the object of the act."[41]

I should note that what would count as a "direct" encounter is becoming increasingly unclear and problematic with the prevalence of virtual interactions, particularly following the global pandemic. Writing before the pandemic, Ezio Manzini, a design educator, points out that, with respect to care activities for the sick, children, and the elderly, "a part of the relationships . . . must have a physical dimension and one of the proximity" because "not recognizing that, in their everyday lives, people also live in their physical dimension and that for a number of reasons physical proximity is crucial, leads to dehumanizing visions and proposals," such as a robot taking care of an elderly.[42] It is difficult to speculate at the time of writing whether the new normal forced upon humanity by the pandemic continues to preclude the possibility of close physical contact that we have taken for granted in the pre-pandemic life and will force us to rethink the notion of "direct human contact." Is the inhumanity and cruelty we feel when one can see the loved one only through a glass window, or worse, through a cell phone or a computer screen, relative to what we have been used to? Furthermore, if such an encounter becomes the only mode possible for care relationships, would we reach a point where such an encounter can be accepted as the "direct" encounter and interaction? As Margus Vihalem argues, along with Rancière, aesthetics is a matter of constituting the realm of the sensible that changes as the social, political, and technological landscape changes, and, as such, "new objects of perception and new fields of action can thus be introduced: for instance, in the age of the internet, social interaction produces new affects and may lead to new affectivities that did not exist before; new elements of culture are discovered that modify the way we understand human culture in general."[43] I shall not explore the implications of the radical change we are currently experiencing that has been forced on us as we deal with the pandemic situation and leave what constitutes the direct encounter with others an open-ended question.

Despite the challenge of determining what constitutes a direct encounter, attending to the particularity of the other person here and now appears in one of the most prominent professions dispensing care: medicine. The medical profession is by necessity goal oriented in giving a correct diagnosis of the patient's ailment and finding a cure. In order to accomplish this goal, all agree that the scientific mode of managing patient care facilitated by rationality, objectivity, and detachment is necessary. However, an increasing number of medical professionals question whether this mode of medical intervention is sufficient. If this is an exclusive way in which medicine is practiced, "while attention to symptoms is critical for medical practice," many worry that they forget that "the patient is more than a medium for disease."[44] Instead, they suggest that, in tandem with the scientific operation of diagnosis and treatment, medicine needs to attend to healing the person in her wholeness, not just as an anonymous molecular host to a specific disease.

Often citing Martin Buber's notions of I-You and I-It relationships, those medical professionals argue for the importance of developing an I-You relationship with the patient.[45] Treating the patient only in terms of the ailment is to regard him as an It in Buber's sense. According to Buber, when experiencing an It, a person "bends down to examine particulars under the objectifying magnifying glass of close scrutiny, or he uses the objectifying telescope of distant vision to arrange them as mere scenery."[46] The objects appear "to be constructed of their qualities," and they can be "put in order" and "become subjected to coordination." In short, to experience a person as an It is to take him as "an object of detached perception and experience."

However, experiencing another human being as an "It" dehumanizes him in that I am not attentive to the very individual endowments that define him. A person is not a sum total of various qualities; instead, he as You integrates all the qualities and categories as an organic whole. Buber describes these different relationships as follows: "When I confront a human being as my You and speak the basic word I-You to him then he is not a thing among things nor does he consist of things."[47] Furthermore, You must be encountered here and now; "I do not find the human being to whom I say You in any Sometime and Somewhere."

Applying Buber's view, Felicia Cohn advocates what she calls existential medicine that is "based on the good of a *specific other*, avoids blind recourse to any given set of rules, and serves as a reminder of the complexity of life."[48] In particular, this kind of medical practice avoids seeing a patient as the sum total of symptoms to be cured but a whole person whose life consists of everyday affairs with a disease making up only one portion of it. The existential medical perspective pays "greater attention to the everyday events of life and the particularity of the involved persons" because "human existence is a complex of many events, all of which form individual identity."[49]

For my purpose, it is particularly important to note that Buber himself draws an analogy between experiencing a person as a whole and an art object in its wholeness. Just as "a melody is not composed of tones, nor a verse of words nor a statue of lines," a person is not "a loose bundle of named qualities."[50] In experiencing a person, "I can abstract from him the color of his hair or the color of his speech or the color of his graciousness . . . but immediately he is no longer You." Focusing on and responding to the singularity of the individual person, You, as the object of care corresponds to the nature of aesthetic experience. I experience and appreciate *this* tree and *that* painting, rather than a specimen of an oak tree and an example of an impressionist painting, by directly perceiving its respective appearance and character. Calling it "participatory epistemology," Josephine Donovan characterizes the aesthetics of care as a mode of perception where "subjects are qualitatively particularized, embedded in specific locales—their unique physical bodies and historically and geographically specific environments."[51] Specifically concerned with the care aesthetics directed toward nonhuman creatures, she continues that "the knowledge of these subjects' ways of being requires experiential attentiveness to their unique shapes, expressions, and patterns, as well as to their contextual habitats"; in short, "it requires listening to their diverse voices."

In his discussion of aesthetic experience, Ronald Hepburn states that the aesthetic experience of a work of art is possible only "when we see it . . . as an inherently valuable, irreplaceable artifact, whose message, if any, is *individualized* by its embodiment in that *unique* object."[52] Full immersion in a work of art is possible when we "think as well as feel our way into *aesthetic particulars*."[53] With respect to art, putting the object in its proper category is needed to correctly and fully appreciate its meanings and value. The category consists of genre, historical and cultural context, technique used in making, artist's intention, and the like, as argued by Kendall Walton.[54] However, putting the object into its proper category does not substitute for experiencing the unique individuality of the object. For both art and persons, Hepburn claims: "we look for meaning in their movements, gestures, and presentations."[55] Although guided by the consideration of its proper category, attentive and direct experience of a particular object is absolutely necessary.

The same point receives a specific emphasis from a noted Japanese art historian, Sōetsu Yanagi (柳宋悦 1889–1961), who promoted the aesthetics of folkcraft (民芸 *mingei*) in Japan. Particularly concerned with the discourse of art history that was established following the sudden and rapid Westernization that transformed Japan politically and culturally in the late nineteenth century, Yanagi advocates the distinction between "seeing" or "intuition" and "knowing." He criticizes the art historical discourse of his day as being preoccupied with "knowing" various facts or what he calls "circumstances" that "surround" a work of art, but not "the thing itself." The former is studied "intellectually" and "knowing with the abstract."[56] In contrast, "seeing is connected with the world of concrete things," and seeing the objects' beauty "means coming into direct and immediate contact with the thing itself."[57] While he doesn't deny that "knowing" will help us develop a fuller understanding and appreciation of an object, it has to be considered a supplement to the seeing or intuition because "seeing cannot be deduced from knowing"; instead, when seeing things, they are "comprehended immediately and directly."[58]

As evidenced by these thinkers, aesthetic experience requires a firsthand and immediate experience. We can gain scientific knowledge secondhand by studying a theory or a set of data collected by others. Although we may miss the thrill of scientific discovery or data gathering, in terms of knowledge acquisition, I don't think we lose anything by obtaining knowledge in this manner. We are also not disadvantaged by not witnessing an event to determine the moral worth of an action in the justice-centric framework. Provided accuracy and thoroughness are guaranteed, we feel we are in a position to make a moral judgment based upon an account given by others, as is practiced in court proceedings. However, when it comes to aesthetic matters, we are disadvantaged if we do not have direct access to the object of aesthetic experience. No matter how detailed, accurate, and thorough, a description of the object does not give rise to an aesthetic experience of the object (although it is possible that the description itself may be so poetic or exquisite that hearing or reading the narrative itself may give rise to an aesthetic experience). It is true that today's technology is increasingly helpful in overcoming this difficulty, but this underscores the critical importance of making the experience as accurate and direct as possible.

It is not only the individual singularity of the object that we need to attend to in aesthetic experience. We also need to attend to it in its entirety.[59] That is, there is no aspect of the object that we can ignore at least in our initial encounter. In his discussion of aesthetic education, Harry Broudy emphasizes the importance of learning to perceive the object in its entirety by contrasting it with scientific observation. In the latter, "we perceive carefully, but only those features of an object that are relevant to the understanding of theory."[60] For example, in a scientific experiment on the phenomenon of ignition, the size, shape, or color of the object used in ignition is not relevant. However, if such a phenomenon is to be perceived aesthetically, all of them become crucially relevant. As such, he claims that "the habit of apprehending the sensory properties of objects in their fullness and richness is the first step in aesthetic education."[61] Thus, a direct and attentive experience of the particularity of the other in its wholeness is the first requirement for both care ethics and aesthetic experience.

4 Open-Minded Responsiveness to the Other

Attentive experience of the particularity of the other and the situation alone, however, does not ensure a caring stance. I may experience my friend with all his specific endowments as a means to satisfying my own end, such as helping me with my project. Or I may have a dream for my child to become a super athlete and attend to her specific strengths and weaknesses to devise a training regimen accordingly. My "interested" mode of experiencing my friend and my child, however, does not constitute a caring interaction with them. The ethics of care requires that I experience others for who they are, apart from their value as a means to satisfy my own interest or expectation.

Similarly, one kind of interested experience of art is using it as a means of satisfying my own fantasy or giving the reassurance regarding the world familiar to me. Hepburn makes clear that the aesthetic failure of experiencing an object as a substitute for my own world or dream is also a moral failure that occurs in our interaction with other people:

> Fantasy falsifies through its overriding desire to minister to pre-existing, pre-formed wants and cravings: shirking the task of helping to re-form desire to a better-grasped reality. It smoothes out the recalcitrant individuality of things and people, making them more compliant to desire, whereas it is often these recalcitrances that prompt moral growth, elicit compassion and a turning away from egoistic ruthlessness, and compel us actually to believe in the full personhood of others.[62]

It is easier to experience art and other people as a means of extending my own world laden with my hope, expectation, and fantasy. Respecting the otherness of art, in contrast, according to Hepburn, is challenging because it demands accepting the "invitations to release one's hand from the banisters of familiar meanings and to leave familiar pathways of perception."[63] Grasping the work's individuality and originality, therefore, "takes much effort, sometimes courage."[64]

In a similar manner, our nature appreciation is often directed toward imaginative association that revolves around self. Hepburn's examples include a stalagmite in a limestone cave seen as the Virgin Mary and a cloud seen as a basket of laundry.[65] Though often amusing and entertaining, such imaginative experiences do not help us appreciate those objects with their own story regarding their origin, history, function, and so on. Of course, one could claim that our understanding of their own story is still imposing our all-too-human framework on nature, but it is hard to deny that activating imagination to feel the energy swirling inside the cumulous cloud is being truer to what it is than to fancy its resemblance to a basket full of laundry. Emily Brady similarly advocates "imagining well" when appreciating nature, which is contrasted with "shallow, naïve, and sentimental imaginative responses, which might impoverish rather than enrich appreciation."[66] Open-mindedness and receptivity work in tandem with the active engagement of imagination so that the flight of imagination takes place with other-regarding restraint and avoids satisfying one's own fancy and expectation.

One of the best-known characterizations of aesthetic experience is disinterestedness, as proposed by Kant. It has generated several interpretations and criticisms. Arnold Berleant is one of the vocal critics of this notion. Briefly put, Berleant's objection to disinterestedness and contemplation as characterizations of aesthetic experience is their implication of disengaged passivity. I shall take up his criticism in Section 5. Here, I should point out that he does acknowledge that there are many important insights involved in the notion of disinterestedness. One of the salient features of aesthetic experience captured by the notion of disinterestedness is "directed attention and open receptivity."[67] He agrees that disinterestedness "urges us to an open-minded acceptance in appreciation, a willingness to accept without prejudice sounds, colours, materials, images, and forms that may be strangely dissonant with our customary experience of the arts."[68] Although he prefers not to characterize this attitude as disinterested or contemplative, it is clear that Berleant regards open-mindedness and focused attention on the object as a necessary aspect of aesthetic experience.[69]

David E. Cooper also characterizes disinterestedness as opening oneself up to what the other can offer us. This can be an interpretation of Kant's claim that "every interest spoils the judgment of taste and takes from its impartiality."[70] As such, a disinterested experience is ethically grounded and "invokes such virtues as openness to and mindfulness of things, of allowing things to show up for what *they* are, independently of our preconceptions and prejudices"; it is based upon "respect for the integrity of things."[71] Such an open-minded stance and willingness to experience the other on its own terms, no matter how strange or even disagreeable, make the appreciation of art from the past or from an unfamiliar cultural tradition both possible and rewarding.

The importance, as well as challenge, of this ethically grounded nature of aesthetic experience is a theme shared by many thinkers from various disciplines. Let me give several examples. Iris Murdoch, for example, calls this notion "unselfing." Concerned with the fact that "our minds are continually active, fabricating an anxious, usually self-preoccupied, often falsifying *veil* which partially conceals the world," she claims that "anything which alters consciousness in the direction of unselfishness, objectivity and realism is to be connected with virtue."[72] Consequently, she regards the appreciation of good art as the reward for successful unselfing, which helps one "transcend selfish and obsessive limitations of personality and can enlarge the sensibility."[73] She uses the term "detachment" to refer to disinterestedness in the sense interpreted earlier and states that "this exercise of *detachment* is difficult and valuable whether the thing contemplated is a human being or the root of a tree or the vibration of a colour or a sound."[74]

Also, consider John Dewey's claim that "the moral function of art . . . is to remove prejudice, do away with the scales that keep the eye from seeing, tear away the veils due to wont and custom, perfect the power to perceive."[75] Specifically, "works of art are means by which we enter, through imagination and the emotions they evoke, into other forms of relationship and participation than our own."[76] In order for good art to take me out of my own familiar world, however, I must be able and willing to practice aesthetic engagement. The invitation of good art for me to enter *its* world, in the words of Joseph Kupfer, places "the burden of entering into an open-ended, indeterminate creative process" without any rules to follow.[77] I gain "responsive freedom," but it also comes with an "aesthetic responsibility."[78]

In her argument for the compatibility of beauty and justice, as well as beauty's role in assisting justice, Elaine Scarry discusses how the experience of beauty is facilitated by "radical decentering."[79] Although the impartiality required by justice is something care ethics questions, I believe that Scarry's description of this shift of one's orientation triggered by the experience of beauty is relevant to care ethics insofar as both require understanding of the other on *its*, not *our own*, terms:

Letting the ground rotate beneath us several inches, so that when we land, we find we are standing in a different relation to the world than we were a moment before. . . . We willingly cede our ground to the thing that stands before us.[80]

For Scarry, beauty can be experienced not only in works of art but also in ordinary objects and persons we meet in our daily life. Furthermore, "the way one's daily unmindfulness of the aliveness of others is temporarily interrupted in the presence of a beautiful person" may also take place "in the presence of a beautiful bird, mammal, fish, plant."[81]

The same theme appears as the most important teaching in Zen Buddhism. A Japanese Zen Buddhist priest, Dōgen (道元 1200–53), characterizes this ethical stance regarding the other as overcoming, forgetting, or transcending one's self and as a process necessary for enlightenment.[82] Specifically, in Zen discipline, the respectful engagement with the other, predominantly natural objects like a rock or a tree and also artifacts such as a broom, requires me to experience its raw individuality or Buddha nature, without applying the usual categorizations and classifications of normal experience. I make myself "slender" and enter into the object and become one with it, experiencing its "thusness" or "suchness."[83] The favored vehicle for Zen discipline is artistic practice that aims not so much at acquiring skills, but rather at becoming a person whose mode of being in the world is other-regarding and ethically grounded. Commenting on Japanese artistic training, Robert Carter points out that "ethics is primarily taught through the various arts, and is not learned as an abstract theory, or as a series of rules to remember."[84]

Heavily influenced by Zen Buddhism, Yanagi advocates cultivating one's capacity of "seeing" or "intuition" by exercising "constraints and constrictions" by "rein(ing) in our tongue."[85] He recommends: "you should first adopt an accepting attitude" and not to "push yourself to the forefront but lend an ear to what the object has to say."[86] As Yanagi himself characterizes this mode of open-minded acceptance of the object of aesthetic experience as "self-education," it is clear from other writers' uniform exhortation of minimizing self in listening to the other on its own terms that the aesthetic stance taken is also a moral stance.[87] We don't bring our world and impose it on the other but we invite the other bring its world to us. Care ethics requires me to listen to the other and to try to understand her experience and situation from her perspective.

It is true that I may not completely succeed in understanding the other on its own terms. But this limitation neither invalidates the effort needed nor does it justify total abandonment of this effort. Marcia Eaton points out that "we must always be aware that there are limits to how much one does or can know about another's interests and intentions," but, she continues, "we can . . . come to know something of the Chinese or African or medieval or Baroque worldviews. With *work*."[88] Both aesthetics and ethics demand work in cultivating this unselfed and decentered stance.

Thus, whether it is called unselfing, radical decentering, respecting the other, appreciating the other on its own terms, or transcending one's own horizon, these thinkers together highlight the ethical dimension of aesthetic experience. It is paramount for both care ethics and aesthetic experience that one experiences the other with an attitude of open-minded acceptance and appreciation without imposing on it any preconceived ideas or expectations. I suspend the world familiar to me and try to transcend my own horizon. I am willing to meet the other, whether a work of art, a natural or manufactured object, a creature, or another human being, on its own terms, rather than making them conform to my own framework. I approach the other as "You" rather than as "It" and render myself receptive to what the other offers.

5 Active Dimension of Care Ethics and Aesthetic Experience

However, this receptivity presupposed in both care ethics and aesthetic experience does not mean passivity on the part of the one-caring and the agent of aesthetic experience. It is a condition underlying the caring attitude that makes a reciprocal and collaborative relationship with the other possible. With attention to the particularity of the other and open-minded stance, my care relationship with him activates the imagination. Particularly when determining the best course of action motivated by my care for him, I need to imagine what the world and the current situation would feel like if I were him.

Providing care for a person requires empathy by putting myself in his shoes and imagining what *his*, not *my*, experience may be in this situation so that I can determine what best serves his need. I have to be sensitive to the particular circumstance and his individuality so that I can be nimble in deciding how I care for him. Recall Peter Goldie's observation that an ethically virtuous act requires a delicacy of discrimination when helping an independently minded but financially strapped person discussed in Section 1. What would be best for me if I were him may not be what suits him best. Milton Mayeroff describes this process as follows:

> To care for another person, I must be able to understand him and his world as if I were inside it. I must be able to see, as it were, with his eyes what his world is like to him and how he sees himself. Instead of merely looking at him in a detached way from outside, as if he were a specimen, I must be able to be *with* him in his world, "going" into his world in order to sense from "inside" what life is like for him, what he is striving to be, and what he requires to grow.[89]

The importance of activating imagination in this way is illustrated by two examples. The first case is when caring includes providing food, shelter, and clothing to the other. What *I* would like if *I* were the recipient of such aid should not be assumed as applicable to others if I am a caregiver serving their needs. Cultural, religious, economic, and other factors such as age, gender, and health status, as well as the recipient's particular character should lead me to understand what would be most helpful for the person in this circumstance. Otherwise, my care act is in danger of being patronizing or even oppressive. As Daniel Engster points out, "since different individuals and groups manifest their needs for food, clothing, and shelter differently, an important virtue of caring . . . is meeting these needs according to the particular circumstances and tastes of individuals."[90] This becomes an issue when well-meaning care activities are provided by various organizations to parts of the world that are in dire need of assistance due to poverty, disease, natural disaster, displacement, and the like. The "help" offered by those organizations with good intentions may backfire because of the insensitivity toward the recipients' religious commitments or cultural practices.

Another example that reveals the importance of imagination is medical practice. As discussed before, many practitioners urge medical practice to be imbued with an affective and empathetic relationship with the patients without losing sight of the purely scientific methodology of diagnosing and dispensing treatment. In advocating care in addition to cure, Neil Pembroke, for example, argues for the importance of "this process in which one imaginatively enters the inner world of the other."[91] He cites Martin Buber's characterization of "encounter" or "meeting" with the other person as You as "making the other present" by "imagining the real."[92] This imaginative projection requires more rigorous exercise than if I were to imagine myself in the patient's shoes. It must involve an empathetic experience of immersion into the patient's inner life with all his anxiety, pain, suffering, insecurity, and so on. This is a departure from the mainstream scientific mode of practicing medicine whereby "'deempathization' is required if physicians are to make sound, scientifically based clinical assessments."[93]

In this respect, it is noteworthy that care ethics is primarily concerned with the first-person experience of engaging in a caring action rather than a third-party onlooker who judges the moral worth of an action performed by others. The latter concern is not excluded, but the first-person account is the focus of care ethics, as stated by Noddings: "Even though we sometimes judge caring from the outside as third-persons, it is easy to see that the essential elements of caring are located in the relation between the one-caring and the cared-for."[94] Furthermore, when comparing care ethics to aesthetics, she refers to artists' accounts of their creative acts, such as those by Mozart and Joan Miró.[95] Their first-person accounts of engaging with the materials, according to her, are often dismissed in the scientific, objectifying discourse that privileges "dominating insistency on objective evaluation" because "we have no way of measuring it."[96] The act of caring is similarly best analyzed from inside, so to speak; hence her insistence that rational justification and rule-governedness are not appropriate for care ethics, and "at times we must suspend it in favor of subjective thinking and reflection, allowing time and space for *seeing* and *feeling*."[97]

This focus on the first-person experience has an equivalence in aesthetics. It takes the form of a challenge to the preponderant orientation of Western aesthetics that is centered on a spectator or an onlooker who forms a judgment. Even with its purported aim of shifting aesthetics from the object-centered orientation to the experience of engaging in aesthetics-related activity, as I indicated in Section 1, the virtue theory of aesthetics is ultimately a judgment-seeking discourse rather than an attempt to understand the matter "from the inside" of the experiencing agent. Friedrich Nietzsche's observation is apropos here. According to him, Western aesthetics "formulated the experiences of what is beautiful, from the point of view of the *receivers* in art," and takes Kant as a representative of this stance that "considered art and the beautiful purely from that of the 'spectator'" who considers himself as someone "placed before the great visual and acoustic spectacle that is life."[98] Although Nietzsche leads this observation as a preparation for his very specific vision of an Übermensch as the artistic creator of his life, he is correct in pointing out that the aesthetics from the perspective of the creator, whether of art or aesthetic experience, has been largely neglected.

More recently, in his proposal for "a new aesthetics" that takes atmosphere as the fundamental concept, Gernot Böhme observes that "the old aesthetics is essentially a judgmental aesthetics, that is, it is concerned not so much with experience, especially sensuous experience . . . as with judgments, discussion, conversation."[99] I suspect that this judgment-oriented aesthetics is a legacy of a long-held modernist project to give some credence and respectability to aesthetics by adhering to the favored scientific model that gives primacy to objectivity. The phenomenological account of aesthetic experience has been neglected in general because it is considered too subjective to allow objectivity and universal applicability.

Experience that occupies a central place in aesthetics has a dynamic content. In the last section, I argued that open-mindedness and listening to the objects' voice are necessary for an aesthetic experience. However, such a stance does not imply that we become a passive receptacle of what the object offers to us. We are not a sitting duck, so to speak, simply "receiving" what the object provides. When describing "undergoing" that, together with "doing," facilitates aesthetic experience, John Dewey states that "it involves surrender." But, he continues, "adequate *yielding of the self* is possibly [sic] only through a controlled activity that may well be intense."[100] Thus, according to him, the receptivity that is necessary for a successful aesthetic experience is not "passivity" that "merely takes in what is there in finished form"; instead, "this taking in involves activities that are comparable to those of the creator." In short, it is "a process consisting of a series of responsive acts that accumulate toward objective fulfilment."[101] These responsive acts stimulate "doing" that activates a discriminating and sharp sensibility, emotional investment, and the exercise of imagination.

When activating the imagination that is other-centered rather than self-centered, in both acting for care and developing an aesthetic experience, I need to tailor my action according to the particularity of the object of my attention and the specific situation surrounding it. One of the reasons why care ethics emphasizes attentiveness to the specifics while de-emphasizing rule-governed decision-making is that the content of caring act varies from person to person, situation to situation. I cannot be considered to act from care if I impose what I think should be the case regardless of what is best for the particular person in a particular circumstance. As a teacher, for example, teaching a student with care requires sometimes holding her hand and gently guiding her, while some other times or with a different student the best course of action is to guide her with tough love by demanding a better performance.

This ability to be nimble and flexible so that our action regarding the other can be person- and situation-specific also underlies a successful aesthetic experience. As Paul Ziff's notion of aspection indicates, a successful aesthetic experience requires experiencing a work of art that best brings out what it has to offer.[102] Individuated action is needed based upon the kind of art object we are dealing with. For example, Ziff illustrates that the most appropriate way of experiencing Venetian paintings is to focus on balanced masses while we should attend to contours in Florentine paintings. Sometimes aspection requires engaging one's body differently in a literal sense, such as moving away from a painting to take in a whole view while with some others we should go up close to see the minute details of the brush stroke. Doing so not only enriches the nature of aesthetic experience but also indicates the other-regarding, respectful attitude on our part. This individually tailored active engagement required for appreciating art is perhaps becoming more prominent with various contemporary art projects. They often involve literal participation, as in participatory art, olfactory art, and environmental art. However, a contrast between more traditional art that does not require the appreciator to literally engage in actions and those recent projects that do does not indicate any qualitative difference between them. The literal physical engagement required in those contemporary art projects simply makes active involvement required in appreciating art more explicit. With either case, we experience the work of art with care.

By far the most forceful account of the active nature of aesthetic experience is given by Arnold Berleant in his notion of aesthetic engagement. For him, aesthetic experience is not contemplation or taking in what the object of contemplation offers. This is why he objects to the characterization of aesthetic experience widely accepted since the eighteenth century as being disinterested, despite agreeing that open-mindedness is an important aspect of aesthetic experience. Rather than being only receptive, aesthetic experience "is equally active, requiring the contribution of the appreciator of art or nature in discerning qualities, order, and structure and in adding the resonance of meanings to that experience."[103] Aesthetic experience is instead "performative" and "participatory" on the part of the experiencing agent who co-creates an aesthetic experience by collaborating with the object by mobilizing focused attention, sensibility, open-mindedness, imagination, and creativity. According to him, "a performative element is present in all art and aesthetic appreciation, for the appreciator who is actively engaged is, by that fact, 'performing' the work by attentively viewing a painting or reading a novel."[104] In short, aesthetic appreciation is "a creative act, one that takes developed skill and thoughtful determination, very much the abilities that the artist employs in her work."[105] An aesthetic experience generated in this way can be characterized as subjective in the sense the experiencing subject's thorough involvement is needed, but it is not subjective in the sense of the experience being wholly personal and idiosyncratic, which makes intersubjective sharing and communication impossible. The attention is fully focused on the object in its particularity and wholeness, and we mobilize relevant knowledge and associations to try to understand and appreciate it on its own terms, instead of using it as a trigger for our own fancy or imaginative flight that is not anchored in the specific quality of the objects. Imagination required for aesthetic experience needs to be disciplined in the sense of being rooted in what the object is; it is object driven.

I have previously discussed Emily Brady's notion of imagining well, in contrast to sentimental imagination that uses the object simply as one's own fancy or self-wallowing. When one assumes the standpoint of an impartial spectator, one practices self-regulation and works to "strike a balance between the character of the aesthetic perceiver and the character of the aesthetic object."[106] Sympathetic imagination involved in the aesthetic appreciation of a beach pebble interweaves the image of waves repeatedly washing it on the beach, resulting in a remarkably smooth surface. This "imagining well" is contrasted with going down one's memory lane associated with the event that unfolded the last time one walked on the beach picking up pebbles with a close friend.[107] Thus, aesthetic experience requires other-centered imagination activated with our engagement with the other, just as in the case of ethical relationship with other persons motivated by care.

What becomes clear from the discussion so far is the temporal dimension of care ethics and aesthetic experience. The care relationship needs to be nurtured and developed through the interaction of the parties involved, even if the roles of carer and the cared for are immediately given, as in a parent and a child or a teacher and a student. As such, it takes time. Christopher Groves reminds us further that it can stretch into futurity as we try to care for the current environment as a practice for intergenerational justice. Similarly, aesthetic experience takes time; it is not a knee-jerk reaction. We may be struck by the beauty of an object but that marks a starting point of the development of an aesthetic experience that goes through various stages that I have outlined in this chapter. Experience by its own nature unfolds in time through our interaction with the world, as Dewey reminds us.[108] In this regard, the often-held distinction between plastic or spatial arts and temporal arts seems irrelevant if we understand aesthetics as an experience, not as an object. Experiencing a painting, a sculpture, architecture, or a garden, despite the fact that they themselves are stationary physical objects, takes time, and its temporal sequence is often critical to the aesthetic experience of them. For example, the way in which we enter an architectural space or a garden contributes to our sequential experience of negotiating between the outer and inner spaces. The legibility of the composition of a painting can be enhanced or compromised if we direct our attention from left to right, or from afar to close-up. Although there may be an interest in the ontology of an object of aesthetic experience, I believe that the core of aesthetics resides in our experience as a first-person account, and it is inseparable from the temporal dimension.

*   *   *

This chapter was devoted to laying out the structural similarities between care ethics and aesthetic experience. These commonalities are not just interesting coincidences. Rather, there is a deep connection as both ultimately address how best to negotiate our interactions with other people and objects around us. They characterize a good, rich, and fulfilling life that results from cultivating and practicing successful relationship with the other, whether humans, nature, or artifacts. The following statement by Noddings sums up the main thesis of this chapter: "the receptivity characteristic of aesthetic engagement is very like the receptivity of caring. Consciousness assumes a similar mode of being—one that attempts to grasp or to receive a reality rather than to impose it."[109] Both care ethics and aesthetic experience remind us that our existence is supported by relationships with others, sometimes caring for them and other times being cared for. The reward of such a way of living offers a deep satisfaction, both ethical and aesthetic. Care ethics and aesthetic experience thus both define our mode of existence as relationality and interdependence. This shared ontology has further ethical and aesthetic consequences, and they will be the subject matter of the next chapter.

2

Relationality

Aesthetic and Ethical Consequences

As presented in the last chapter, care ethics starts with recognizing and embracing the interdependence and relationality of self and other-than-self. This view of the human mode of existence is offered as an alternative to the autonomy and independence advocated by justice-centric ethics and the liberalist view of human existence. As delineated in the last chapter, aesthetic experience is also facilitated by the relationality and collaboration of the experiencing agent and the object of aesthetic appreciation. This chapter explores further the relationality and interdependence as a faithful account of our authentic mode of existence. At the same time, I shall also argue that a successful and satisfying care relationship with the other, whether human beings, nature, art, or artifacts, and whether in an ethical or aesthetic context, presupposes certain conditions, including the worthiness of the other to merit the care given, as well as self-care of those who do the caring.

1 Relationality as Mode of Existence

As we have seen in the last chapter, care ethics emphasizes the relationality of human existence over autonomy, independence, and self-sufficiency that are favored by justice ethics and the Western liberalist tradition. According to Noddings, "taking *relation* as ontologically basic . . . means that we recognize human encounter and affective response as a basic fact of human experience."[1] Relationality, rather than independent autonomy, defines the mode of human existence, according to her: "It is not just that *I* as a performed continuous individual enter *into* relationships; rather, the *I* of which we speak so easily is itself a relational entity. I really am defined by the set of relations into which my physical self has been thrown."[2] My identity is dependent upon the relationships I have with others, whether they are my family, friends, colleagues, or even nonhuman creatures and material objects around me, and such relationality does not compromise autonomy. As Milton Mayeroff puts it:

> autonomy does not mean being detached and without strong ties; that would imply that attachments and strong ties necessarily tie me down and enslave me. Again, autonomy does not mean being self-enclosed and "free as a bird." On the contrary, I am autonomous because of my devotion to others and my dependence on them, when dependence is the *kind* that liberates both me and my others.[3]

While not specifically implying care in the sense used in care ethics but instead referring to "a purely ontological and existential way," Heidegger's notion of "care" as a mode of Da-sein suggests relationality as its mode of being-in-the-world.[4] We are thrown into this world, find ourselves in the present predicament (being-in-the-world), and project ourselves into the future (being-ahead-of-itself). Throughout this process, we are entangled with the world (being-together-with) through care and concern. We are not alone; we cannot but engage with the world. "Being-ahead-of-itself does not mean anything like an isolated tendency in a worldless 'subject,' but characterizes being-in-the-world. But to being-in-the-world belongs the fact it is entrusted to itself, that it is always already thrown *into a world*."[5] Care is "a primordial structural totality" or "an existential *a priori*" that defines our mode of being in the world prior to any specific action or position.[6] So, "when we determine something objectively present by merely looking at it, this has the character of care just as much as a 'political action,' or resting and having a good time." For Heidegger, therefore, although the term "care" is used, it characterizes the basic human condition of being-in-the-world and negotiating with the world, rather than a certain attitude or ethical commitment. As such, his notion of care differs from those held by the advocates of care ethics insofar as it is more ontological and existential. However, his characterization of the mode of being of Da-sein as care is essentially a relational account of existence, a foundation of humanity shared by the ethics of care.

Similarly, advocates of care ethics maintain that interdependence and relationality should define the human mode of existence, although their discussion is based on concrete experiences of living in the world compared to a more abstract ontology offered by Heidegger. After all, in order for me to be able to exercise freedom, autonomy, and independence, I had to be nurtured in the first place by those who care for me, most typically, though not exclusively, represented by the mother. Furthermore, in order for me to achieve important goals, work or otherwise, the accomplishment is made possible not only with help from my mentors and colleagues but also by those who support me behind the scene, such as a secretary, an assistant, and even a janitor who cleans the office space overnight so that I can work there the next day.[7] Citing Annette Baier, Daniel Engster reminds us that "moral theories such as liberalism . . . that do not give proper moral recognition to caring display a form of bad faith, since caring forms the necessary ground of all moral practices and sustains these practices across generations."[8] Dependency is most recognized when one needs to be cared for, such as in sickness and in old age. However, even without such life circumstances, we all participate in a web of dependency relationship. In short, Engster concludes out that "human life is deeply implicated in relations of dependency and caring."[9]

This interwoven and interdependent nature of our existence characterizes not only interpersonal relationships but also our relationships with the material world. As Christopher Groves reminds us, "subject and object are interdependent: the subject is 'held together' by the object; the subject tends to and protects—cares for—the object."[10] It will be a form of bad faith to think of our existence as a monad-like autonomous, atomistic, independent entity divorced from the world. We are sustained by, and in turn sustain, others, whether other humans, natural world, or material world.

The move from a worldview and practice premised on discrete entities to that which consists of relationality between various players and participants is advocated by some noted contemporary designers. For example, Ezio Manzini and Carla Cipolla suggest reconfiguring the design profession heretofore defined as designing objects for clients/users into "designing series that are deeply rooted in relational qualities."[11] In the standard design model, "[agents] and [clients] are performing predefined roles" so that any possible interpersonal relationship that may develop between them is adventitious to the transaction mediated by the proposed design.[12] The transaction between the agent and the client is thus rather mechanical, following a script; there is no genuine encounter between them. Interestingly, they invoke Buber's I-It relationship to characterize this standard design model.

In contrast, Manzini and Cipolla see a potential of I-You relationship facilitated by a circular interaction design where "benefits are reciprocally produced and shared by the participants, who collaborate in a way that favor the perception of each other as a 'Thou'—not as an 'It'—in their interpersonal encounters."[13] Examples given are walking bus and living room restaurant. Instead of a school bus which transports students, walking bus offers a service to chaperone students by walking together local streets, thereby encouraging conversations between the chaperone and students, as well as with passersby and others out on the local streets. Instead of dining at a restaurant where chefs, waitstaff, and eating guests each play an assigned role and the interactions are prescribed and predictable, dining as guests at somebody's house would render people's interactions more intimate, spontaneous, and improvisational. The guest may help set and clear the table, for example.

These "relational services" promote "an approach that focuses more on 'actions' and 'relations' than on 'things.'"[14] They encourage collaborating with the other, whether the service provider or the client, by being fully present to the other's presence, improvising one's action as the situation and relationship unfold. As endemic to I-You relationship, there is no rule or script that dictates one's act, and it requires each party's full and active participation.

As relational services are qualitatively oriented to favor "I-Thou" encounters, these services are those that more radically present a limitation to a direct design intervention in interhuman interactions. "I-Thou" relational encounters happen in present time; they are immediate, i.e., this specific interpersonal interaction needs to be favored by a solution that does not impose the interposition of any predefined procedure between participants. Each participant, for the others—and for the designer himself—needs to be perceived as a presence, not as an object.[15]

Unlike the standard design practice in which the client/user is a receiver of the service provided, in relational services they are coproducers of the experience.

I submit that, while not using the term, Buber's I-You relationship characterizes the care relationship and interdependence. He declares that "without It a human being cannot live. But whoever lives only with that is not human."[16] Here again the practice of medicine illustrates this point. On the one hand, medicine as a branch of science by necessity objectifies a patient in terms of his condition and applies various rules and principles in figuring out the best course of treatment. This is what conventional medical training largely consists of. To achieve the goal of finding the cure and best treatment, a patient is abstracted into a sum total of symptoms and the medical professionals' approach has to be objective and rational with an attitude of detachment. The practitioners describe this conventional mode as follows: "There is little space for personal emotion or personalised compassion within either instrumental or value rationality. . . . the principles of value rationality rule out embodied and emotional responses at the level of individuals. . . . The emphasis is on the quantifiable rather than the experiential."[17] In fact, medical professionals admit that it is much more comfortable to regard the patient as an It, a patient with this disease, than as a You, a person with her anxiety, fright, as well as dignity, because the world of It can be made to be well ordered. An acquaintance of mine who is an ER doctor admitted that it is easier to practice medicine if he distances himself from the patient by thinking, "it's not me who is in pain and suffering." Furthermore, the emphasis of the whole enterprise is on the future outcome, that is, a successful treatment of the illness resulting in the restoration of the patient's health and the interaction with the patient is relegated to the expectation of the future outcome, characterized by one professional as "disease-centered" rather than person-centered.[18]

However, this kind of I-It relationship is not sufficient in the doctor-patient relationship. Those who advocate I-You relationship by adopting what they call the "philosophy of the present tend to view their lives as *relational and ongoing* rather than focusing on future objectives."[19] Indeed, such advocates cite feminist ethicists' challenge by pointing out that "women's voices have been stifled in the public sphere, and qualities deemed suitable for professional life, such as detachment and objectivity, are generally those traditionally associated with a 'masculine' standpoint."[20] They summarize the complementarity of both approaches in medicine thus: "biomedical preoccupations with future outcomes—for example, the restoration of health— would be accompanied by a greater recognition that compassionate care requires a focus on the dignity and well-being of people in the present."[21] Bringing us back to aesthetics, Fisher and Freshwater cite Roslyn Wallach Bologh's notion of "aesthetic rationality" that is "a mainly unacknowledged female form of rationality (in the sense that it is associated with domestic and communal relations), which is in the broadest sense appreciative of and responsive to beauty."[22]

2 Relational Aesthetics

The intimate relationship with the other is also required in an aesthetic experience, whether of a work of art, nature, artifact, or other people. What is crucial in the relationship between the experiencing agent and the experienced object is that the relationality between them trumps the autonomous, independent existence of each party. That is, the aesthetic experience is possible when the separation between the subject and the object is overcome by "doing" and "undergoing" in the Deweyan sense, as well as by the activity of engagement proposed by Arnold Berleant. The aesthetic experience is neither subject based (in the sense of being generated by the subject with no anchoring in the object) nor object driven (in the sense of the object providing all the qualities for appreciation). It emerges from the interaction between the two.

If care ethics advocated by Noddings can be characterized as "a relational ethics," which she suggests as a preferred alternative to "a feminine approach,"[23] it is noteworthy that the term "relational aesthetics" was proposed by Nicolas Bourriaud primarily to account for the relatively new forms of art that makes people's everyday life and social interactions art projects, such as Rirkrit Tiravanija's and Liam Gillick's social and participatory art.[24] Bourriaud created this term to account for their art projects that create a setup where the visitors freely engage in actions and conversations, whether they be cooking and eating, sleeping, or reading and writing on a table. He defines relational art as "a set of artistic practices which take as their theoretical and practical point of departure the whole of human relations and their social context, rather than an independent and private space."[25] There is no finished product, and the so-called art is open-ended and improvisationary, consisting of the relationship that is spontaneously generated by participants' interactions with each other and the environment.

However, it should be noted that such openness and relationality characterize experience of any art. Citing Umberto Eco, Claire Bishop points out that "every work of art is potentially 'open,' since it may produce an unlimited range of possible readings; it is simply the achievement of contemporary art, music, and literature to have foregrounded this fact."[26] In fact, Bourriaud himself does admit that art-making has always been relational, first between humans and deity, then between humans and objects, and, most recently, between humans.[27] He characterizes this relationality as "transitivity," "encounter," and "dialogue" by pointing out that "at the outset of this, negotiations have to be undertaken, and the Other presupposed . . . . Any artwork might thus be defined as a relational object."[28] In short, "each particular artwork is a proposal to live in a shared world."

While Bourriaud may be credited for coining the term "relational aesthetics," the idea is by no means new, nor the examples illustrative of this idea.[29] Furthermore, this model applies not only to our relationship with art but also with nature. For example, Ronald Hepburn characterizes our aesthetic appreciation of nature as the experience thus: "I am both actor and spectator, ingredient in the landscape and lingering upon the sensations of being thus ingredient, rejoicing in their multifariousness, playing actively with nature, and letting nature, as it were, lay with me and my sense of myself."[30] In short, aesthetic experience of nature is co-created by us and nature.

By far the most comprehensive view of relationality that applies to aesthetic experience of any object, whether art, nature, environment, objects, or social interaction, is Arnold Berleant's notion of aesthetic engagement, sometimes presented as participatory aesthetics. Without specifically calling it such, aesthetic engagement *is* relational aesthetics. His notion of aesthetic engagement attempts to overcome one of the dominant frameworks governing the Western philosophical tradition: the dichotomy and separation between a subject and an object. The reach of this dualistic framework, no doubt paralleling other dichotomies such as mind and body, humans and nature, and male and female, has been deep and extensive, including in aesthetics. The persistent paradigm of aesthetics is accordingly that there is an object distinguishable and separable from an experiencing agent and that the subject takes in whatever is provided by the object. However, in aesthetic engagement, "there is no separation between components but a continuous exchange in which they act on each other."[31] In other words, "humans' relation to things is not a relation between discrete and self-sufficient entities. On the contrary, just as people impose themselves on things, so, too, do things exercise an influence on people."[32] Aesthetic experience is a dynamic process of negotiation and collaboration between an open-minded I and a You that invites me to enter its world and engage in a dialogue with ample reward for my willingness to dance together. Ultimately, "the world in which humans participate cannot be entirely separated from the human presence. There is rather a reciprocal relation between people and the things and conditions with which we live. And when environment involves human interests, it must necessarily be understood in relation to humans and not as an array of independent objects."[33]

Although this relationality between the experiencing agent and the object facilitated by aesthetic engagement is meant to apply to all aesthetic experiences, it may be best illustrated by the aesthetic experience of things that lack the usual sense of clearly defined or framed object-hood. Environment is one such example. Berleant specifically refers to "environment" instead of "the environment" because "to speak of 'the' environment turns environment into an object separate from the perceiver."[34] Of course environment consists of discrete objects such as a landscape, built structures, objects, and human activities within, but objectifying them as constituents of "the" environment will mislead us into thinking that we as the experiencing agent are somehow separate from it. The fact is that we are part of our environment interacting with other constituents and, more importantly, in having an aesthetic experience we are very much part of the creative force.

In this regard, the notion of atmosphere is gaining more attention today. Though atmosphere is constituted by identifiable items, such as a spatial environment and its ingredients, including nonmaterial factors like sound, light, smell, and temperature, as well as human interactions, an atmosphere *itself* lacks object-hood. Atmosphere is sensed and felt by an experiencing agent who contributes to its formation by unifying various ingredients into a harmonious whole. As such, atmosphere effectively illustrates relational aesthetics by emphasizing the interdependence of all the elements and parties involved. Advocating atmosphere as the fundamental aesthetic concept, Gernot Böhme claims,

atmospheres are neither something objective, that is qualities possessed by things, and yet they are something thinglike, belonging to the thing in that things articulate their presence through qualities. . . . Nor are atmospheres something subjective . . . and yet they are subjectlike, belong to subjects in that they are sensed in bodily presence by human beings and this sensing is at the same time a bodily state of being of subjects in space.[35]

What is particularly noteworthy is that Böhme compares atmosphere, "the prototypical 'between'- phenomenon," to the Japanese notion of inbetween, "*aidagara.*"[36] Indeed, the Japanese worldview, particularly reflecting Buddhism, characterizes reality as consisting of relationships rather than discrete individual beings and objects. Robert Carter characterizes the Japanese worldview as a "declaration of interdependence," that is, "a recognition that we are not only inextricably intertwined with others but with the entire cosmos."[37]

The best illustration reflective of this worldview is the Japanese term for human beings, *ningen* 人間. The first character designates "human" and the second one "between," indicating that an individual is defined by the relationship she holds with others. The Japanese ontology, therefore, does not subscribe to the Western dichotomy of the subject and the object; instead, its foundation is relationality. Tetsurō Watsuji (和辻哲郎 1889–1960), one of the most influential Japanese thinkers of the twentieth century, refers to human existence as "betweenness" (*aidagara* 間柄 as referenced by Böhme), leading one commentator to remark that the precise translation of *ningen* should be "human being in betweenness."[38] I find this primacy of relationality over individual entities to be a recurrent theme in many aspects of the Japanese cultural tradition, whether it regards humans and nature, interpersonal relationship, humans and objects of aesthetic appreciation, or artists and the materials or subject matters of their creation. For example, Sōetsu Yanagi claims that "considered as a form of activity, the seeing eye and the seen object are one, not two. One is embedded in the other."[39]

That relationality and interdependence characterize the foundation of many East Asian traditions is pointed out by Lorenzo Marinucci. He argues that the primacy of relationship, interdependence, overcoming of object-subject dichotomy is long-held and well-entrenched among East Asian traditions by citing Daoist texts and many Japanese terms that include the character for *ki*, meaning air or atmosphere. He worries, however, whether the notion of atmosphere, mood, or air as the primary reality will be dismissed as "exoticism" or "anthropological curiosity."[40] Marinucci's own response to this possible dismissal is to point out that a similar worldview exists in the Renaissance notion of humor theory.

Let me offer another example from the Western tradition: the organicist theory regarding human health advocated by Paracelsus (1493–1541). His writings on medicine today may be characterized as holistic. He recommends the physicians to attend carefully not only to the patient's ailment but also to the region of his residence (with specific soil, climate, food, customs, and the like), his "innate nature—harsh, crude, hard, gentle, mild, virtuous, friendly, tender," astronomical condition, and the time of the year.[41] Essentially, the physician has to be a "cosmographer and geographer" as well as knowledgeable in philosophy, physics, alchemy, astronomy, mineralogy, and herbology, because what is outside of human body, namely nature and environment, and "inner firmament" are inseparable and mutually reflective of each other.[42]

Martin Buber develops a similar view in his discussion of "interhuman."[43] By advocating the I-You relationship as the authentic mode of human existence, Buber is essentially locating the locus of one's being in what he variously characterizes as the meeting, contact, encounter, conversation, dialogue, or partnership one experiences with the other. In an almost uncanny resemblance to the Japanese notion of human betweenness, Buber characterizes conversation as an event "whose meaning is to be found neither in one of the two partners, nor in both together, but only in their dialogue itself, in this 'between' which they live together."[44] Dialogue is located in the inbetween, rather than two monologues combined. I believe the following statement by Buber summarizes the authentic mode of human living in the world underlying Berleant's aesthetic engagement, Böhme's new aesthetics, and the Japanese worldview: "Man exists anthropologically not in his isolation but in the completeness of the relation between man and man; what humanity is can be properly grasped only in vital reciprocity."[45]

One's self is not a monad-like isolated center of the world but exists and is defined only in its interaction with others. The relationality in aesthetic experience thus has an existential dimension, bringing us back to the comparison of care ethics and aesthetic experience. Both prioritize relationality between self and others over their independent, autonomous existence and identity. The priority placed on relationality over discrete existence of the subject and object has further consequences. Berleant's notion of aesthetic engagement challenges another time-honored tradition of Western aesthetics: disinterestedness. I have given one interpretation of disinterestedness that is helpful in characterizing the open-minded attitude required for aesthetic experience. Here, however, disinterestedness is interpreted as a hindrance to the proper understanding of aesthetic experience.

The notion of disinterestedness emerged in the eighteenth century with Shaftesbury and was given a prominent role in Kant's aesthetic theory. Shaftesbury was particularly concerned with separating a personal interest in the functional or economic value of an object from its aesthetic value. For example, the beauty of a tree is independent of the shade and fruits I enjoy, the enjoyment of a landscape separate from my pride of owning the land, and the majesty of the ocean is appreciated apart from my prideful anticipation of commanding it.[46]

This experience of appreciating something for its own sake, irrespective of my personal, vested interest, receives a thorough treatment by Kant. He defines the judgment of taste as the satisfaction we take in the "mere representation of the object . . . however indifferent I may be as regards the existence of the object of this representation."[47] He calls such satisfaction "disinterested" and distinguishes it from "the pleasant" and "the good."[48] The ideal mode for experiencing an object aesthetically is a spectator who is detached from the reality of the object, despite the fact that its existence is actually enmeshed in the web of material relations with other objects, as well as social relations due to our expectation, hopes, and associations. The object is bracketed from the world of existence and apprehended as a pure form.

Despite crediting disinterestedness by calling attention to open receptivity as I discussed previously, Berleant is critical of this notion for mischaracterizing aesthetic experience as distanced by removing practical interest, concerns, and affairs and requiring "separating and isolating the art object or excluding our purposes and goals."[49] Furthermore, the disinterested mode of experiencing the object is modeled after a cognitive approach that is based upon the dualistic structure of the perceiver and the perceived, regarding "the object of aesthetic perception as separate and independent."[50] However, the aesthetic experience is not a passive reception of what the object offers us, nor is it a totally subjective apprehension based upon one's self.

> Both perceiver and object are important but are incomplete in themselves. Neither is a discrete element in the aesthetic field but both combine in mutually creative and dependent ways: no aesthetic perceiver without a perceptual object; no perceptual object without a perceiver who activates it in experience.[51]

Aesthetic experience is thus possible only with relationality and interdependence.

Josephine Donovan also criticizes the Kantian disinterestedness for lacking any emotional involvement or investment: "Kant's aesthetics is . . . an impassive, impartial, formal judgment stripped of all emotional or qualitative aspects."[52] This is illustrated by the privileged mode of landscape appreciation according to the aesthetics of disinterestedness: "[W]hen we step back to get a better view we create not only a physical distance but a corresponding psychic aloofness. The landscape perspective gives rise to (or is symptomatic of) a sense of detachment and spectatorship, for we become disengaged observers of rather than participants in the reality depicted."[53]

This emphasis on engagement rather than disengagement and distancing as a foundation of aesthetic experience brings us back to care ethics that focuses on the first-person account of intimate relationship between the carer and the cared for. Detachment that may be necessary for justice ethics is not suitable for care ethics, as explained by Gilligan:

> Seen as responsive, the self is by definition connected to others, responding to perceptions, interpreting events, and governed by the organizing tendencies of human interaction and human language. Within this framework, detachment, whether from self or from others, is morally problematic, since it breeds moral blindness or indifference—a failure to discern or respond to need.[54]

We can thus conclude that both care ethics and our aesthetic life emerge from the relationality and interdependence of our existence, and that enhancing this mode of existence through our ethical and aesthetic interaction with others leads to a good life.

3 Unsuccessful Relationality

The preceding characterizations of relationality involved in the care relationship and aesthetic experience suggest that both parties to the relationship need to participate in making it successful. I have argued that in both endeavors, as the one who cares and the one engaged in aesthetic experience, I am an active agent and I need to meet the various demands placed on me. Namely, I attend to the other's particularity in its wholeness, open myself to be receptive and respectful to the other's reality, actively interact with the other by marshaling utmost sensibility, sensitivity, and imagination, and perform a certain action or create an experience. The discussion so far, however, has been one-sided in the sense that it focused on what I am supposed to do as the one who cares and the one who enjoys an aesthetic experience, without examining the demands placed on the object of care or aesthetic experience.

However, if the care relationship and the aesthetic experience are sustained by relationality, as I argued in the last section, both parties to the relationship need to contribute to make it a success. It takes two to tango, and no matter how much effort one party makes, without the cooperation and collaboration by the other party, the relationship fails. With respect to the care relationship, one of the questions often raised regards the wisdom of dispensing care for a person who is not worthy of receiving care, who never acknowledges or reciprocates in kind, or who wields unequal power over the carer to demand a certain action. The first of these cases occurs when the recipient of care is somebody who lacks moral integrity or an evil person, such as an abuser, rapist, or sadist. Here we do need the justice perspective to recognize that not all relationships merit sustainment through care. One critic points out that "a conception of the self as defined not through separation from but through interconnection with others is oddly unhelpful in deciding what is morally wrong with rape, abuse, and sexual harassment."[55] Furthermore, some critics point out that by caring for an evil person, such as a Nazi officer, the caregiver damages her own moral integrity. These criticisms indicate that care ethics cannot be the sole bearer of ethical framework; it needs to operate in conjunction with justice ethics.[56] Advocates of care ethics do not address the issue of what moral obligation one should fulfill if one's caring act is known to support and even strengthen the cared-for's evil deeds. I would imagine that this is the kind of dilemma experienced by medical professionals who are providing life-saving measures to a mass murderer or a serial rapist. I suppose that in such cases it makes sense for them to adopt the I-It attitude and treat the patient purely objectively and scientifically. Requiring them to make an effort to develop an I-You relationship seems not only cruel but also morally inappropriate. Thus, at the very least we can claim that there should be a limit to one's responsibility as a carer.

Even if considerations of justice ensure that the cared-for is worthy of receiving care, some critics question further if the care relationship is unidirectional, that is, one-caring always giving and the cared-for always receiving. The worry is whether a morally viable relationship can be sustained if the caregiver's care is one-sided without some sort of reciprocity. As we have noted previously, an act of care is performed without any expectation of reward or repayment. However, a certain kind and degree of reciprocity is rightly expected. As Noddings points out, "we do not expect cared-fors . . . to do for us what we do for them, nor do we expect payment of some sort. Instead, we look for signs that our caring has been received."[57] Provided that the receiver of care is capable of showing some kind of acknowledgment and appreciation, failure to show appreciation by the care receiver may be due to indifference, a feeling of entitlement, or a lack of sensibility in recognizing the value of care received. Either way, it shows a lack of care on the receiver's side. That is, the successful care relationship requires a sensibility on the part of the receiver. This is particularly pertinent when care is expressed indirectly through material objects, as I shall discuss in the next chapter, such as the way in which a gift is wrapped or the food is served.

Reciprocity in this context does not necessarily mean an equivalent action. A sign of acknowledgment and appreciation may suffice, as sometimes the cared-for may not be in a position to return any favor. The only thing they can do to "reciprocate" for the care given may be to express appreciation by uttering "thank you" or even just by smiling. Of course, all of these possibilities are premised upon the assumption that the cared-for is able to recognize and express appreciation in some way, and this excludes a newborn, a person with a severe mental defect, and a comatose person. Excepting these cases, without any kind of reciprocity, care ethics ends up promoting self-sacrifice, implicitly endorsing and perpetuating the traditional feminine virtue in a patriarchal society. Slavish dedication to another person does not make for a successful interaction motivated by care. When describing a genuine interhuman relationship based upon I-You interaction, Buber admits that "it is true that my basic attitude can remain unanswered, and the dialogue can die in seed."[58] A genuine dialogical experience is possible only when willing partnership is formed. Daniel Putman thus points out that "caring opens the agent up to possible exploitation" and "caring may reach a point where it is personally destructive to the agent."[59] Because of this possibility, Putman suggests that in care ethics "applied wisdom—the well-balanced person applying intelligence to a situation—takes a central role in judging the appropriateness of particular virtues." Practical wisdom must accompany care ethics.

A similar concern regarding the worthiness exists for the object of aesthetic experience. The notion of reciprocity in one's experience of beauty provides Elaine Scarry with an argument for the implied equality of parties that is part of the support for the notion of justice based upon fairness. She invokes a justice language in characterizing the relationship between the experiencing agent and the object as "a reciprocal contract," that is, between "the beautiful being (a person or thing) and the perceiver" where "each 'welcomes' the other" and both "exchange a reciprocal salute."[60] The object must be an equal partner in giving rise to an aesthetic experience of beauty.

The same reciprocity is expected in the aesthetic experience of art. Some works of art are worthier than others of our attempt at experiencing with attentiveness, respect, and willingness to interact, in short, with the attitude of care. For example, a work of art may be too esoteric, elitist, or idiosyncratic to be capable of inviting me to enter its world. As a result, my readiness and willingness to engage with the object does not receive a commensurable response or reward, and I may have to decide that it is not worth the effort. It may also be the case, as Ronald Hepburn points out, that the work lacks artistic merit or is dominated by theorizing: "If much is said about it [the art object], yet little or none of that can be read back into the look or the sound of the work itself, but remains external to it, we are entitled to suspect that theorizing has supplanted art."[61] In these cases, our attempt at greeting, saluting, or engaging in a dialogue is one-sided with no responsive collaboration, and it does not lead to a successful aesthetic experience.

Or a work of art may be what Joseph Kupfer calls "cheap" or "vulgar" art, which "dulls the sensibility, inhibits imagination, and disposes toward intransigence" because it merely presents a world all-too-familiar and all-too-comfortable to me and exacerbates my complacency and lethargy.[62] Iris Murdoch also condemns bad art for providing forms that are "the recognizable and familiar rat-runs of selfish day-dream."[63] Fine aesthetic sensibility is not required for "the mystery story, the soap opera, the popular fiction that deliberately dramatizes extraordinary episodes of life," Harry Broudy points out, but "to go beyond stereotyped dramatics requires cultivation, as it does to go beyond stereotypes in any other type of experience."[64] It is noteworthy that this problem was already mentioned by Friedrich Schiller more than two centuries ago:

> We see crude taste first seizing on what is new and starling, gaudy, fantastic and bizarre, what is violent and wild, and avoiding nothing so much as simplicity and quiet. It fashions grotesque shapes, loves swift transitions, exuberant forms, striking contrasts, glaring shades, pathetic songs. In this age beautiful means simply what excites a man.[65]

Of course, these observations can be criticized for being elitist and possibly too moralistic. Furthermore, the experiences of these art objects described by these thinkers may be those with which we embark on our life-long journey of practicing aesthetic education, just as children start with appreciating colorful images, simple story lines, and amusing movements. However, parents and educators expose them to a wider variety of visual arts, music, theater, and literature of increasing difficulty that helps nurture a finer and more sophisticated sensibility. Aesthetic education aims at cultivating a capacity to appreciate monochrome images, complex stories without happy endings, music with a different tonal structure, and subtle actions on the stage. The aesthetic life of those who refuse to cultivate sensibility and stick with what may be called easy pleasure must be impoverished because they are missing out on a large swathe of a fertile source of aesthetic experience, such as subtlety, understatement, silence, fine nuance, and the like.[66] Their moral life may also be compromised for being closed-minded and refusing to widen their horizon by going beyond their comfort zone and venturing into a world heretofore foreign to them.

In this regard, the aesthetics of nature is instructive in that a case can be made that every part of it, even if unattractive or (seemingly) useless, is worthy of respect because it is not "ours."[67] Humility may be required more in our interaction with nature, not only in the practical sense of questioning the anthropocentric and exploitative attitude toward nature, which regards nature as It rather than You, but also in the sense of engaging with it aesthetically. Specifically concerned with those parts of nature that do not present immediate aesthetic appeal, Aldo Leopold calls for the need for "perception" when developing a "conservation esthetic."[68] He characterizes such development as starting with "the pretty" and the "under-aged brand of esthetics" consisting of scenic places with "proper mountains with waterfalls, cliffs, and lakes."[69] With cultivation of more mature perceptive faculty informed by ecology and natural history, according to him, we will be able to overcome what he calls "underdog bias" and appreciate "values as yet uncaptured by language," such as brush, weeds and bush, and Kansas plains.[70]

With respect to the aesthetic experience of artifacts, built structures, and environments, I believe some are worthy of our caring attitude, while others not. As I discuss in Chapter 4, the care relationship with artifacts implies our literal engagement with them to promote their longevity through acts of maintenance, such as cleaning and repairing. Particularly if we reject disinterestedness understood as isolation and detachment as a requirement for aesthetic experience and instead encourage full engagement with various dimensions of the object that have real-life significance and consequences, not everything we experience and interact with can partner with us in creating a satisfying and successful aesthetic experience.

One kind of such object are those which literally harm human well-being, such as weapons of mass destruction and torture devices. Those whose view can be called autonomism or separatism are clear in making a sharp distinction between functional beauty and the morally problematic function of an object. For example, Glenn Parsons and Allen Carlson state that

Functional Beauty . . . is as morally neutral as the function of artefacts are, and sometimes odious artefacts possess it. We do not need to endorse or support the existence, or use, of any object simply because it is functionally beautiful, but it would be an over-reaction to deny that an object is functionally beautiful simply because the object's function discomfits us.[71]

Their view is shared by Jane Forsey, who cautions, when considering our disapprobation of things like Scud missiles, to "be careful to distinguish moral, political, economic, cognitive, or practical judgments about design from . . . the specific aesthetic appraisals."[72]

This kind of clear distinction between the aesthetic and the moral feels counterintuitive and is difficult to realize in our lived experience. At the same time, they are making a conceptual claim, rather than reporting from our common experience. But is it possible to give a conceptual account that captures better our intuition? Let me suggest the following in response to their autonomist view. It may be the case that a certain torture device fulfills its function of inflicting as much pain as possible effectively and efficiently. However, if we regard the overarching function of any artifacts as protecting and promoting human well-being, whether through providing safety and comfort or through assisting in our tasks, a case can be made that a brilliantly designed torture device or a weapon works against the ultimate purpose of serving humanity. If we consider the ultimate function of artifacts this way, it is questionable whether we can attribute an aesthetic value on the basis of how it functions to fulfill its immediate goal—to inflict as much pain and harm to humans as possible, let alone develop a care relationship with them. Developing a care relationship with these objects can be considered equivalent to caring for an evil person who acts to harm others. Though indirectly and possibly unwittingly, we become a coconspirator in harming others and in turn damage ourselves.[73] However, the concern here is more ethical than aesthetic, because the object's sensory qualities are irrelevant and our negative judgment refers solely to the end it is supposed to serve.

In comparison, there are cases in which the *aesthetic* concerns discourage care relationship with certain artifacts, built environments, and social phenomena. They are what Arnold Berleant calls "negative aesthetics," what Katya Mandoki calls "aesthetic poisoning," and what Harry Broudy calls "aesthetic poverty." Unfortunately there are many examples from our everyday life. Berleant cites examples most notably experienced in urban life, such as "aesthetic intrusion" of omnipresent unwanted noise; "aesthetic pain" from air pollution; "aesthetic distortion" caused by strident colors of signage and billboards; "aesthetic deprivation" felt by dwellers of cramped urban housing with inadequate exposure to natural light, sun, and wind; and "aesthetic depravity" resulting from exposure to hard core porn and vulgar amusement.[74] In her argument against the art- and beauty-dominated aesthetic discourse's fetish with what she calls the "Pangloss Syndrome" whereby negative aesthetic experiences are "either only mentioned superficially or swept under the rug," Mandoki calls for aesthetics to pay equal attention to aesthetic poisoning.[75] It includes "the disgusting, the obscene, the coarse, the insignificant, the banal, the ugly, the sordid" that "our sensibility confronts . . . every day." For examples of what he calls aesthetic poverty, Broudy gives typical buildings on American Main Street with "no surprises, no contrasts, no conflicts, no resolutions—in short, no life" and nothing "intrinsically interesting to perception."[76] He also laments that people today do not devote more attention to the aesthetics involved in conversation and wishes they devoted "more care to the sound of their speech and its qualities of expression."

These objects and phenomena dull, impoverish, offend, harm, or assault our aesthetic sensibility, and they should be called out for the negative aesthetics that they are, instead of ignoring them in favor of the Pangloss Syndrome or marshaling the theory of disinterested attitude as a way of deriving positive aesthetic experience. Recognizing them for constituting negative aesthetics calls for their elimination, modification, or improvement. It is true that we may disagree over specific examples of aesthetic harm and negativity. Is Las Vegas an example of crude and vulgar amusement, or is it appreciable for its eloquent presentation of one kind of Americana? Do poverty-stricken parts of Detroit and New Orleans indicate aesthetic deprivation, or is it rather a judgment made by white middle-class people looking on from outside while the residents may feel a sense of attachment accrued over time? How about plastic pink flamingos decorating the front yard or a velvet wall decoration featuring Elvis? For my purpose here, we don't need to settle disputes over these examples. The point is that I believe most of us would agree that we don't live in an aesthetic utopia with no room for change or improvement. Some aspects of our lives and environments are not good candidates for aesthetic engagement, and some of them are downright harmful.

Just as we should not be blind to the immoral and evil character of the other person when developing a care relationship, we should not ignore the aesthetic harm that affects the quality of life and the state of the world. I grant that developing a positive aesthetic experience of these objects and phenomena through adopting a disinterested or distancing attitude can sometimes serve as a heuristic strategy to diversify our aesthetic sensibility. However, they are ultimately not a good candidate for developing an aesthetic relationship based on care because such a relationship implies protecting them. Instead, negative aesthetics calls for a full-fledged condemnation of their existence. One could say that it is still motivated by the caring attitude in protecting oneself and others from being exposed to harmful aesthetic experiences, but the care is directed toward the experiencing agents rather than the object itself. In Chapter 4, I will argue for a default position of care relationship with the material objects, but equally important as its corollary is what Broudy calls "*enlightened* cherishing," which he defines as "a love of objects and actions that . . . are *worthy* of our love" which creates in us "a desire to preserve and care for the object."[77]

Relationality as the foundation of care relationship and aesthetic experience thus suggests that we need to be judicious as to with whom or what we develop a care relationship. Even Buber, who advocates I-You relationship, recognizes that "without It a human being cannot live."[78] Particularly with respect to the literal "It," that is, objects of daily use, in order for us to function by using them, we cannot but regard them as "It"; we cannot afford the time or energy to attend to and develop an appreciation of every particular object's specific individual identity. Furthermore, while aesthetic experience involves care, as I have been arguing, and helps cultivate an attentive, respectful, and responsive engagement with the other, its potency gets compromised if one's life is over rife with aesthetic experiences. Consider the strategy called artification utilized in organizational life and business that promotes maximizing aesthetic experiences at the workplace as a means to increasing productivity and efficiency, as well as improving the quality of the workers' life. For example, advocates of arts in industry encourage us to adopt the "I-want-to -just-experience-life-to-the-maximum mindset."[79] Particularly because "in an office environment, experiencing life to the maximum is not always easy," they recommend bringing "the same intensity (of experiencing art) in one's job." Referring specifically to organizational life, another commentator makes a similar observation: "The ordinary . . . is easily strange enough" but it is eclipsed by "the atypical" which "can fend for itself," so we need to make an extra effort to illuminate "the ordinary" to make it "strange."[80] Artification strategy fully recognizes and utilizes art's power for sharpening one's perception. Referring to the workplace participants in photography sessions who testified that their visual experience became fuller, richer, and more intense, one commentator remarks that "when life is full of activity and information, we tend to switch on the 'automatic pilot,' which means that we do not really take in the world with our senses. Life becomes dull, but actually it is not life that is to blame, but rather our outlook on life that is poor."[81]

However, even if it were possible for every aspect of our life to become art-like, the potency of "strangeness" that artistic vision entails becomes diluted. To put the matter differently, if our life becomes a continuous series of "an experience," as characterized by Dewey, can we even make sense of the notion of "an experience"? While increasing the occasions for having "an experience" may enrich our lives, this notion has significance *precisely because* it stands out against the background of the humdrum. He announces at the outset of *Art as Experience* that his aim is to "restore continuity between the refined and intensified forms of experience that are works of art and the everyday events, doings, and sufferings that are universally recognized to constitute experience" by making an analogy that "mountain peaks do not float unsupported."[82] If we continue this metaphor, if every inch of the earth's crust becomes a mountain peak, there will be no more mountain peaks. Dewey's characterization of the humdrum is rather negative, just as artification advocates describe a typical, un-artified working life as mechanical and dehydrated. However, it is not clear whether Dewey would advocate turning every humdrum aspect of our lives into "an experience." Indiscriminately increasing art-like experience will end up diluting the very intensity and special-ness we seek. It is possible that we may start suffering from aesthetic fatigue, or aesthetic overdose. Instead, I think what needs to be pursued is a balance between such intense experience and the mundane.[83]

4 Problem of Universal Caring and Significance of Self-Care

There is another sense in which there needs to be a limit to one's care, even if the objects of one's care are worthy of receiving caring attention and action. The relationship that matters in care ethics must be based upon a direct and lived experience of interaction. Noddings thus rejects "the notion of universal caring—that is, caring for everyone—on the ground that it is impossible to actualize and leads us to substitute abstract problem solving and mere talk for genuine caring."[84] I don't think care ethics excludes from the moral sphere my remote caring for indeterminate others through making donations, for example. In addition, a case can be made that there is a moral responsibility for cultivating a relationship with the other with whom I have not formed any relationship; otherwise, there will be too many humans without anybody who cares about and for them. However, a personal, intimate, concrete, and emotion-laden relationship I have with the other is central in care ethics, and I believe that it forms the core of our moral life. Indeed, there is something inhuman about a good utilitarian who considers every human being equally so that sometimes tending to the needs of a child with whom I have no relationship should take precedence over the needs of my own child, if fulfilling the needs of the former results in more utility. Thus, Daniel Engster justifies the need for selectivity of care actions, such as toward family and loved ones:

> Caring is, however, best practiced in particular relationships where the care giver can be attentive, responsive, and respectful to the dependent's needs and abilities. As such, care theory itself supports a particular distribution of our general caring duties, since

caring will usually be most effectively and excellently performed in particular personal relationships.[85]

Furthermore, if a caregiver's life is dominated by caring for as many people as possible, her life will be overwhelmed by constant commitment to caring for others. Such a life exacerbates the traditional model of caregivers, predominantly women, that often results in sacrificing their own well-being. As much as such devotion to the others may appear admirable, judicious selection of caregiving actions, as well as self-care, needs to be folded into care ethics. As Andrew Sayer states,

> the well-being of the carer also matters, and while care-giving can be a source of fulfilment in itself, it can become oppressive for the carer if she has no escape from the burdens it involves because no-one else is willing to do it, so that it makes her little more than a means to the ends of the person for whom she is caring.[86]

Thus, care ethics needs to be supplemented by practical wisdom that helps select who benefits most from one's care, what is the end of care, and how best to go about dispensing care.

Here we should address the notion of self-care that is garnering increasing attention in both popular and philosophical discourses. As a practical matter, as well as in care ethics, self-care is encouraged. We know from real-life experience that self-care is a precondition for other-directed care, because if we neglect care for ourselves we cannot care for others. This is often the case of a caregiver whose caregiving task is so all-consuming that self-care gets neglected to the point that she burns out and cannot be an effective caregiver. This situation often happens with those who are singlehandedly caring for aging parents, or a sick or disabled family member. As I write, we are witnessing the extreme mental and physical distress among medical professionals caring for extremely ill patients infected with Covid-19, leaving no time or energy for self-care.

At the same time, however, self-care suffers from the popular image promoted by various self-care industries, particularly related to beautification, that it is a form of narcissism, self-absorbed obsession, or self-indulgence. It tends to conjure up a picture of someone who fusses over her health and appearance by being excessively preoccupied with all kinds of diets, exercises, spa treatments, facials, and the like. The implication is that she is exclusively focused on herself without any concern for other-than-self. This kind of image unfortunately gives the notion of self-care a bad name.

However, self-care in the context of care ethics suggests how it is necessary to sustain a successful relationality between self and the other. In various philosophical traditions, including Buddhism, Confucianism, Greek philosophy, Stoicism, and more recent Western philosophies, self-care is an ethical practice based upon relationality as a mode of human existence. What I am and how I am is inseparable from my place in the world and relationship with others.

Those who advocate the importance of self-care as a philosophical stance often refer to Socrates's commitment to cultivating virtues as a life-long project even when the death penalty is imposed on him. In defending himself in front of the Athenian court against the charge of promoting the wrong deities and corrupting the youth, he admonishes Athenians by challenging: "are you not ashamed of your eagerness to possess as much wealth, reputation and honours as possible, while you do not care for nor give thought to wisdom or truth, or the best possible state of your soul?"[87] He continues by defending his teaching: "I go around doing nothing but persuading both young and old among you not to care for your body or your wealth in preference to or as strongly as for the best possible state of your soul."[88] His well-known exhortation of conducting an examined life can be understood as self-care in the sense of leading a life that is worth living. Thus, it is clear that what Socrates advocates is not self-care in the sense of maximizing pleasure for oneself in isolation from others. His concern is rather with the kind of self-care by which one develops a virtuous self that leads to a good life, which includes virtue-based interactions with others.

Buddhism in general is well known for its emphasis on compassion toward others, while also renouncing one's self. It may therefore appear contradictory to associate Buddhism with self-care. However, consider what is perhaps the most rigorous of the edicts on self-discipline issued by Zen Buddhism. This includes not only reading scriptures and engaging in meditation but, more importantly, the mindful practice of daily activities, ranging from cooking and eating to the cleaning of oneself and the environment, in short quintessential self-care activities. These practices are an indispensable part of cultivating an ethically grounded interaction with the world, whether regarding the materials used for cooking, the cook who prepares food, the corridor of the temple, or rocks in the garden. Concerning cleansing oneself in the lavatory, for example, Dōgen (道元 1200–53), arguably the most important Zen thinker in Japan, makes clear that it is also an occasion to purify the world: "Even though our body and mind may be impure there is a method that can purify not only our own body but the entire world," and "after the dirt is washed away, pray for all sentient beings, vow to maintain true equanimity and then no impurities or dirt will remain."[89] Similarly, when washing one's face and mouth, not only does one clean oneself but "the inner, outer, and middle of the universe" and "venerating oneself, venerating others, and venerating things all reveal the nature of one's enlightenment and detachment," clearly indicating the intertwined nature of self-care and care for the world.[90] While Zen emphasizes overcoming, forgetting, or transcending oneself in order to develop a respectful relationship with the others, such self-overcoming training and discipline can be interpreted as a form of self-care. Becoming a certain kind of person is inseparable from developing a capacity to serve the well-being of others and the world around.

Heidegger's notion of care as an ontological and existential mode of Da-sein is not specifically put forward as an ethical commitment, as explained in Section 1. However, in claiming that "The *perfectio* of human being—becoming what one can be in being free for one's ownmost possibilities (project)—is an 'accomplishment' of 'care,'" he seems to suggest that projecting one's self by freely developing an authentic mode of existence is our task. In other words, we are tasked with self-cultivation as a form of projecting oneself through working with the world into which we are thrown.[91] Since our mode of being cannot be separated from care, that is, interactions with the others and the world, self-care cannot be separated from our relationships with nonself. The way in which one fashions oneself cannot but affect one's relationship with others and the world. Although Heidegger does not seem to specify what the character of such care relationship should be, such as following a justice-centric approach that privileges abstract rule-governed decision-making or an ethics of care that motivates actions born out of one's personal relationship with the other, he is clear that our entanglement with the world around us is a basic human condition which is recognized when practicing the authentic mode of being.

Inspired by the Greek notion of self-care, the fashioning of oneself or "techniques of the self" advocated by Michel Foucault, encourages an authentic mode of existence in which one is empowered to shape oneself. It is, however, a disciplined creative act in the sense one aspires to lead a virtuous and beautiful life, rather than simply following whims or what has been deemed a particular society's and period's moral laws. For Foucault, then, self-care is not a self-enclosed project in itself in terms of caring only about oneself; instead, it is a commitment to cultivating a virtuous life which invariably gets expressed in the way in which one interacts with others. There is no separation between developing a care relationship with the other and cultivating one's self. In fact, self-care is a precondition for care for others.[92] In Richard White's summary, Foucault's notion of inventing oneself "suggests a return to virtue ethics, in which the cultivation of specific virtues—including courage, justice, temperance, and wisdom—is a form of self-fashioning that helps to orient our basic attitudes toward other people."[93] Care for others, according to care ethics as we have seen, is not just going through the motions but it has to be a genuine expression of my commitment to relating to others through acknowledging and respecting their reality. Hence, cultivating and practicing virtues so as to fashion oneself is inseparable from caring for others.

It is noteworthy that aesthetics plays a critical role in this project of self-creation. For example, while self-discipline through mindful engagement with everyday activities is specifically practiced by Zen trainees, the Buddhist cultivation of a virtuous self as a form of self-care is practiced by laypeople more commonly through artistic practices. The ultimate aim of training oneself and striving toward artistic achievement is to become a kind of person whose virtues permeate not only his artistic practice but also his way of being in the world.[94]

For Foucault, aesthetics also provides a strategy for self-creation. He uses the metaphor of sculpting oneself, and he doesn't mean body-building practice, although tending to one's body is inseparable from self-care. He observes that "art has become something which is related only to objects and not to individuals or to life. That art is something which is specialized or which is done by experts who are artists."[95] He then asks, "couldn't everyone's life become a work of art? Why should the lamp or the house be an art object, but not our life?" While art as objects is concerned with appearance, for him creating life as art is an ethical project by determining "how the individual is supposed to constitute himself as a moral subject of his own actions."[96]

Finally, consider Nietzsche's discussion of creating oneself. The task here is "to 'give style' to one's character," which he calls "a great and rare art" that is "practiced by one who surveys everything his nature offers in the way of weaknesses and strengths, and then fits it into an *artistic plan* until each element appears as artistic and reasonable and even the weaknesses delight the eye."[97] As such, "in man *creature* and *creator* are united: in man there is material, fragment, excess, clay, dirt, nonsense, chaos; but in man there is also creator, form-giver, hammer hardness, spectator divinity, and seventh day."[98] Moreover, a man who cannot fashion himself in this way poses a threat to others, for "whoever is dissatisfied with himself is continually ready for revenge, and we others will be his victims if only by having to endure his ugly sight."[99] His acceptance, even the celebration, of weaknesses in one's character may appear problematic, because it seems counter to self-improvement. However, I interpret Nietzsche to be encouraging shaping oneself that respects the integrity of self. While it is important to correct one's weaknesses, it is also important to retain one's individuality. Commenting on Nietzsche's notion of self-fashioning, Graham Parkes points out that "rather than eradicate the tendencies in the soul that are branded as vices, one can work with them in a wide variety of ways, such that they ultimately become not only aesthetically pleasing but also fruitful."[100] Artistic integrity and the unity of an object is not generated by making every part of it beautiful, as Plato demonstrates by arguing against attempting to make a sculptural piece beautiful by applying gorgeous colors to various parts, as well as criticizing democracy by analogizing it to "a cloak embroidered with every kind of ornament."[101] Instead, Nietzsche's favorite image of a beautiful whole is classical music in which dissonance, unpleasant to the ear if heard in isolation, plays a crucial role in generating a unified whole. Just as care ethics encourages me to accept and respect the other person with her particularity with warts and all, I have to practice accepting my individuality. My so-called weakness could be an integral part of the sculptural piece I am trying to make of myself. So, instead of self-coddling, Foucauldian and Nietzschean self-creation can be understood as a discipline to cultivate a virtuous self, an integral part of care ethics.

*   *   *

The last chapter explored what is expected of a person in care ethics and aesthetic experience. This chapter explored the notion of relationality that is foundational for care ethics and aesthetic experience. Relationality characterizes our mode of existence in this world, and such interdependency and entanglement with others should be acknowledged and celebrated. It also reveals that successful development of relationality is made possible when both parties to the relationship have the capacity and willingness to meet and work together. Care for others thus requires both self-care and practical wisdom. The next chapter delves further into the inseparability of ethics and aesthetics of interpersonal relationship.

3

Expression of Care in Social Aesthetics

This chapter explores how the notions of care, interdependency, and relationality underlie our interpersonal relationships. A fulfilling social engagement based upon care requires aesthetic manifestations. This can range from creating *an* experience in the Deweyan sense, expressing care through body aesthetics, to conveying care through the design, arrangement, and handling of environments and objects. Here, the ethical commitment to care cannot be separated from its tangible aesthetic embodiment, largely through nonverbal communication. Furthermore, a successful social interaction supported by care requires not only for the active agent to practice expressing care through aesthetic means, but also that the recipient of care to be able to discern the expression of care and to respond appropriately. Cultivating aesthetic sensibility is thus an indispensable dimension of care ethics.

1 From Objects to Persons

In our daily life, our social interactions are often mechanical and rule-governed as we play the role of a store clerk, customer, medical professional, patient, lawyer, client, teacher, student, employer, employee, and so forth. Of course, there is a good reason for not getting personally involved with the other person and keeping a proper

distance in our interaction. Not everyone I interact with is my friend
or family, with whom my relationship is (or should be) motivated by
care. Does this mean that aesthetics and care have no role to play in
the bulk of our daily life as we interact with different people?

In Chapter 1, I discussed aesthetics in light of care ethics
and vice versa. If we start from care ethics, we move from our
interpersonal relationships to our interactions with objects of
aesthetic experience. If we start from aesthetic experience, we
realize what is typically involved in such an experience of objects also
applies to interpersonal relationships. This latter move from "objects
into persons" is articulated by Arnold Berleant.[1] Since the aesthetic
field and aesthetic engagement, the core notions of his aesthetics,
refer to the occurrence and nature of experience, there is no limit to
what constitutes the arena of aesthetics. Thus, according to him, the
same notion of the aesthetic field and engagement can characterize
social interactions between and among people. Aesthetic factors are
present in "environments of all sorts, including human situations and
social relationships."[2] The same desiderata of aesthetic engagement
with objects, namely the focused attention to the individual
specificity, open-minded responsiveness, and active and imaginative
engagement that is based upon collaboration and reciprocity, apply to
successful social interactions that are premised upon, and promote,
respect for the others for who they are, appropriate response to what
they offer, and the spirit of collaboration and reciprocity.

> the aesthetic field describes the context of interacting perceptual
> forces, and aesthetic engagement may at times characterize the
> perceptual experience of a social process. When it is an integral
> part of social relations, aesthetic engagement transforms that
> process, turning relationships governed by a utilitarian standard that
> objectifies people into a perceptual context of interdependencies.[3]

Accordingly, the aesthetics of social interactions cannot but determine,
and be determined by, the ethical mode of human relationship. In
short, "ethical values lie at the heart of social aesthetics."[4]

Berleant refers to the medical arena as one of the areas of our
experience, besides education, business, and workplace, that tends
to be dominated by more mechanical and scripted role-playing.

These occasions that generally give rise to I-It relationships have the potential for I-You interactions by adopting the aesthetic engagement model.

> A professional who is aesthetically aware performs a function by actively pursuing a plan of treatment designed to take into account not only the standard protocols but the particular characteristics, needs, and perceptions of the person being treated. . . . When aesthetically engaged, the individual undergoing treatment becomes an active participant, a collaborator in the process, understanding and appreciating everything that is done and making every effort to promote the optimum conditions for successful treatment. In this situation, as in all instances of aesthetic engagement, a human exchange takes place on a perceptual level, with eye contact, shared feeling, and interest that is palpable.[5]

As we have seen in Chapter 1, there is an increasing recognition among medical professionals themselves that the conventional mode of practicing medicine, to regard and treat a patient as a bundle of symptoms, an It rather than a You, is inadequate and misguided. They would agree with Berleant that the relationship between a medical professional and a patient should be first and foremost a humane and fulfilling human relationship, despite, or in addition to, the role expected to be played by each party. Berleant's claim is that such relationship requires *aesthetic* engagement, which I have argued is characterized by care, not in the usual medical sense whereby the professional is expected to dispense care to the patient but in the sense of the ethical mode of negotiating with the world including people.

When both parties are fully engaged with each other, the social interaction itself takes on a certain aesthetic form. A successful conversation, for example, makes for an aesthetic experience. Following John Dewey and Donald Davidson, Kalle Puolakka characterizes a successful conversation as having an organically developing sequence with various rhythms, such as suspense, surprise, cohesion, culmination, and conclusion.[6] Such texture and form of the conversation are based upon mutual understanding of what the other understands, activation of imagination regarding what form and direction the conversation may take (that is separate from conjuring a pictorial image related to the content, although I would suppose it is not excluded), and improvisation of how to respond to the other party's utterance. It becomes a collaborative and spontaneous venture, and the whole enterprise reminds one of jazz performances. There is no script or score but only a loose outline of what we talk about or play, and we build upon each other's contribution while maintaining a general structure and organization.

In this regard, Puolakka makes a useful distinction between making a conversation and having a conversation: "In *making* a conversation, we are not fully engaged in the situation and the conversation lacks a sense of direction, sometimes proceeding only with great effort . . . . In contrast, *having* a conversation involves an inner movement and accumulation of the conversation that Dewey finds typical in aesthetic experience."[7] The former can be characterized as going through the motions. In contrast, when an exchange builds up the conversation to its fulfillment, we have a very satisfying experience, *an* experience in the Deweyan sense. While it may appear to happen naturally, in a way such a conversation results from much effort on both sides who are willing to take a risk, open oneself up to vulnerability, and take a chance in hoping that the other is willing to engage. At the same time, a certain degree of spontaneity is needed, as a strenuous effort to create what is characterized by Jean-Paul Sartre as "a perfect moment" between Roquentin and Anny in *Nausea* compromises the possibility of its aesthetic appreciation as they are experiencing it. Whatever the nature of a particular relationship between the parties may be, perhaps friends or total strangers who happen to strike up a conversation, it is a microcosmic case of developing a care relationship. I must attend to the other person fully, open myself to whatever he offers, and actively engage in responding with an appropriate response that is worthy of his offer. The primary step is both parties' willingness to listen to the other with open-mindedness.

In this regard, it is noteworthy that one of today's foremost designers in Japan, Kenya Hara, advocates the importance of emptying one's mind:

"Emptiness" (*utsu*) and "completely hollow" (*karappo*) are among the terms I pondered while trying to grasp the nature of communication. When people share their thoughts, they commonly listen to each other's opinions rather than throwing information at each other. In other words, successful communication depends on how well we listen, rather than how well we push our opinions on the person seated before us. People have therefore conceptualized communication techniques using term like "empty vessel" to try to understand each other better.[8]

It should also be noted that the aesthetically satisfying conversation is derived more from the form rather than the content. Whether a business transaction or sharing one's private life, the emphasis on the content makes conversation more of a means to an end. Georg Simmel claims that sociability is rather generated by "good form . . . since in sociability the concrete motives bound up with life-goals fall away, so must the pure form, the free-playing, interacting interdependence of individuals stand out so much the more strongly and operate with so much the greater effect."[9] In order to ensure what he calls "the democratic structure of all sociability," where there is an equal and reciprocal back and forth without one party unduly dominating the relationship, and to ensure the focus on form, Simmel suggests restraint on bringing in overly personal and individual-oriented content to the conversation.[10] The content of the conversation from the sociability point of view is relevant only as "a mere means to maintain the liveliness, the mutual understanding, the common consciousness of the group."

A similar observation is made by Andrew Sayer, who describes sociability as follows: "A sociable evening with friends can best be enjoyed not by worrying about how you are feeling or what you are getting out of it, but by letting go and melting into an 'imaginative unity with the affective life of others.'"[11] The conversation is experienced as satisfying and fulfilling when it is woven into an aesthetically appreciable tapestry through mutual collaboration, whatever the content may be. One could characterize such an experience as a kind of participatory art premised upon equal and caring engagement with each other.

It is important to emphasize that the aesthetics of conversation and interpersonal relationships does not necessarily guarantee like-minded agreement. Such harmony of content may enhance the aesthetic experience. However, it is more challenging but also rewarding to engage in a dialogue with somebody who holds a differing view on political issues or assessment of art. If each party simply throws their view at each other, spinning their respective wheel without creating any traction, such disagreements do not result in meaningful communication and exchange of ideas, as warned by Hara. It ends up being a juxtaposition of two monologues. Other times, even if in the end the dialoguers agree to disagree, the conversation can be satisfying when there is a genuine back and forth, each party willing to be open to the other's view while taking the time to explain their own view. This underscores that the aesthetics of conversation has more regard for the nature or form of interaction than the content. At the same time, this aesthetic concern with form does not mean it lacks social significance. On the contrary, it suggests a model of civil discourse that is sustained by the participants' commitment to uphold a caring and respectful relationship with others that leads to a collaborative venture.

In this regard, consider Claire Bishop's criticism of art projects that Nicholas Bourriaud touts as representing relational aesthetics: Rirkrit Tiravanija and Liam Gillick. While their art offers a space in which the audience is free to engage in various actions and conversations with others, this invitation for seemingly democratic participation is compromised by the predisposition of the like-minded audience, art lovers, who already know how to play this artistic game, so to speak. Naturally a convivial and harmonious atmosphere is generated because there is an implicit agreement that they are participating in a collaborative art-making venture, and they will cooperate, rather than challenge or question the setup, meaning, and value of the whole enterprise. According to Bishop,

> the relations set up by relational aesthetics are not intrinsically democratic, as Bourriaud suggests, since they rest too comfortably within an ideal of subjectivity as whole and of community as immanent togetherness. There is debate and dialogue in a Tiravanija cooking piece, to be sure, but there is no inherent friction since the situation is what Bourriaud calls "microtopian": it produces a community whose members identify with each other, because they have something in common.[12]

Essentially, these examples of relational art are experienced by a kind of cliquish group of the members of the artworld, disenfranchising those who are outside of the artworld, such as street vendors, manual laborers, factory workers, illegal immigrants, refugees, and the like, whose experience of such art may be very different from those had by art lovers and afficionados. Relationality in this context is already predetermined rather than generated through participants' efforts. It is too easy, not hard-won.

In addition, James Thompson points out that Bourriaud's emphasis on relationality in those art projects eclipses the social significance of its outcome. He points out that Bouirraud's concern "to patiently restitch the relational fabric" and to "turn beholders into neighbours" is ultimately a concern with "the formal aspects of this trajectory than the potential that new relational practices have for announcing or creating a fairer world."[13] Thompson's critique stems from his acknowledgment that the relationality cultivated through artistic means has a potential to be developed into care relationship that provides the foundation for a just society in which the well-being of every member is intricately enmeshed and intertwined rather than each member exerting autonomy, freedom, and independence. He thus calls for the rethinking of the usual model of actors- and performance-focused theater performance that makes rehearsals, backstage helping hands, and the human relationship between and among people involved in the production invisible. Successful participatory, relational theater art projects embrace the whole process including the so-called practice and the interpersonal relationships generated through the process.

> The emerging connections between individuals coalescing in this process have an aesthetics—a shape, feel, sensation and affect. This does not exist within one particular person or object of the work, but appears in-between those involved, so that there is a sensory quality of the process and outcome that cannot be disaggregated from the collective effort.[14]

Art that is based upon care aesthetics, thus, is process- and relationship-oriented and the aesthetic value is found in "co-created moments" instead of a certain display or outcome: *the show is not always the thing.*" [15] Participation in such art project affords a sense of caring, being cared for, mutual respect, and concern for each other, and helps to "cultivate the understanding that regard for others is central to making the world a better place." [16] It may appear that the same criticism lodged against the like-minded participants in Tiravanija's and Gillick's can apply to this kind of theater production. However, I think the difference is that the former presents an appearance of open invitation with an emphasis on spontaneity, while the latter is clear from the outset that all the participants are cognizant of their roles in creating this relational experience.

Thus, the aesthetics of conversation and relationality in art suggests that democratic discourse that is premised upon the equality of all the participants and respectful regard for each other does not encourage facile agreement among the participants. If anything, it encourages reasoned disagreements and exchange of different ideas. It is the form of and the attitude toward the exchange that matters, not necessarily a harmonious content. We can disagree without being disagreeable or disrespectful, and the experience can be aesthetically satisfying despite lack of agreement or consensus.

2 The Role of Body Aesthetics

Now, any kind of direct, face-to-face human interactions, conversations or otherwise, are always experienced perceptually, mediated by voice, facial expression, and body movement. As such, their aesthetic features play a crucial role in determining the nature of interactions. From the point of view of care ethics, it is not sufficient that a certain goal gets accomplished, such as carrying on a conversation, agreeing on a treatment plan, driving a friend to a store, cooking a meal for a sick neighbor. The manner in which these goals are accomplished is as important as, or sometimes more important than, achieving the goal. That is, body aesthetics plays a critical role in promoting care-driven human interactions.

The ethics of care requires that one's care be expressed through embodiment. The "same" action can be performed gently and kindly, indifferently, or spitefully. As mentioned in Chapter 1, Noddings points out, "I cannot claim to care for my relative if my caretaking is perfunctory or grudging."[17] I also referred to Peter Goldie's observation on the same point, although he seems to consider this as a strictly ethical matter. Others make the role of aesthetics in our ethical life explicit. For example, citing Seneca, Nancy Sherman remarks that "we spoil kindness . . . if our reluctance is betrayed in inappropriate 'furrowed brows' and 'grudging words'" and concludes that "playing the role of the good person . . . has to do with socially sensitive behaviour—how we convey to others interest, empathy, respect, and thanks through the emotional expressions we wear on our faces (or exhibit through our body language and voices)."[18] Marcia Eaton also points out that "we have to pay attention to the tone with which something is said, as well as to the content, and to the relations between the speakers, or to meanings of other words spoken earlier or later."[19] When expressing virtues, according to David E. Cooper, it is not enough that one makes a charitable contribution or writes a morally uplifting book. It "must show up in an aesthetically charged way—in gestures . . . or demeanour, 'style' and presence—that draws others, sensitive to the 'energy' being radiated, to the person."[20] Consider the difference between the way in which the then president Donald Trump threw paper towels to the Puerto Rican victims of hurricane as if they were a football and another action whereby they were handed to the people gently and carefully. Despite accomplishing the mission of handing out paper towels, an action carried out in a rather indifferent and nonchalant manner, as if it were a game, seems to compromise, or even nullifies, the value of the action's end result. I believe we often experience in our everyday life that the aesthetics of an action can make or break its moral value.[21]

One may dismiss body aesthetics regarding social interactions as a matter of etiquette or manners, which is often criticized for being superficial, or worse, a means of stereotyping and exclusion. Gender stereotyping particularly has a powerful force in dictating people's behavior which leads to a criticism of a person who does not conform to the expected way of conducing herself.[22] We are also all-too-familiar with the way in which a "respectable" mode of behavior has been codified as a means of exclusion. Invariably those who are considered to act contrary to a respectable manner tend to be the society's oppressed groups based upon race, ethnicity, economic status, national origin, and sexual orientation. We certainly need to be cognizant of this danger as we judge other people's actions. Sometimes, what may appear to me to be a callous or rude behavior may not be so because of the other person's different cultural upbringing or an unusual circumstance. This reinforces the need for adjusting our judgment of others rather than indiscriminately imposing a preconceived standard of respectable behavior, bringing us back to the open-mindedness required in care ethics and aesthetic experience. At the same time, like the possibility of failed care relationship and a failed aesthetic experience, my effort in bending over backward to cast a positive light on a seemingly rude behavior has its limit. Unfortunately, the world is full of attitudes and actions indicative of indifference, rudeness, and hostility expressed through the aesthetics of actions.

Thus, there is no denying that aesthetics has a significant role to play in facilitating successful social interactions. They require both moral and aesthetic sensibility and sensitivity. Ossi Naukkarinen points out that tactful behavior is neither rule-governed nor prepared in advance, because "it is always an art of acting in the here-and-now," and, as such, "tact and its ethics approach the debates in aesthetics. When viewed like this, both tact and aesthetics are essentially about the sensory, context-specific evaluation of things."[23] Marcia Eaton similarly points out that "both *aesthetic and moral* sensitivity are demanded in making judgments such as 'This situation calls for bold action' or 'This situation calls for subtlety.'"[24] Whether called tact, sensitivity, flexibility, nimbleness, or responsiveness, this attention to the specifics of the other individual and the situation, as it is with the aesthetic experience, is a necessary condition for a successful human interaction. So are the open responsiveness and active, imaginative, and creative engagement with the other person. Ultimately, Eaton points out that there is a "connection between being a person who has aesthetic experience and being a person who has sympathies and insights of a kind required for successful social interaction."[25]

In Chapter 1, I discussed how care ethics requires both the process/ motivation and the actual act. My care for another person needs to be actualized in some form of action. No matter how much I insist that I care about my mother, if I never lift a finger to do anything for her even if I am able, my so-called care remains empty, invoking the common criticism, "talk is cheap." At the same time, my action needs to be motivated by genuine caring. Simply performing an action in conformity with what care ethics requires does not make the action one of care. This is perhaps best illustrated by a polite, pleasant, and smiley demeanor of those who play the role dictated by what is expected of that role. Daniel Putman claims that "salespersons consistently act in a way characteristic of the virtue and deciphering how much a particular salesperson might genuinely care about a customer is difficult" and concludes: "We seem to have accepted that a certain amount of pseudo-caring is inevitable in business and politics but the distrust of these institutions may be indicative of the fact that we know such actions are only a form of mimicry done for ulterior reasons."[26] Perhaps what we can say is that, in this role-playing performance, we expect the salesperson to behave in a polite manner and we are jolted when such façade of politeness does not exist or, worse, when the behavior exudes rudeness or even hostility.

But the problem of performance is not limited to role-playing. Without any specific role to play, one can be putting on a performance of how one wants to be regarded by others. Buber thus distinguishes "being" and "seeming," or "what one really is" and "what one wishes to seem," that is, putting on a performance in order to give a favorable impression to the other.[27] Such a show amounts to a kind of lie, according to Buber: "The lie I mean does not take place in relation to particular facts but in relation to existence itself, and it attacks interhuman existence as such. There are times when a man, to satisfy some stale conceit, forfeits the great chance of a true happening between I and Thou."[28]

This concern with mere performance is also addressed in Confucianism, well known for its insistence on the importance of expressing virtues by observing decorum through body aesthetics. Eric Mullis points out that "Confucius often expressed concerns about individuals whose embodied aesthetic expressions were not rooted in internal psychological states," and their actions, no matter how they conform to the societal expectation of proper behavior, are regarded as "an empty ritual that has no ethical import because it is not motivated by morally appropriate sentiments and broader moral dispositions."[29] In terms of judging the moral worth of someone's action, there is no sure way of ascertaining whether his seemingly caring interaction with me is genuinely motivated by his caring attitude or a mere show. However, this unknowability can be mitigated to a large extent if we consult our everyday experience. I believe that it is rather commonly experienced that, if I am familiar with other things about him, I can place his particular interaction with me within a holistic frame, or what Mullis calls his gestalt, that provides consistency and coherence across the span of time. This enables me to make a more informed judgment. If he consistently acts in a similar manner toward everyone around him, there is a good reason to believe that his seemingly caring attitude toward me is genuine, although of course there is no absolute guarantee. Or someone's seemingly indifferent or callous manner may not be an indication of lack of care, because he is generally rough and gruff, like one of my uncles. His seemingly uncaring interaction with me can be mitigated by everything else I know about him, including his generosity and affection toward me though not expressed in the normally expected way. On the other hand, if my interaction with a person happens for the first time or only once within a limited time frame, there is no telling what motivated his seemingly caring interaction. But if I develop my knowledge and understanding of him through a continuing relationship, I will be in a better position to gauge his action in the broader context of his way of relating to the world around him.

3 Practicing Body Aesthetics

My discussion so far has been concerned primarily with a spectator's judgment on the moral value of the other person's action expressed through body aesthetics. While this judgment-making is an important aspect of care ethics and aesthetics, the primary concern for both is the first-person account as an active agent participating in social interactions. Social aesthetics through bodily engagement brings to light that we are both capable of and responsible for creating an ethically grounded and aesthetically satisfying experience for all concerned. This active role we play in shaping the social landscape does not receive due attention by the spectator-oriented discourse that has dominated Western aesthetics. I mentioned in Chapter 1 that the so-called virtue theory of aesthetics still adheres to this spectator mode of judging the product of art-related acts. The account of virtue-driven aesthetics I am developing here can be considered a virtue theory of aesthetics that truly redirects the focus of inquiry to the account "from the inside." Just as we can sharpen our sensibility for aesthetic experience as a spectator, we can also cultivate and practice aesthetically sensitive social engagement. The ethical way of being and living is not merely a matter of conceptual understanding and acting according to a rule or performing. It has to do with conducting our life in such a way that the caring attitude and its expression in actions become who we are, and this needs cultivation and practice.

This emphasis on cultivation and practice of ethical life through aesthetic means is prominent in Confucianism with its emphasis on bodily expression of virtues and the importance of practice and cultivation. Nicholas Gier points out that "bad manners are wrong not because they are immoral but because they lack *aesthetic* order: they are inelegant, coarse, or worse," and "Confucian *li* [the good] makes no distinction between manners and morality, so an *aesthetic* standard rules for all of its actions."[30] In particular, artistic training provides a model for cultivating embodiment of moral virtues. For Confucianism, artistic training is not meant primarily as sharpening one's skills and creativity. Though they are not irrelevant, training in the arts is a means of self-cultivation. Eric Mullis explains: "learning and practicing an art form entails intentionally cultivating, refining, and expressing an integrated system of habits: motor habits necessary for the performance of artistic actions . . . as well as habits of perception."[31] This provides a model for cultivating a virtuous self, as "the process of ethical self-cultivation also includes self-awareness, a commitment to continued education, and the intentional cultivation and refinement of habits associated with virtuous disposition." Body engagement in art-making, such as calligraphy, dance, and music, in particular, offers an effective model of embodied expression of one's habits and perception. Through repeated performance and practice, one internalizes artistic training and a virtuous mode of being, and in turn they flow naturally into outward bodily expression. Thus, despite a possibility of performing a virtuous action as an empty gesture or going through the motions, performance and practice are indispensable to cultivating an ethical way of being in the world and interacting with others.

The cultivation of moral virtues through bodily practice is also prominent in the Japanese aesthetic tradition. For example, the art of tea ceremony, a kind of participatory art established in the sixteenth century, consists of a host entertaining a guest by serving tea and snacks in a tea hut. Although highly prescribed and choreographed and requiring repeated practice, the slow and elegant body movements of the host making tea and the guest receiving and savoring the drink are a silent but eloquent expression of the care and respect for the other party. While this art takes place apart from everyday life, the participants are expected to carry the aesthetic experience thus gained over to their everyday life. Various body movements expressive of respect and care toward objects and people are supposed to become the participants' second nature and inform their daily activities, such as eating, receiving a gift, and interacting with people. Kristin Surak describes the expression of care, respect, and gratefulness involved in the tea ceremony as "vigilant consideration of others," while Eiko Ikegami observes that the aesthetics of tea ceremony promotes "silent aesthetic communion . . .through artistry of motion and gesture."[32] It provides a model of ethical life conducted with the vehicle of aesthetics.

A Japanese geisha, literally meaning a person accomplished in the arts, practices classical instrumental and vocal music, dance, and the art of entertaining guests. The arduous physical regimen of all these activities, according to a first-person account, is "as much a discipline of the self as the technical mastery of an art form" and "if art is life for a geisha, then her life must also become art."[33] Accordingly, "a geisha's professional ideal is to become so permeated with her art that everything she does is informed by it, down to the way she walks, sits, and speaks."

The point of citing the training for tea practitioners and the geisha, as well as the Confucian practice of the arts, is not to claim that they all become virtuous through their training and participation in the respective arts. Rather, they demonstrate the efficacy and importance of bodily training through which personhood and artistry are cultivated. You "become" a certain kind of person who would naturally display the artistry gained. Cultivation of an ethical mode of being in the world and interacting with people and objects within it similarly requires embodied practice. As Robert Carter reminds us, "correct ethical action most often grows out of concrete, physical training, or repetition, and is best described as a cluster of attitudes about who one is in the world and how to properly and effectively interact with others. Ethics is not a theoretical, intellectual 'meta' search, but a way of walking (or being) in the world." [34] Particularly in the Japanese tradition, according to him, "ethics is primarily taught through the various arts, and is not learned as an abstract theory, or as a series of rules to remember," and by being taught through arts, he means practicing arts oneself rather than being an onlooker or spectator who appreciates them, the favored mode of aesthetics in the Western tradition.

The importance of the care relationship and body aesthetics in interpersonal interactions raises a question as to how much gets compromised or changed in technologically mediated interactions. Many aesthetic features present in a face-to-face interaction, such as the tone of voice, facial expression, gestures, and general comportment are either not available or presented differently in the electronically medicated communication. Furthermore, this mode of communication often encourages people to simply vocalize what they want to say without engaging in a true dialogue or conversation with other people, as in Twitter. I raised a similar question regarding what counts as a direct experience of the other person during the time of pandemic in Chapter 1. Although I will not explore it here, I think it is worthwhile to speculate on whether and how different modes of communication and interpersonal relationships unfold both with technological advancement and in a situation such as the pandemic and what the moral and aesthetic implications of those modes will be.

4 Expressing Care through Objects

So far, my discussion of social aesthetics concerned the direct personal interactions through conversation, body movement, facial expression, and the like. However, my interactions with others are not limited to such direct encounters. The expression of care (or lack thereof) can be mediated by the design, creation, placement, arrangement, or handling of the physical objects, that is, nonverbally and nonbodily. This section explores this aspect of social aesthetics by examining a number of examples, many of which, though not all, are taken from contemporary everyday environment in Japan. As I mentioned in Introduction, it is not my intention to idealize the Japanese culture or claim its superiority. For my purpose here, they are helpful in exemplifying my point about expressing care through objects. This kind of expression seems to have appeared quite early in Japan, as indicated by the aesthetics of garden and the tea ceremony, dating back to the eleventh century and the sixteenth century, respectively. In my observation, the aesthetic sensibility formed by them still has a considerable impact on people's lives today outside of these specific art forms.

The ethos of expressing care and consideration for others through objects has a long lineage in Japanese culture. The earliest writing on this subject is found in the eleventh-century manual for garden-making, *Sakuteiki* (作庭記), which lays the foundation for subsequent garden design in Japan. In addition to the principle of "obeying the request" that stresses respecting the individual characteristics of materials used, such as rocks or trees, another cardinal principle is changing the axis, meaning avoiding symmetry. Reminding us of Alexander Pope's criticism of formal gardens that adhere to strict symmetry where "Grove nods at Grove, each Ally has a Brother, And half the Platform just reflects the other," the absence of a central axis recommended in *Sakuteiki* is meant to honor and enrich the owners' and visitors' experience of walking through the designed space.[35] By avoiding symmetrical design, the garden provides a continuous source of stimulation, such as meandering paths, partially hidden vistas, and "borrowing" a distant landscape as a part of the garden (*shakkei* 借景). This other-regarding attitude toward garden-making that is designed to delight the visitors is alive and well in contemporary Japan. It can be seen in their everyday environment, such as gently curved entrance pathways into buildings.[36]

In addition to the body aesthetics discussed in the last section, the Japanese tea ceremony provides this object-mediated expression of care in a concentrated manner. The host carefully chooses, prepares, and arranges tea implements and decorative items like a hanging scroll, an incense burner, and flowers in a vase, in order to provide the utmost comfort and delight for the guest. He takes into consideration not only each guest's interests but also the season, the time of the day, and the weather. The extreme details attended by the host are quite stunning. They include clearing the snow only from the stepping-stones in the garden and sometimes leaving snow in the water basin for winterly aesthetic delight, the nonchalant and labor-unintensive look of the knot of the string tied to secure the lid onto the tea container, the geometrical proportion that directs where to place various implements without giving an impression that the placement was belabored (*kanewari* 曲尺割) while at times breaking such proportionality (*minesuri* 峯摺), and highlighting the changing pattern of drying water droplets as the wet kettle surface dries by being heated.[37] While there are basic rules that guide these considerations, the ultimate decisions are made by the host according to the specific occasion. Just as the care relationship is developed when the carer attends to the singularity of the cared-for in a specific situation, orchestrating various aspects of the tea ceremony also requires being attuned to the specific occasion, referred to as *ichigo ichie* (一期一会), one time one meeting. It requires utmost sensibility, flexibility, and improvisational skills. Robert Carter thus remarks that "true mastery in practice is, while encountering new situations, dealing with any difficulties which might arise with an ease and spontaneity which displays, at the same time, imperturbability."[38]

This expression of care is also embodied in the simple meal and snack served along with the tea. It is often remarked that Japanese food serving is like a visual art. Each morsel is arranged strategically to enhance its native aesthetic appeal, rather than everything mixed and heaped together. A serving vessel, whether a plate or a bowl, is chosen not only to highlight the food inside but also to reflect the season. A Japanese dish thus provides both gustatory and visual feast, delighting the guest. Of course, the degree of meticulous attention is most prominent at a fancy restaurant or in a tea ceremony, but I can speak from my personal experience of growing up in Japan that a similar attention is also given for home-cooked and -served meals.

We appreciate the manifestation of care expressed by the aesthetic delight offered by the objects outside of Japan and occasions prompted by art such as a garden and the tea ceremony. For example, passengers walking on the corridor of Seattle-Tacoma Airport are treated to an enjoyable experience of tracking the whimsical images of the school of salmon inlaid onto the floor (Figures 1–4). Their winding direction is fun to track, from the fry to the emaciated old ones, sometimes swimming individually and sometimes gathering in a pool, sometimes transforming into recognizable decorative salmon figures of the Northeast first nations and tongue-in-cheek salmon traveling with a suitcase or

FIGURE 1 *Seattle-Tacoma Airport.*

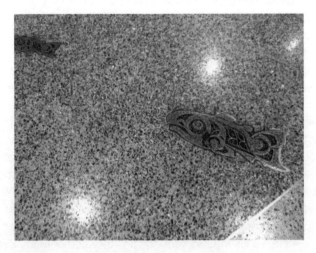

FIGURE 2 *Seattle-Tacoma Airport.*

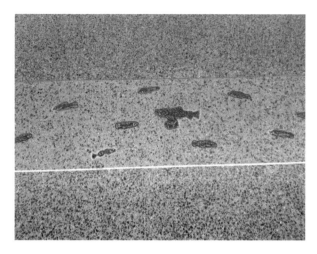

FIGURE 3 *Seattle-Tacoma Airport (note the middle salmon carrying a suitcase).*

FIGURE 4 *Seattle-Tacoma Airport.*

transformed into an airplane shape! These figures on the floor are not simply decorative; they break up the monotony of walking on an airport corridor, welcome the visitors with the local flavor as well as delightful fun. After a long tiring flight, the passengers feel properly greeted and cared for.

What is underfoot often escapes our attention. However, as in this airport corridor, sometimes we find not-so-hidden gems on the street pavement. One of the fun experiences of visiting different places for me has become finding various patterns on the manhole covers. This quintessentially utilitarian objects from our everyday surrounding can be a source of enjoyment as well as the enhancement of the sense of place. Japan has a project concerning manhole covers that is well known by now, in which each municipality features the objects and landscapes associated with the place (Figures 5 and 6).[39] But Japan by no means has a monopoly over such a project. From my travels within the United States, I was heartened to be greeted with the similar sense of place and the pride in cities such as Portland featuring a rose, Phoenix a phoenix, and Seattle a map of its waterfront (Figures 7 and 8).[40] Seattle in particular offers delightful greetings with a wavy pattern at every corner of its urban environs, such as the pavements, the bus stop shelters, and other street furniture. Such unified patterns are certainly pleasant to behold in themselves, but their effect goes beyond straightforward sensory pleasure by integrating the sense of pride in the city and a sign of welcoming greetings to the visitors, in short an expression of care for the city, residents, and visitors.

FIGURE 5 *Manhole cover featuring Osaka Castle (Osaka, Japan).*

FIGURE 6 *Manhole cover in Ueno Park noted for cherry blossoms (Tokyo, Japan).*

FIGURE 7 *Manhole cover (Phoenix, Arizona).*

FIGURE 8 *Manhole cover (Seattle).*

In contrast, let us consider the opposite case where the objects exhibit lack of care. A glaring example is the train station in Providence, Rhode Island, which I sometimes use to go to Boston or New York. It is an embarrassment. Its platform with bare concrete structure has few signs indicating where it is or which way is Boston or New York, let alone any welcoming greetings for the visitors or indication of the sense of place. It exudes thoughtlessness, indifference, and carelessness.

I mentioned in Chapter 2 that a successful care relationship is based upon reciprocity, not necessarily in terms of the receiver of care returning a similar favor but in terms of returning a sign of grateful acknowledgment. The train station is an example of the other party not offering care for the passengers and visitors. On the other hand, let us consider the case in which the other party is offering an aesthetic manifestation of care for us, but we are not reciprocating by not even acknowledging, let alone appreciating, the aesthetic gift offered. Suppose I hurry through a garden without paying attention to the thoughtful ways in which the rocks and trees are arranged, gobble up a beautifully arranged dish, and never notice the aesthetic presentation of a sense of place at every street corner and literally underfoot. It is not only that my aesthetic life is impoverished by remaining oblivious to the aesthetic bounty offered but most likely my moral life is probably not as richly endowed as it could be. Even if I am the "recipient" of an aesthetic expression of care, the relationship will not be fulfilled if I lack the sensibility, perceptive power, and moral sensitivity to be able to discern, appreciate, and reciprocate by full engagement.

Commenting on Japanese food, Graham Parkes remarks that "the care with which the food has been prepared and presented invites corresponding care and attention in the handling and eating of it."[41] In a similar manner, a successful experience of tea ceremony makes demands not only on the host for setting it up and executing it but also on the guest who needs to attend carefully to various details that express the host's care. Today's tea master, Sen Genshitsu XV, thus explains that the primary purpose of the tea ceremony is a tacit communication, "contagion," whereby "the guests will 'feel' what the host intended to 'give' them in and through the ceremony. An intense level of kindness prevails, and the guests learn through this enveloping atmosphere to be kind to one another in turn."[42] As previously mentioned, the vehicle of this contagion is aesthetic: body movements, selection and arrangements of various objects, the singular atmosphere resulting from the integration of all the elements including those beyond human control, such as the season, time of the day, and weather. The aesthetic sensibility necessary to recognize and appreciate such aesthetic manifestation of care *is* a moral sensibility as well. As summarized by Carter, the tea ceremony "is an event of a 'Thou' interacting intimately with other 'Thous.'"[43] As such, it is an aesthetic activity that promotes cultivation of kindness and respect for others, and "learning to be kind is not just the intellectual recognition of what kindness is, but through mind and body as unified, one actually practices being kind."[44] Aesthetic experience, as discussed in Chapter 1, thus is not something we as recipients passively take in, but is generated by our active engagement requiring an ethically grounded and mindful entanglement with the world.

So far, the aesthetic gifts offered or denied by the examples have been fairly obvious. With respect to the tea ceremony, gardens, and food, we expect aesthetically charged experiences and are predisposed to gain an aesthetic pleasure. In cases of the objects underfoot, their decorative elements are added specifically for aesthetic delight. In both cases, the expression of care is forefronted because there are a number of ways in which objects could have been created and handled differently, such as the tearoom prepared only according to what is most convenient for the host, the food served haphazardly on a plate, and the manhole covers featuring a generic geometrical pattern merely to prevent slippage. Hence, it will take an extremely dull sensibility not to notice and appreciate these gifts.

In comparison, the need for perceptual acuity and imaginative engagement become more pressing for the following examples, because their aesthetic expression of care tends to be invisible, either because we take them for granted or because they address special needs not shared by everyone. It is a common sight in Japan that a small shelf is placed below a counter at stores, banks, post offices, hotels, airports, and ATM machines, where one can put a pocketbook and other belongings while tending to the transactions (Figures 9 and 10). An even smaller shelf with a half circle cut out is often seen at the same places for resting a cane and an umbrella, while sometimes an umbrella stand is located at the entrance (Figures 11 and 12). The subway hanging straps are often of different lengths to accommodate people with differing heights (Figure 13). Public bathrooms are equipped with a baby seat attached to the wall where a baby can be placed while the parent tends to her needs (Figure 14). Some clothes

FIGURE 9 *Airline counter with tables (Shinchitose Airport, Japan).*

FIGURE 10 *Bank ATM machine with a table in front (Sapporo, Japan).*

FIGURE 11 *Post office table with a cane holder and umbrella stand (Sapporo, Japan).*

FIGURE 12 *In-store ATM machine with a cane and coffee cup holders (Sapporo, Japan).*

FIGURE 13 *Subway car (Sapporo, Japan).*

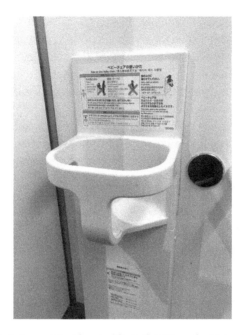

FIGURE 14 *Baby seat inside a public toilet (Haneda Airport, Tokyo).*

feature big buttons with diagonal buttonholes for easy maneuver for those who are dexterity-challenged, such as children, senior citizens, and people suffering from arthritis. Finally, a well-known children's tune or a bird's chirping is used to announce safe crossing of a street to the visually challenged.

   None of these objects provide aesthetic delight the way the objects in the previous group of examples do. However, they provide care by addressing specific needs, sometimes of a certain group of people while other times of all of us when we find ourselves inconvenienced by situations like carrying too many things. From the aesthetic point of view, we may further distinguish those which provide care by their sheer existence regardless of the sensuous features, such as the baby seat, a shelf under the counter, and a cane holder, from those which provide care by their specific design, such as the buttonholes and the tune for safe street crossing. That is, the former responds to people's needs not so much by their specific design features because there cannot be that much variation for fulfilling their function; the important thing is that they are placed where they are. In comparison, the safe crossing signal can be conveyed by different sounds such as a series of mechanical staccato sounds often heard in the cities in the United States and Europe. However, the sound of a bird chirping, or a familiar children's tune, creates a gentler and more pleasant soundscape compared to the harsh mechanical staccato sounds.[45]

In this regard, consider the final example originally from the United States but now available globally: OXO brand of kitchen utensils. Its vegetable peeler is a redesign of the basic metal peeler. It has an enlarged handle made with a nonslip polypropylene plastic and rubber material for easy grip that is further enhanced with flexible fins that can conform to individual grip, preventing the peeler from slipping. In addition, an oversized hole at the end of the handle makes it easy to hang, particularly for the visually impaired. It turns out that the designer of this redesign was inspired by watching his wife with severe arthritis struggle with a conventional metal peeler to peel a potato. Akiko Busch characterizes this peeler's "kind of funky elegance that made it appealing to everyone" as embodying "consideration, empathy, and comfort."[46]

But when we characterize an artifact as expressing or embodying care and consideration or indifference and neglect, what are we doing exactly? Are we making a judgment of the attitude or motivation of the designer? After all, an object cannot be held responsible for lack of care or credited for being considerate. Although we often do criticize an object or a built structure for being thoughtless or praise it for its care toward us, it is a shorthand way of making a judgment on the designer, according to this line of thinking. In the next section, I will argue for the legitimacy of attributing moral characters to an object.

5 Moral Agency of Objects

Let's consider again the example of the Providence train station. Nigel Taylor's criticism of those objects or structures that appear to be put together carelessly and shoddily without any consideration of its relationship to the surroundings is apropos here. Such structures, Taylor states, "would offend us aesthetically, but, more than that, part of our offense might be ethical. Thus we might reasonably be angered or outraged, not just by the look of the thing, but also by the visual evidence that the person who designed it didn't show sufficient *care* about the aesthetic impact of his building."[47] He concludes that "to care . . . for how something looks, and thereby for the people who will look at it, is to exhibit not just an aesthetic but also a moral concern. Or rather, it is to exhibit an aesthetic attentiveness which is itself moral."

Taylor seems to suggest that there is an ethical demand on architects and designers to design their objects with care which should be manifested in the specific features. If we regard this object-regarding demand as a code of professional ethics, it is rather unique. Professional ethics regarding other disciplines, such as medicine, science, business, journalism, law, education, social work, and the like, primarily concerns what constitutes professional conduct, such as confidentiality, honesty, whistleblowing, conflict of interest, humane treatment of nonhuman animals, and relationships with clients, patients, or students. This reflects a widely accepted belief that ethics deals only with our interactions with members of moral community, typically other humans, but today with the establishment of environmental ethics nonhuman creatures, plants, inanimate objects of nature, and arguably nature in general. In this framework, artifacts are placed outside of the moral community.

When ethical considerations are directed toward objects, they often concern art or objects of some special historical or social significance. For example, as mentioned in Chapter 1, in art appreciation and criticism we debate about the aesthetic relevance of the moral character of the artist or performer, controversial subject matter, such as regarding race, religion, and political ideology, and the problematic process involved in the creation, such as harm to humans, animals, or environments. In addition, particularly in recent years, questions have been raised with increasing frequency about public monuments and memorials associated with problematic past. Finally, street art and graffiti are sometimes criticized as an act of vandalism. In these last examples, ethical considerations are derived from extraneous factors associated with the objects, not generated by their sensuous qualities. The problematic historical significance of a statue and the graffiti's perceived disrespect for public property are regarded as affecting their aesthetic value, if judged from a moralistic perspective, irrespective of their sensuous appearance.

In comparison, relatively absent is ethics regarding artifacts themselves. Warwick Fox, for example, observes that "Western ethics has . . . overwhelmingly focused on our obligations in respect of people."[48] While Fox recognizes the development of environmental ethics has ramifications for the artifactual world, he points out that environmental ethics' primary focus has been nature and "the built environment constituted the major blind spot in theorizing associated with the development of environmental ethics to date." Furthermore, he claims that it is not sufficient to address sustainability and carbon footprint in the ethics of built environment. It should include *aesthetic* considerations such as a structure not fitting in with its surroundings even when it is otherwise sound in virtue of satisfying human needs and minimizing its carbon footprint, and he develops his architectural ethics by virtue of what he terms "responsive cohesion."[49]

Ezio Manzini also points out that, in comparison with macro-level examination of grand programs such as energy systems and artificial intelligence, "we continue to lack . . . an ethics of design" of "the diffuse production of material and immaterial artifacts from which we build the daily environment."[50] The recent decision by the American Institute of Architects to censure those architects who knowingly design spaces intended for execution, torture, and solitary confinement is noteworthy in the sense that it takes a clear position against the ethics of the intended use of some built structures. Even then, this code of professional ethics addresses the intended function of what they design, regardless of the particular aesthetic features of the designed space.[51] In general, therefore, I agree with Fox and Manzini that ethics regarding artifacts' aesthetics has been largely absent in Western philosophy and design discourse.

When it comes to many everyday objects and structures whose designers and creators are largely unknown, let alone their intention or attitude in creating the object, the physical objects themselves often take on the moral attributes such as care, thoughtfulness, consideration, and kindness, or indifference, neglect, callousness, and hostility. Such judgments we make may be interpreted as an indirect judgment of the anonymous architects and designers. Taylor's previously cited criticism of a structure that seems to have been created without care applies both to the object itself and the designer behind it: "we might reasonably be angered or outraged, not just by the look of the thing, but also by the visual evidence that the person who designed it didn't show sufficient *care* about the aesthetic impact of his building."[52] Although we often curse the unknown designer for creating such an object, it seems to me that the anger is also directed toward the object itself, because the fact is we as users are negatively affected by the sensuous features of the object. Unlike when we interpret and evaluate art by considering the artist's intention and her *oeuvre*, we normally judge an artifact on the basis of the object itself alone: the proof is in the pudding.[53] It may be the case that the apparent lack of care in the train station resulted from the designer's failed attempt or his lack of skills, rather than from his indifference. Or, conversely, the apparent evidence of care may not guarantee that such a stance was assumed by the designer. However, regardless of the intention or ability of the designer, the notion of care is often invoked when judging designed objects and structures in our everyday life.

Those who embrace the Western ontological framework may resist attributing moral qualities to objects. They lack sentience, free will, and the kind of agency we humans exercise, which makes them ineligible for being assigned a moral blame or praise. Criticizing an object for being disrespectful or praising another for being thoughtful seems to be a quintessential case of a category mistake. So, when Juhani Pallasmaa, himself an architect, characterizes the ethos defining much of contemporary architectural structures variously as "arrogance," "narcissism," "impudence," "ego trips," and "showiness," he must be referring to larger-than-life so-called starchitects.[54] When he instead calls for "an architecture of humility" based upon modesty, courtesy, responsiveness, and care, he must be calling for a character transformation of his fellow architects, so the objection goes.

It is easy to turn criticisms of starchitects' showcase pieces into a criticism of the architects' personality, but Pallasmaa's criticisms *are* referring to the structure's aesthetic features comprised of size, shape, spatial configuration, relationship with the surroundings, materials used, negotiability, comfort for the dwellers/visitors, and the like. We often make these judgments, even *despite* what we know about the architect. For example, I believe we will be hard-pressed to characterize Frank Lloyd Wright's prairie-style buildings as being arrogant and showy, despite his rather messy personal life and dictatorial personality.

The attribution of moral virtues or vices to artifacts is voiced not only by those who are involved in design profession. David E. Cooper, for example, advocates virtue-centric aesthetics: "Beauty will surely have significance for us if we see in it the exemplification and expression of the virtues we admire."[55] He illustrates this by taking Japanese gardens and French formal gardens like Versailles as an example. He argues that it makes sense to attribute virtues (or their opposite) to gardens insofar as the former exhibits or embodies virtues of being "'unpretentious,' 'graceful,' 'dignified,' 'free and open,' 'generous,'" and the latter "the artificiality, pretentiousness, vainglory, and the 'enslavement' of nature."[56] Some may not agree with these characterizations of these gardens, but his main point, which is also my point, still remains. That is, Cooper concludes that "I find it neither puzzling nor awkward to ascribe to buildings, say, qualities such as austerity, boldness, humility, friendliness, and generosity."[57] The moral virtues and vices are aesthetically relevant as features of the object insofar as the design features embody them. In locating virtues or vices in the qualities of the object, Cooper's virtue-centric view differs from the virtue theory of aesthetics which locates them in the creator behind the objects.

There has been an increasing attention to the possibility of attributing agency to artifacts, particularly in the field of technology studies. According to those who argue for the agency of objects, they *shape* our actions. For example, while agreeing that artifacts lack intentions, claims, and responsibility, Peter-Paul Verbeek points out that artifacts often play a role in shaping or mediating the users' actions, regardless of whether the designers explicitly designed the object to guide the users' actions that have moral significance. This leads him to claim that "moral community can also be defined in terms of the ability to *shape* morality."[58] Designed objects' agency is found in their "mediating role—one with an ethical dimension in that moral considerations are transformed, shaped, or even taken over." For example, the shape of a table determines the relationship between and among the people around it. A round shape enhances nonhierarchical equality, while a rectangular shape promotes more hierarchical relationship with someone "at the head of the table," and each seating arrangement carries a certain moral significance.[59]

There are other examples offered by thinkers from various fields that demonstrate how an object's design shapes or guides people's action, sometimes for paternalistic reasons: speed bumps, an inwardly curved fence along the bridge and overpass to prevent suicide and throwing things, and a black image of a fly at the strategic point on the urinal to prevent spillage at Schiphol Airport in Amsterdam. Variously characterized as "actant," "commendable closure," and "libertarian paternalism," these objects "nudge" people toward or away from certain actions without closing off the possibility of engaging in different actions like not slowing down when driving over a speed bump, scaling the fence to jump, or aiming at a different part of the urinal.[60]

While these paternalistic design strategies may be innocuous enough, particularly because they do not fully determine our actions, thus not depriving us of the freedom to act otherwise, there are other examples of artifactual design that shape our actions completely through measures of exclusion. One of the most egregious historical examples of exclusionary design is the New York's Long Island parkways' overpasses built early twentieth century. They were designed too low to allow busses used by beachgoers who are mostly from the racial minority and economically disadvantaged population. Although the overpasses themselves do not possess an intention and irrespective of whether Robert Moses specifically commissioned a racist agenda, the overpasses act as a de facto agency for exclusion.[61]

A more contemporary and increasingly common example is urban furniture in many cities around the world that are specifically designed to deter what many societies consider to be undesirable actions. Such urban furniture invariably targets marginalized population, namely unhoused (commonly known as homeless) people and skateboarders who are, at least initially, predominantly urban youths from depressed neighborhoods. Variously characterized as "hostile architecture," "defensive architecture," "callous objects," or "obstinate objects," they include "anti-sleep benches" with armrest partitions or curvy shapes (Figures 15 and 16), "anti-homeless spikes" in front of store windows to prevent people from seeking refuge from inclement weather and loitering, "antipick garbage cans" that prevent people from fishing out food debris and recyclable items, and "skatestoppers" on a low wall with small metal nubs, sometimes called "pig ears," placed on the ledge (Figures 17 and 18).[62]

FIGURE 15 *Outdoor seating (downtown Providence, Rhode Island, USA).*

FIGURE 16 *Outdoor bench (New York City).*

FIGURE 17 *Bench outside a hotel (Phoenix, Arizona).*

FIGURE 18 *Outdoor seating (downtown Boston).*

Although sharp spikes may signal their function to everyone loud and clear, anti-sleep benches, antipick garbage cans, and skatestoppers are innocuous enough not to be noticed at all by those who use benches, garbage cans, and walls only for their intended primary functions of sitting and disposing of garbage. The benches' armrest, curvy shape, locked lid for garbage cans, and pig ears thus remain invisible to them. Robert Rosenberger describes a typical commuter's perception of these objects as "a phenomenology of political occlusion":

> Imagine that the commuter . . . is not herself living unhoused and rarely, if ever, thinks about things like trash picking, sleeping on benches, or navigating antiloitering ordinances. Despite using this bus stop every day, it is possible that this person will at most times be barely—if at all—aware of the antihomeless agenda built into this setting. . . . The utter normalcy of the experience itself keeps the politics occluded from view.[63]

These examples may pose extreme cases fraught with problematic moral, social, and political significance, but if we attend to our everyday environment with a critical eye, we may realize that many of its parts are designed to suit the dominant segment of the society, usually consisting of the economically advantaged, able-bodied, regularly sized, relatively unencumbered, cis-gendered, and literate. These assumptions regarding targeted users render negotiating public space challenging for the unhoused, the physically challenged, short or obese people, those carrying babies (in particular more than one)[64] or many large and heavy packages (typically those without cars who need to do grocery shopping using public transportation), transgendered, and those who are not proficient in the local language. Or, conversely, those objects mentioned in the last section, such as a cane holder and the different lengths of the subway hanging straps, that address some of these people's needs remain unnoticed by those without special needs. What can pose challenges and obstacles to some segments of society, as well as their solutions, remain invisible to the dominant group. Rosenberger points out that part of what may prevent us from seeing the politics built into the world around us is the basic fact that we are each limited by our own personal history of experience. . . . [W]hat each person knows is limited by the fact that she is an individual body in the world with a particular vantage point and a particular restricted set of life experiences.[65]

This brings us back to the main tenet of care ethics and aesthetic experience discussed in Chapter 1: the importance of experiencing the other, whether a person or an object, on its own terms through unselfing and decentering while activating the imagination.

While these examples of hostile architecture or callous object are clearly meant for an exclusionary purpose, there are others that are not intended but act as a de facto means of exclusion or oppression. Calling them "oppressive things," Shen-yi Liao and Bryce Huebner argue that artifacts can be racist, with or without the creator's intention. An example like the Kodak's Shirley card, which was "the standard tool used by professional photographers to calibrate skin-color balance during the printing process," constitutes "light-skin bias."[66] Designed to take light-skin color as the norm, thereby skewing the resultant colors of dark skin, they show how such objects help normalize whiteness while nonwhiteness as deviation. Racism is not just an idea or attitude held by people. It can be enacted by objects; hence the notion of "racist objects" which they define as follows:

> racist things are material artifacts and spatial environments that partially constitute the stability and structure of this racial frame, while also shaping the habits of attention and categorization and the attitudes that are typically adopted by people who live and act within this racial frame.[67]

Unlike in the case of defensive architecture, the examples of oppressive things are even more insidious and below the radar of most people because of the absence of explicit racist intention. It is a difference between Robert Moses having a racist intention in the construction of the parkways and the case in which the intention is to exclude large vehicles like busses and trucks from being on the parkways to create a more relaxing and leisurely atmosphere befitting the name, parkway, without giving a thought that most passengers on the busses are black people.

The point of gathering these examples is to show that artifacts can be considered to exert agency by shaping human actions, often with moral consequences, even though they cannot be held responsible, and their agency is thereby different from the agency attributed to human beings. If agency in the sense explained can be attributed to artifacts, it is not far-fetched to endow them with moral qualities and evaluate them accordingly. Given the fact that artifacts are designed and created by humans, their expression of moral qualities can be considered as belonging to the realm of social aesthetics. Just as the aesthetic dimensions of my action helps determine its moral quality, the aesthetics of artifacts can be morally charged.

We should note that for the view that artifacts can be assigned agency because they shape human actions, thereby making sense of the moral attributes given to them, it is critical to keep in mind the fact that artifacts are designed and created by human intentional acts. Natural objects also shape our actions. For example, a steep mountain makes us walk around it to reach the other side, an apple tree invites us to pick its fruits, and the rain forces us to cancel an outdoor event. But we don't normally attribute moral qualities such as thoughtlessness or generosity to nature.[68] With the framework surrounding the view I have been discussing, the difference is due to the fact that nature works for or against us independently of us, while the way in which artifacts shape our actions could have been otherwise, either through a different design or by not creating the object in the first place. However, this distinction between artifacts and nature may be endemic to the Western philosophical framework. In other cultural traditions, such as some of the indigenous American traditions, it is not strange at all to assign generosity to a natural phenomenon or an object by thanking the rain for watering crops or a buffalo for giving up its life to feed its human siblings. I will explore this issue more in Section 1 of the next chapter.

When reviewing the examples used to illustrate the agency of artifacts, we note that they tend toward directing us *not* to do or *stop* doing certain things: sleeping on the bench, skateboarding, taking the bus to the beach, speeding when driving, spilling when urinating, and rummaging through garbage bins. Perhaps it is the most effective way of illustrating the agency of artifacts because the result is fairly clear. One cannot sleep on the anti-sleep benches, skateboard on skatestoppers, or drive fast over a speed bump (I suppose one can but with a big price to pay for the damage to the car, not to mention an unpleasant jolt).[69] The design of these objects is *reactive* in the sense that they are addressing what is perceived to be a problem that needs to be corrected.

What deserves more attention, I believe, is the way in which artifacts are characterized as exercising agency in *proactively* exhibiting care for others, illustrated by many Japanese practices and the design of things underfoot that I mentioned before. If some artifacts are considered to exercise moral agency by shaping our behavior, as Verbeek suggests, it should include not only those that change our behavior that is deemed undesirable for the society at large and our own well-being but also those which facilitate and enhance the good for the society and our well-being. Guiding us to stop risky behavior such as speeding on the street can be considered a sign of care for our safety. However, care can be expressed in a more positive way by facilitating a delightful aesthetic experience, such as the meandering path in the Japanese garden, the salmon decorations on the airport floor, the meticulous arrangement of food, and the like, as well as easing the minor nuisances and inconveniences of daily life like not having a place to rest a cane or buttons that are too small to handle.

Care ethics and aesthetics help encourage proactive measures to promote not only social relationships and actions based upon care but also the creation of objects and built environment that give outward expression to the fact that care is given to every member, particularly the vulnerable, of the society. A humane and civilized society requires building the living environment for its members that provides tangible signs that the quality of their experience is taken seriously and responded to. Artifacts such as the OXO peeler, Busch states, "are instruments not simply of food preparation, but of human behavior, coordinates that can help us calibrate our place in human relations," and they "can be the small agents of *human decency*."[70] If I am surrounded by such small agents of human decency indicative of the care given to my needs, comfort, and well-being, I become disposed to pay it forward by spreading the gift of care. Unlike the care relationship between two people which requires reciprocity in some form, when care is mediated by artifacts with unknown designers or creators, I cannot reciprocate in the same sense. Even when I know the designer or creator of the object, it seems beside the point to convey my appreciation to that person, although such a gesture may be welcome. Rather, when I am favorably affected by the expression of care in my everyday objects and environments, I believe my sensibility, both aesthetic and moral, becomes sharpened so that I become more sensitive to other people's well-being and needs and act accordingly. For example, by noting the different lengths of hanging straps in a subway, I become more attuned to how people of different statures are faring in a crowded subway. If someone with a short stature is struggling to keep balance, I may try to yield my space to her so that she can hang on to a longer hanging strap or a nearby pole.

Or, as Joan Nassauer, a landscape architect, states, visible evidence of care elicits an aesthetic response that is "potent in affecting behaviour. Sometimes the look of a well-cared-for landscape makes us feel good, and we may act to get or to share that good feeling, an aesthetic response."[71] Such a landscape gives a cue that it is worth maintaining and caring. This recognition will inspire me not to damage it, at the minimum, but furthermore to turn me into a literal caretaker by helping with tending the landscape. No matter how ecologically sound a landscape may be, if it appears to be neglected and unkempt, it is difficult to inspire a caring response from the onlooker. Thus, she argues for some recognizable cues of care, such as a neat border or a well-maintained fence, even if the garden itself consists of wildflowers growing freely and profusely, which is more ecologically sound compared to the monoculture of green lawn that is dependent upon heavy use of water and chemicals for its maintenance.[72] The "visible evidence of care and stewardship often elicits a response that is not only normative . . . but also aesthetic," and, as an immediate response, "it may be even more potent in affecting behavior."[73]

While the fact that recognition and appreciation of the signs of care inspire care and stewardship in the onlooker may be globalized, Nassauer points out that what are considered signs of care are culturally contextual and locally based. Hence, as in any aesthetic experience, it is critical that our aesthetic response to the sign of care is focused on the particularity of the constructed landscape with its specific local conditions and cultural context. She suggests: "Care may be a global construct of aesthetic quality that is exhibited in different forms in different local conditions. If so, identifying forms of care and introducing new forms of care may be a useful tool for landscape ecology and sustainable development."[74]

The social relationship supported by care that I explored in this chapter is on an individual, personal level. It may appear that such micro-level matters pale in comparison to macro-level considerations such as the societal care for its members and the humanity's care for the global environment. Such pressing social, political, and environmental issues certainly need a macro-scale exploration from various perspectives: politics, law, sociology, anthropology, psychology, science, agriculture, and environmental management, to name some obvious ones. However, insofar as aesthetics can play a role in expressing and inspiring care for the other, whether it be another human being, object, or environment, the nature of aesthetic experience that requires direct experience of the singularity of the other necessitates focusing on the micro-level. However, Nassauer is optimistic that "bringing the immediacy of aesthetic satisfaction and neighborhood concern to a planetary community of care may be within our reach" because "our propensity to care for small places and familiar people may extend and aggregate across and beyond landscapes."[75]

This optimism regarding how appreciation of care and active participation on the micro-level can extend to the macro-level is shared by those who are engaged in participatory art projects that embody care acts and relationships. For example, by analyzing case studies of theater projects that are constituted by people's participation based upon developing and engaging in care relationships and acts with each other, James Thompson states: "Intimate care . . . can be connected to an affective solidarity and felt sense of justice, and ultimately might be foundational to the ethics and aesthetics of a theatre and arts practice that seeks to engage with communities."[76] As a theater experience which is public, the presumably private realm of care that is usually invisible, unnoticed, and taken for granted is given an explicit expression, blurring the so-called distinction between the private and the public. Furthermore, as a theatrical event, the aesthetic dimensions involved in reciprocal relationships, a collaborative venture, and interpersonal interdependencies are made visible, such as the orientation and movements of participants' bodies in relationship with the others, not to mention their facial expression and the tone of voice. The embodied care relationship experienced from within, so to speak, as participants rather than spectators, it is expected, will lead them to be attuned to the communal ethos based upon respect and care for one another. Such a feeling forms the foundation of a just society where everyone's voice is respected and heard, interdependent and collaborative relationship is encouraged rather than regarded as weakness that compromises individual autonomy and independence, and empathetic responsiveness to one another is promoted and practiced. According to Thompson, "felt, embodied, careful collaborative acts of mutual reliance are the minute building blocks of that more caring, just society," and "an aesthetics of care can be a demonstration, a showing of caring, but . . . it can be the actual moment of building a more just distribution of caring and increase participants' capacity to care and be cared for."[77]

Insofar as care-driven ethical actions requires aesthetic engagement, which in turn requires direct perceptual experience, the focus should be on the micro-level: a personal relationship with the other. Just as care ethics practiced by an individual cannot extend to universal care for all the starving people, individuals' care for the environment cannot be directed on the global scale. Those large-scale issues must be addressed by political discourse that by necessity depends upon a generalized approach. However, this is not to diminish the significance of our personal engagement with the other that is driven by care and mediated by aesthetics. Just like Nassauer, I believe that the cumulative effect of our individual care activities helps shape the world. Similarly, as James Thompson claims in relation to theater arts that involve all the participants in developing embodied care relationship with each other, such small-scale movements "suggest something grander as potential sources for gentler, kinder forms of inter-human relations" and "hints of a more hopeful, equitable way of being together."[78] In short, the aesthetics of care provides an effective means of cultivating the ethics of care that can promote a just society and a sustainable world.

* * *

This chapter was devoted to exploring various aspects of interhuman care relationships, whether through direct interactions or mediated by objects. Objects in this context were regarded as a vehicle for expressing care for other humans. But what about our interactions with objects themselves for what they are? In the next chapter, I shall explore the ways in which we individually interact with the material world motivated by care.

4

Care Relationship and Activities with the Material World

I argued in the last chapter that the aesthetics of care can easily accommodate social aesthetics, that is, the aesthetic dimension of interpersonal relationships and interactions. By focusing aesthetic concerns on the nature of experience rather than a specific kind of objects, social interactions are very much within the purview of aesthetic inquiry. Although I also argued that the aesthetics of social interactions can be medicated by objects, the primary focus of social interaction is interpersonal relationships. Hence, it marks a shift from the object-centered framework that has dominated Western aesthetic discourse.

If we view the matter from the perspective of care ethics, we can also pursue aesthetics in the reverse direction: from persons to objects. That is, care ethics primarily concerns the nature of human relationships, but I have argued in Chapter 1 that it can also explain the nature of aesthetic experience in general. While I referred to Arnold Berleant's social aesthetics as an "objects into persons" previously, his notion of aesthetic engagement encompasses the reverse move from persons to objects as well:

Aesthetic engagement is an experience of aesthetic appreciation that transforms a physical juxtaposition into a social relationship in which a personal encounter takes place. It projects the aesthetic connection we can experience in the arts into our engagement with other people and with *things*, as well, turning our encounter with separate, *impersonal objects* into personal relationships.[1]

While the aesthetic experience of art has been extensively analyzed in aesthetics discourse, relatively less discussed is the nature of the aesthetic experience of the material world in general, in particular artifactual objects with which we interact daily. In this chapter, I shall explore various ways in which care ethics can guide our relationship and aesthetic interaction with the material world.

1 Relationship with Material Objects

It may appear that ethical care is incompatible with objects in light of Martin Buber's I-It relationship, which typically characterizes human-object relationship. Although Buber's main concern is to lift human-human relationship from I-It to I-You, were he to have explored the implications of his view further, it is possible that he may have considered the application of I-You relationship to human-object relationship. In his 1957 "Afterword" to the original publication of *I and Thou* in 1923, he considers and responds to a possible question regarding the human-nature relationship. He points out that "we occasionally encounter a similar contact between men and animals: some men have deep down in their being a potential partnership with animals."[2] Though not specifying any person, he may have in mind somebody like St. Francis of Assisi, as he characterizes such a person as "spiritual." He admits that a plant "cannot react to our actions upon it, that it cannot 'reply,'" thereby seeming to indicate that it cannot be treated as You.[3] However, he speculates further:

> this does not mean that we meet with no reciprocity at all on this sphere. We find here not the deed of posture of an individual being but a reciprocity of being itself—a reciprocity that has nothing except being. . . . The living wholeness and unity of a tree that denies itself to the eye, no matter how keen of anyone who merely investigates, while it is manifest to those who say You, is

present when *they* are present: they grant the tree the opportunity to manifest it and now the tree that has being manifests it.

He is tentative in applying I-You relationship to plants, as he characterizes this possibility as the "pre-threshold."

I believe it is relatively easy for humans to relate to living things in nature, namely nonhuman animals and plants, particularly with contemporary environmental ethics' expansion of the moral domain to include them. Caring for our animal companions is very much like caring for our children, and caring for plants is also commonly practiced by many of us working in our gardens. All our care activities for living things in this regard make sense because we can more or less figure out what constitutes their good. We try to help them grow and thrive by contributing to their own good.

Beyond caring for our animal companions and plants in our gardens, we are witnessing an increasing number of tangible projects specifically designed to protect wildlife. For example, animal crossing corridors and tunnels above or below busy highways have been constructed to secure the safety and well-being of wildlife whose habitats have become increasingly jeopardized by human expansion.[4] In addition, some contemporary artists create objects for the benefit of wildlife. For example, Lynn Hull's "trans-species art" provides sculptural structures on trees and electric poles for easy roosting and nest-making for birds, carved patterns on stones in the desert to retain water for drinking, and duck islands with wood and mixed media. Other projects which are dubbed as "equal opportunity housing" by Elizabeth Lynch include bat houses, nesting boxes, and foundations for artificial coral reefs. Lynch explains that "these projects supply homes for animals while attending to human aesthetic concerns."[5] The aesthetic appeal of these projects is critical in promoting the ideal of coexistence of humans and nonhumans so that their utility value to animals does not sacrifice the aesthetics of the environment for humans, thereby indicating that care for nonhumans and the care for humans can be integrated.

Even for nonsentient things like plants, sometimes we treat them as if they were sentient with a capacity to receive our caring attention. Consider the indigenous Americans' practice of signing to the corn related by Buffalo Bird Woman: "We cared for our corn in those days as we would care for a child, for we Indian people loved our gardens, just as a mother loves her children, and we thought that our growing corn liked to hear us sing, just as children like to hear their mother sing to them."[6] Regarding some gardeners who talk to their plants to encourage their growth, David E. Cooper comments: "when this is viewed, not as a horticultural experiment but as expressive of a sense of being engaged with the plants in a mutual enterprise—of a shared good—it is no more to be derided than the 'conversations' people have with their pets."[7] A contemporary Japanese master gardener, Masuno Shunmyo, similarly bases his practice by paying attention to what each material is "requesting" and engaging in a dialogue with it.[8] However, we cannot dismiss these care acts for plants for being "weird" or "flaky" because talking, having a dialogue with them, and singing to them does not work like a fertilizer. Instead, such seemingly inane acts manifest a care relationship we develop with plants while tending to the needs of the specific plant growing with a specific soil condition and local climate, and, by adjusting our care action accordingly, sometimes coming up with a creative and imaginative solution. Plants in return often reciprocate by bearing beautiful flowers or bountiful crop.

The care for plants is also manifested by the design of some protective devices seen in Japan. While protecting tree branches from the weight of snow or their root system from various elements, their elegant appearance exudes a gentle and caring attitude (Figures 19 and 20). These devices caress and embrace the trees; at the same time, their design shows care for the passersby whose environment is graced with this elegant display. They also illustrate the cues to care proposed by Joan Nassauer discussed at the end of the last chapter.

Thus, application of care relationship seems generally unproblematic for nonhuman animals and plants which we regard as having a good of their own. However, what about nonliving things in nature, such as rocks and icicles, and artifacts, in short inanimate objects? Buber does seem to suggest the possibility of developing an I-You relationship with inanimate objects in nature by issuing a cautionary statement: "we should do justice with an open mind to the actuality that opens up before us" that is provided by "this huge sphere that reaches from the stones to the stars."[9]

FIGURE 19 *Tree with snow protection (Sapporo, Japan).*

FIGURE 20 *Tree root protection (Osaka, Japan).*

Now, among inanimate objects, nature may allow for a fairly easy extension of his vision of I-You relationship because it is not "ours" in the same way another person is not "mine." As we reflect on the harmful environmental legacy of anthropocentrism, we could regard members of nature, both animate and inanimate, sentient and nonsentient, as belonging to the moral sphere subject to our ethical treatment. The so-called environmental holism holds that nature as a whole demands moral consideration. Aldo Leopold's land ethics can be interpreted in this way.[10] For the purpose of the discussion here, I set aside various views and controversies over according moral status to inanimate objects of nature, species as a whole, or nature as a whole.

However, what about artifacts that are our creations? The second formulation of Kant's categorical imperative that we should treat humans as an end but never merely as a means seems to imply that this ethical imperative does not apply to artifacts which can be treated solely as a means, our typical interactions with them. This difference is often justified by the fact that a thing, unlike humans or natural objects, does not have a good of its own that can be damaged by our uncaring attitude or careless handling. The damage to artifacts that cripple their functionality or compromise their appearance harms their owners and users, not the objects themselves. The conventional framework in Western moral discourse would categorize artifacts as a typical example of those entities *to which* we humans do not have any obligation, although we may have an obligation *with regard to* them. There may be a number of reasons why we should treat an artifact with care, such as its value to other humans, the duty we have toward its owner, a danger posed to others if we do not handle it with care, and so on. But it is generally assumed that we don't owe *the object itself* anything; we don't wrong *it* if we neglect its care, handle it roughly, or damage it. Magdalena Hoły-Łuczaj points out that artifacts in general thus suffer from ontological inferiority compared to nature, and certainly humans, because their existence always depends upon anthropocentric reasons and human activities.[11] Furthermore, they are not self-generative and lack their own internal telos. Does this mean that artifacts are outside of the moral sphere, hence demanding no moral treatment from us?

There are two possible ways care ethics can address this issue. One is to enfranchise artifacts into the moral domain. The other is to change the entire orientation and focus on the way in which we carry ourselves in the world and interact with entities within, rather than adjusting our conduct based upon the moral status of the entity. I shall argue that this second possibility is more promising. However, let me first explore the first strategy.

Within the Western ontological framework, it may indeed be difficult, if not impossible, to attribute any moral status to artifacts, because they lack sentience, free will, and agency, long thought to be the requirements for moral considerability. The prime example of members of a moral community on the basis of these attributes is human beings. Moral considerability of other entities is determined by how much of these attributes they have in common with humans. Steven Vogel characterizes this familiar move as follows: "criteria for moral considerability such as sentience or life involve emphasizing points of commonality between humans and certain groups of nonhumans and then extending the moral concern we unquestioningly grant each other to nonhumans to which we are significantly similar."[12] In addition, as Andrew Light and Holmes Rolston III state, moral community membership consists of two factors: "moral patienthood" and "moral agency."

> Many ethicists accept a distinction between moral *agents* and moral *patients*. The class of moral patients is that class of beings to whom we consider that we owe ethical obligations . . . and are deserving of . . . moral considerability. Moral agents are defined as that class of moral patients, usually only persons, to whom we owe obligations and who, in turn, are held do be morally responsible for their actions. All moral agents are moral patients but not all moral patients are moral agents. When we accord moral agents moral recognition we can expect them to live up to certain duties related to the respect of those obligations. On the other hand, if a being is only a moral patient and not a moral agent we do not expect it to be morally responsible for its actions.[13]

The debate then focuses on the criteria for moral patienthood, and they usually include sentience, life, or existence independent of humans (such as inanimate things of nature). The consensus seems to be that all humans deserve moral considerability based upon moral patienthood, although some humans, such as infants, mentally deficient members, and patients in a vegetative state, lack moral agency. In contrast, artifacts lack moral patienthood because they lack sentience or good of their own, let alone personhood. Where does this leave artifacts? If we attribute agency to artifacts by shaping our actions, as I argued in the last chapter, can they be enfranchised into the moral domain? The fact that artifacts cannot be held to be responsible for intentionality or free action does not pose a problem for their moral considerability, as the same holds for babies, mentally deficient humans, and nature.

In a provocative discussion, Steven Vogel makes a case for the possibility and importance of "thinking like a mall," just as Aldo Leopold argues for the land ethic by "thinking like a mountain." Despite the obvious fact that a mall is an artifact and its existence is wholly dependent upon a human creative act, he points out that it is endowed with autonomy, like a mountain, in the sense of "being *left alone*" without involving "some sort of internally directed teleological self-development" as in the case of biological organisms.[14] Just as a mountain goes through many changes brought about by climate conditions, growth and decay of fauna and flora, and human activities, a mall is not fully determined by the architect or builder. It goes through vicissitudes due to social and natural forces. Despite the commonly regarded view that an artifact like a mall is completely dependent upon humans, hence lacking autonomy, and cannot be a genuine "other" to humans, Vogel concludes that "to think like a mall would be to see that it, too, might know something that we do not, and to realize that the social world, too, can be autonomous of us, just as beyond our understanding, and beyond our wishes, as a mountain."[15]

A similar point is made by a different approach suggested by Anne Eaton, whose main concern is to define the function of an object such that the function depends neither upon the maker's intention nor how an object happens to function as or is put to use. The intentionalist view cannot account for the unintended or unforeseen way in which the object comes to be used, while the conventionalist view cannot distinguish between the object's genuine function and the fortuitous way in which an object is put to use. She instead offers an evolutionary account of the object's function. Just as the biological evolution proceeds whereby an organism evolves in response to its environment and simultaneously changes the environment, an artifact is also intimately entangled with its environment, which is the historical and cultural context. Hence, "we should conceive of functions not as performances or activities that once-and-for-all meet pre-existent environmental demands but, rather, as a dynamic feedback loop where continually shifting performances shape the demands that these performances meet."[16] Her evolutionary account can be interpreted as a challenge to human-dependent definition of artifacts, whether by reference to the maker's intention or the user's use. It is then possible that the commonly held gap between humans with free will, intentionality, and autonomy and artifacts that are not endowed with any of these capacities is not as wide as it may first appear to be. If so, it paves the way for reconsidering the ontological inferiority of artifacts that is invoked to exclude them from the moral community.

It should also be noted that the ontological inferiority of artifacts is not shared universally, as I briefly mentioned in the last section. Various forms of religious and cultural traditions accord something akin to a spirit or a soul to even inanimate objects, not only from nature such as rocks and mountains but also from the artifactual realm. For example, Japanese culture has a long tradition of honoring artifacts such as knives, needles, and dolls and expressing respect and gratitude toward them when retiring them by giving them to temples or shrines for a proper service and disposal (*kuyō* 供養), instead of throwing them in trash. Today, seal stamps (*hanko* or *inkan* 印鑑) used for certifying official documents in Japan seem to have joined the rank, as Japan moves toward digitization.[17] In fact, Sōetsu Yanagi characterizes innocuous and humble everyday objects made by unknown craftsmen as having a heart:

> But to think of them as nothing but physical objects would be an error. They may simply be things, but who can say that they don't have a heart? Forbearance, wholesomeness, and sincerity—aren't these virtues witnesses to the fact that everyday objects have a heart?[18]

He describes their way of being in the world with us as "loyal companions" and "faithful friends" who "work thoughtlessly and unselfishly, carrying out effortlessly and inconspicuously whatever duty comes their way."[19] Their presence and the usefulness offer "an expression of humility."

So as not to imply that this view of the artifactual world is limited to non-Western thinking, consider the following lovely poem by an American poet, Pat Schneider, titled "The Patience of Ordinary Things":

It is a kind of love, is it not?
How the cup holds the tea,
How the chair stands sturdy and foursquare,
How the floor receives the bottoms of shoes
Or toes. How soles of feet know
Where they're supposed to be.
I've been thinking about the patience
Of ordinary things, how clothes
Wait respectfully in closets
And soap dries quietly in the dish,
And towels drink the wet
From the skin of the back.
And the lovely repetition of stairs.
And what is more generous than a window?[20]

These characterizations of objects may strike those who are versed in Western ontology as a form of anthropomorphism or a quaint form of animism. But also consider Heidegger's ontology of "things." While the existence of a jug is made possible by human making, he claims that "the jug's thingness resides in its being *qua* vessel" and "the vessel's thingness does not lie at all in the material of which it consists, but in the void that holds."[21] Because of its void, the jug can take in and retain what is poured into it. When pouring out, the jug gives a gift of whatever is poured out.

The holding of the vessel occurs in the giving of the outpouring. Holding needs the void as that which holds. The nature of the holding void is gathered in the giving. But giving is richer than a mere pouring out. . . . The jug's jug-character consists in the poured gift of the pouring out. Even the empty jug retains its nature by virtue of the poured gift.[22]

Strictly speaking, the jug itself is an inert object, and it is us humans who do the pouring in and pouring out. However, he attributes the identity of this object to these acts; furthermore, he characterizes this feature of the jug as giving gift rather than a mechanical action of pouring out. Somewhat similar to both Yanagi and Schneider, he characterizes the jug's mode of being as "modestly" and "inconspicuously compliant."[23]

Ultimately, however, if this way of understanding artifacts is interpreted as determining their moral considerability, which in turn determines a basis for our care relationship, I believe it is unhelpful. The assumption behind this strategy is that our moral duties are determined by the moral status of the other. The assessment of the ontology takes precedence over moral deliberation. This makes our moral life reactive and fragmented by "making calculations and deliberations concerning each separate action, which would be quite alien to our everyday practices," as pointed out by Hoły-Łuczaj.[24] Furthermore, our moral life becomes compartmentalized between the spheres of "on-duty" and "off-duty," as pointed out by Cooper with reference to Joel Kupperman's work.[25] Iris Murdoch also points out that "the moral life . . . is something that goes on continually, not something that is switched off in between the occurrence of explicit moral choices."[26] Although such occasions of moral choices constitute perhaps the most dramatic dimensions, our moral life concerns our way of being in the world in general that supports the occasional "one-off" moral decisions and choices. Finally, this way of determining our moral duty rests on the same logic that led us in the past (and many would claim is still the case today) to justify acting differently toward various oppressed beings, due to their race, gender, sexual orientation, age, ethnicity, disability, culture, and species membership, among others. Our actions toward them, according to the view under consideration, is conditional upon whether we grant them moral considerability (and, of course, the crucial question is, who is "we" that makes this judgment?).

One could claim that if we enfranchise artifacts into the moral sphere, every being and thing we interact with demands moral considerability so there will be no "off duty" time in our moral life. However, this result is conditional upon accepting the moral considerability of artifacts, and, although I have given some reasons in support, it is far from clear whether such a view will be widely accepted. Instead, I propose that it is more promising and faithfully reflective of our moral life as we live it to focus on how we conduct ourselves in the world and interact with the other, regardless of what the other may be. As I have argued, the care relationship is primarily concerned with our mode of being in the world, as we interact with others. Although I have also argued against universal care by pointing out not all "others" are worthy of our care, it is meant as a corrective or secondary consideration to the cultivation of open-mindedness, respect for the singularity, and collaborative relationship with the other. I suggest that the attitude of care should be the default stance which may be overridden through practical wisdom by some cases of nonworthy others, rather than starting with classifying others based upon their moral considerability.[27] The next section will outline an argument in favor of this stance.

2 Human Actions on Artifacts

In discussing how we should conduct ourselves with the material world, Simon James contrasts two strategies.[28] One is "moral pull" that bases our actions on the moral considerability of the object. The other is "moral push" that puts primacy on our attitudes and actions. Although he does not specifically mention care ethics, James invokes virtue ethics to argue for the stance of "moral push" toward inanimate things. Rather than reacting to the "moral pull" of the other in response to its moral considerability, care ethics promotes a proactive approach to the other as a way of being in the world and relating to the world, including inanimate objects. He regards "gentleness" as a virtue that should accompany our interaction with objects. If someone "routinely and gratuitously breaks, chips, rips, shatters, splinters and dents inanimate things," we judge that such a person "must have fallen short of the ideal of moral goodness."[29] Indeed, there is something odd about a person, if such a person exists, who may act morally and caringly toward sentient beings while treating nonsentient objects callously or even violently with no good reason even when such an action does not indirectly harm other sentient beings.[30] For this perspective, it is irrelevant if those objects that are handled without care or, worse, do not have good of their own or rights. The focus is on the human agent's character:

"a morally good person would be disposed to treat certain things gently" and "one must do more than simply appeal to the natures of the things in question."[31] In short, "part of what makes someone morally good or virtuous is the fact that she will tend to exhibit . . . a 'delicacy' towards her surroundings, taking care not to damage the things with which she deals, even when those things are neither sentient nor alive."[32]

The strategy based upon "moral pull" is thus reactive. The commitment to care in this case is conditional and we first need to assess the other's worthiness of our attention and care before adjusting our moral stance toward it. The strategy based upon "moral push" in contrast is proactive. We first decide on what kind of person we want to be and practice and carry out our aspirations in our interactions with the world, whatever the particular other we are interacting with at a specific moment. The default position is to lead a life of respectful, gentle, caring attitude toward the people and the world around us. The primacy is placed on the way of being in the world rather than assessing the moral status of the other. Only with the secondary judgment do we make a discrimination between those which deserve our care relationship and those which do not, including some persons, works of art, and artifacts, as mentioned in Chapter 2.

In light of this notion of "moral push," consider the following examples from Japanese artistic practices. Robert Carter reports on the making of a garden for the Canadian Museum of Civilization in Ottawa by a contemporary Japanese master gardener, Masuno Shunmyo:

> The work began on a cold, rainy day, and as the sand and rocks were being positioned by the Japanese crew under Masuno's detailed instructions, the Canadian workers were surprised by the way in which the Japanese crew entered and left the actual site by walking in the footsteps of a single pathway, which had already been established in the mud on the site, rather than tracking mud all over the newly placed sand, or on or around the rocks, keeping tracking and foreign markings to a minimum. It was a degree of *caring and concern* for the state and cleanliness of the site that was itself quite foreign to the Canadians on hand.[33]

When emphasizing the gentleness, it is irrelevant that mud does not damage the sand or rocks and that it can be cleaned away after the work is completed. Carter concludes how "landscape gardening brings about a *gentleness* in the designer, the builders, and the caretakers."[34] Furthermore, Masuno reports that designing the garden with trees and rocks results from engaging in "a kind of dialogue with them," and Carter characterizes them as "Thou" rather than as "It."[35]

Carter also remarks on a similarly respectful attitude that informs the Japanese art of flower arrangement. While this art form begins paradoxically by cutting off a live flower or branch, initiating its death, its primary aim is to "let flower live," literally the translation of *ikebana* (生け花), or to "let flower express itself" (*ikasu* 生かす).[36] The materials used in this art are thus no longer living nature. However, Carter observes "the *tender* way in which the materials for flower arrangements are handled," which includes carefully unwrapping the bundle of flowers to be used, gently bending and twisting when shaping the branches and stems, and neatly arranging unused remnants of flowers for disposal.[37] The last action is particularly noteworthy because the remnants are disposed of, so it is not as if they will be visible to others, unlike those parts that are arranged for display. Hence, one could say it is an inane gesture, unless one is concerned to treat even those remnants with care and respect. Ultimately, Carter states that the aim of flower arrangement is "not just to teach techniques and basic skills, but to convey attitudes which would apply both to flower arranging and to living one's life generally."[38]

Also consider Carter's description of how a master potter, Shōji Hamada, designated in 1955 as a Living National Treasure of Japan by the Japanese government, handled a pottery piece:

He would sit down on the floor . . . carefully unwrap a piece. . . . We would talk about each piece, touch each piece in order to get the feel of it, and then he would slowly and carefully rewrap it, for this, too, was part of the journey of appreciation that he had taken me on . . . for Hamada, the rewrapping, the care of each piece, was part of being drenched in the beauty of each object. It was done as a sign of respect and appreciation.[39]

Hamada's careful handling is no doubt partly motivated by a desire not to break the piece, but it is clear that his relationship with the piece goes beyond "handle with care" typically observed by shipping clerks.

It is true that none of the rocks, flowers and a carefully wrapped prized object in these examples is objects of daily use and the actions regarding them take place within a framework of art-making and art-handling. However, with the adoption of "moral push," we can extend the gentle, tender, and care-full handling to our everyday objects, such as a teapot, a bicycle, and a broom, examples given by James, not simply for the purpose of "handle with care" or "keep it clean" but, more importantly, for practicing our way of engaging with the material world. I believe it is meaningful and, as I shall argue, important and pressing particularly today, to develop a care relationship with the material world in general.

In this regard, let us revisit Yanagi's characterization of objects having a heart, Schneider's notion of patience of things, and Heidegger's description of a jug pouring a gift. I suggest that Yanagi and Schneider are not so much making an observation on the ontological status of artifacts but rather suggesting a way for us to relate to them. Yanagi's characterization of them as "companions" and "friends" implies how we should relate to them, as these terms describe relations. For them to be our friends, we need to hold our end of the bargain by honoring and appreciating the relationship by treating them with care. By characterizing the way in which a cup, a chair, a floor, and other things of daily use patiently serve us, Schneider is encouraging us to experience the world somewhat paradoxically, from an unselfed, decentered position. That is, although they are described as serving our needs, the poem orients us to view the world from their perspective. Instead of being inert objects that fulfill their function, they are actively doing things to serve us. As such, we have a relationship with them, as if they were our faithful and patient companions. Although Heidegger is making an ontological claim about the jug, characterizing what it does not as a mechanical movement of pouring but rather as gift-giving, we as the recipient of what gets poured become implicated in a relationship with the jug.

Here we can reframe Heidegger's two notions regarding our relationship with things: ready-to-hand (*zuhanden*) and present-at-hand (*vorhanden*). When things are functioning as they should, the objects themselves become an extension of ourselves, such as a hammer as a part of our hand, hence invisible: ready-to-hand. Only when they break or malfunction do we become aware of their existence as a material object. They confront us with their reality, present-at-hand, that is conveniently ignored by us most of the time. "The familiarity itself becomes visible in a conspicuous manner only when what is at hand is discovered circumspectly in the deficient mode of taking care of things. When we do not find something in its place, the region of that place often becomes explicitly accessible as such for the first time."[40] I do believe that these two different ways in which we experience the material objects capture our experience. Our usual mode of experiencing the material objects is taking them for granted. However, this "taken-for-granted" mode of existence relegates objects to a category of second-class citizens compared to us humans who are considered to be the true movers and shakers of the world, including being creators and operators of these objects.

In light of our ethically grounded engagement with the world including inanimate objects that I have been developing, I find this commonly experienced hierarchical perspective problematic. That is, we feel no need to tend to the material world with care until or unless something happens to force us to confront the objects asserting their existence. Our attention to and engagement with objects are reactive rather than proactive; our attitude and action are determined by a version of the "moral pull" rather than the "moral push" strategy. Furthermore, their "taken-for-granted" status makes the objects of daily use invisible, preventing us from exploring the potential aesthetic experiences afforded by them.

3 Care Activities for Objects

The invisibility and "taken-for-granted-ness" of everyday objects is paralleled by the relative invisibility of care activities regarding them. In particular, cleaning and maintenance work are indispensable for the smooth operation of supposedly more "important" and "productive" activities, such as conducting various forms of business, teaching, and dispensing medical care. We take it for granted that the rooms, desks, buildings, and bathrooms are cleaned, garbage taken away, and everything is in working order the next morning.[41] As Steven J. Jackson points out, "think . . . of the differential visibility of faculty and nighttime cleaning staff on American university campuses and its relation to the highly skewed distributions of income that follow."[42] Just as objects normally experienced as "ready-to-hand" become "present-at-hand" when they malfunction, these care activities for objects and built-environments challenge us with their invisible "taken-for-granted-ness" when such activities are not performed as usual. Most of us have experienced the havoc and inconvenience when cleaning crew and garbage collectors go on strike. This hierarchy of visibility and accompanying structure of prestige and reward are also apparent today as many people work under the challenging condition imposed on them by the pandemic. Among the so-called essential workers, those featured as "heroes" are primarily the medical professionals but rarely the cleaning crew whose work is as essential and dangerous as those heroes. Hospitals cannot operate if things are not cleaned and sanitized or if their garbage does not get picked up.[43] As Sandra Laugier points out, when our normal life is disrupted by disaster, such as the pandemic, our dependencies and "radical vulnerability" become revealed, rendering the heretofore invisible care work at the forefront of visibility.[44]

It is noteworthy that some art projects shed light on these "invisible" acts of care and maintenance. One of the most prominent examples is the works by an American artist, Mierle Laderman Ukeles. Guided by her *Manifesto for Maintenance Art 1969! Proposal for an Exhibition "Care,"* her performance and installation projects with New York City's sanitation department, such as *Touch Sanitation* and *Maintenance Work*, highlight those works that support and maintain the city's operation. Maintenance work, such as cleaning, washing, repairing, and picking up the garbage, Ukeles complains, "is a drag; it takes all the fucking time . . . the mind boggles and chafes at the boredom. The culture confers lousy status on maintenance jobs = minimum wages, housewives = no pay."[45] Such work, which is "never done" and mostly carried out by the underprivileged and women, is absolutely necessary in order for a presumably more important "development" work to proceed.[46] Ukeles thus asks rhetorically: "after the revolution, who's going to pick up the garbage on Monday morning?"[47] Her works help illuminate and dignify such invisible and detested dimensions of everyday life. One critic reports that, when viewing her ballet piece performed by the sanitation workers, he marveled at their beautiful 360-degree turn as they picked up and threw the garbage bags into the truck.[48]

Similarly, in a series of paintings and installations, Ramiro Gomez features those laborers, such as domestic help, gardeners, and garbage collectors, whose largely invisible work is essential in keeping the society functioning. Regarding one such painting, *On Tenth Avenue (Chelsea)* (2018), he comments: "the labor and repair performed by the workers on 10th Avenue . . . play an absolutely necessary, vital role to the survival of our society. My paintings . . . make visible labor that otherwise is not recorded."[49] Similar activities in other parts of the world, such as garbage picking and dismantling defunct objects in search of parts that can be repurposed, are also documented in the media of photography and film. Vik Muniz's 2010 film, *Waste Land*, documents garbage picking of the world's biggest garbage dump at the outskirts of Rio de Janeiro. Edward Burtynski's *Shipbreaking* (2000) records the process of breaking apart aging ocean vessels in Bangladesh with a series of photographs.[50] Finally, a 2013 film, *Koolhaas Houselife*, documents the hardships as well as resilience, ingenuity, and patience of a cleaning lady who is tasked to clean an unusual house Rem Koolhaas designed for a French family.[51]

By shedding light on the activities that are often invisible and carried out by the socially and politically marginalized population, these art projects illustrate how "the sensible" can be redistributed in the sense discussed by Jacques Rancière. For him, the politics of aesthetics refers to what he calls "the distribution of the sensible," that is, "what is seen and what can be said about it, around who has the ability to see and the talent to speak."[52] These art projects can be considered as examples of how the organization of the sensible framed by the social and political power relationships can be challenged so that the invisible can gain prominence and the distribution of the sensible becomes more just.[53]

We can go even further by exploring this redistribution of the sensible from a first-person account, rather than as a spectator looking at Ukeles's and Gomez's art projects. We ourselves engage in activities of care and maintenance of objects in our daily life all the time, but we tend to regard them as chores and do not assign prominence as we do with more presumably important aspects of our lives, usually our occupation, studies, and parental care work. However, a case can be made that the care work for objects defines our self-identity as much as these latter works. Furthermore, despite usually not requiring sophisticated knowledge, those chores involve tacit and embodied knowledge that result in skills and at times artistry. Jayne Lloyd points out that "the processes undertaken to care for objects in everyday life are embodied experiences and the tacit skills and knowledge required to complete them are rarely consciously considered, voiced, shared or even acknowledged or understood," despite "the complex multi-sensory actions, skills and knowing."[54] In a case study of a woman in a care home suffering from dementia, Lloyd describes how this woman retained her self-identity and engaged in a form of self-care by performing the act of folding a sheet. The laundering task at the care home is performed by its staff, depriving her of the previous role as a caregiver for herself and others through caring for objects, namely laundering. Lloyd comments that "one way to conceptualise the relationality between people and processes that care for objects is to include objects as an integral part of the existing concept of a relationship-centred approach to care."[55] This example illustrates the challenge of giving care for people whose ability to care for themselves is compromised by physical or mental disability. On the one hand, caregivers must take over such care activities to ensure the care receivers' health and safety. At the same time, rendering them completely helpless and dependent deprives them of their sense of identity and self-ownership, which may compromise the genuine act of care for them.

4 Cherishing Objects

If it is agreed that there is an ethical dimension to our relationship with material objects, as I have tried to argue so far, what exactly does it entail? How do we engage with them through care? What is the role of aesthetics in this regard?

Perhaps the most prominent case of relating to an object as You rather than It is where the object is associated with personal memories and special meaning. We all have a special item that we cherish because it was a gift from a friend, a family heirloom handed down through several generations, or commemoration of a special occasion or a life-changing event. Even if it was mass-produced, the associated history and significance "singularize" it with its own biography, the term proposed by Igor Kopytoff, who draws a parallel between mass-produced, commodified things and slaves who were denied singularized individual identity, biography, and dignity.[56] Following this notion, Shannon Dawdy characterizes souvenirs thus:

> biography of the commodity, as soon as it enters the hands of a purchaser and travels home, becomes entangled with the biographies of individual humans, with their life passages of birth, marriage, and death. Adopted into a household, the object begins a process of singularization by means of a relationship with particular human handlers and a unique series of events resulting in the marks of wear and tear.[57]

However, such singularized objects tend to be things that we display or keep, rather than use daily. As such, we are more prone to think that they stop their life after the point of purchase or being gifted, and our care for the object is generally geared toward maintaining its "frozen" state. Furthermore, the significance of the resultant attachment is something external to the features of the object and the personal value is derived entirely from its associated (hi)story.[58] While we all have objects to cherish and are familiar with the special affection we have toward them, from the point of view of aesthetics these examples tend to lack what George Santayana refers to as "union," "fusion," or "incorporation" of "two terms:" namely "the object actually presented" and "the object suggested, the further thought, emotion, or image evoked, the thing expressed."[59] He claims that "the mementos of a lost friend do not become beautiful by virtue of the sentimental associations which may make them precious" because the division between the object itself and his memory continues to be unbridgeable, rendering its value not aesthetic.[60] I am not sure whether I would go so far as Santayana by denying any beauty to the object of sentimental attachment, but certainly whatever aesthetic value the object may have for me is not intersubjectively sharable.

But what about a more challenging case in which the objects are used, rather than just being kept or displayed, and lack any personal significance, such as a family history? Are they not worthy as objects for developing the care relationship? The problem is that today, at least in the developed nations, our lives are flooded with things we buy, incentivized by consumerism, and they typically end up not being cared for or kept. Their longevity as an object of use tends to be rather short. In the words of Peter-Paul Verbeek, their "psychological lifetime" is truncated because they get discarded even if the functionality is intact, thereby compromising "cultural durability."[61] Lacking a special story as in family heirloom, he recommends that those objects be designed to possess certain features to encourage a strong bond and affection by the user. Rather than relying on memories and stories extraneous to the object to make it an object of affection, Verbeek argues that the design strategy "must take place in a way that stimulates an attachment between people and the artifacts *themselves as material objects*. The bond that arises between people and products will have to concern the *concrete* object that *is present in the here and now*, and not only the meaning or symbols it carries or the functions it fulfils."[62]

Such design strategy includes what Verbeek calls "transparency," whereby the functionality of the object is made clear and legible, enabling easy repair by a layperson, and encouraging active engagement in its operation. Such a design contrasts particularly with today's hi-tech products that hides the functioning parts behind a slick and opaque exterior shell, which leaves the users clueless and completely dependent upon professional repairers. Although I suppose I can still develop and nurture an intimate relationship with my laptop, the impossibility of engaging in its care through repair compromises such a relationship. In short, even without a prior special personal association, active engagement, both perceptual and literal, encourages our experience of the object as Heideggerian "present-at-hand," in addition to something "ready-to-hand" that tends to recede from our experience as long as it is performing its assigned function.

While the symbolic import of an object, such as an associated memory and family history, certainly enhances our attachment to the object, which in turn encourages a caring relationship with it, it does not concern the particular features of the object itself, as noted by Santayana. In order to facilitate cultural durability and longevity of psychological lifetime of an object, it is more important that the object's materiality becomes the vehicle. And I contend that this is an aesthetic concern, not in the sense of a beautiful or elegant design but in the sense of giving tangible evidence of the object's invitation to engage us in interacting with it and experiencing it more as a You than an It. We continue the object's history through its own aging process and our interaction with it, each stage exhibiting a unique characteristic rather than compromising or damaging the original integrity of the object. It is no longer the anonymous other simply serving my needs but also something that grows together with me and shares a life and history with me.

In this context, it is interesting to hear that Naoto Fukasawa, one of the leading designers in contemporary Japan, characterizes his design philosophy called "Super Normal" as facilitating the longevity of the object as the user lives with it through repeated use: "Super Normal's about how things work in relation to our living with them. Not just in one-off use but interactively over the long term, in relation to everything else we own and use and the atmospheric influence all these things have on our lives."[63] Through repeated use, the object in one sense becomes imperfect by showing wear and tear, *shutaku* (手沢), but looked at from another point of view, it shows "the deepening of a relationship" with the user, which he identifies as *wabi-sabi*.[64] He summarizes this relationship as follows: "We come to appreciate an object through using it, and the more we use a good object, the more we are able to appreciate its qualities, and we may discover its beauty not just in how it ages but in *how we age with it*."[65]

This ongoing entanglement with the material world as a basis for our care relationship with it suggests that its temporal dimension is both backward-looking and forward-looking. That is, my relationship with an object is situated both in its past and in its ongoing story. I may not have shared its history because I did not take part in its making or I have not lived with it in the past, although I can take part in its past through imaginative engagement. Now that it is in my possession, I expect to share my life with it by going through various stages of vicissitude together through use, breakage, and repair, and at some point I may delegate its future life to my family, friend, or stranger, unless I put it to rest. Thus, my care relationship with this particular object is both past- and future-oriented, as well as present-engaged.

There is an intuitive sense that, as Simon James observes, "many old inanimate things are thought to deserve respectful treatment."[66] He suggests that a virtuous person respects the narrative associated with an object's history, such as the geological history that has shaped a mountain, and refrains from certain actions like hammering in many climbing bolts on its rock surface. Such an act drastically alters the narrative in a relatively short period of time. He concludes that "old objects, *qua* old, will typically embody, indicate, or in some other way relate to, certain stories or narratives, and humble persons will take these narratives into consideration in their practical deliberations."[67]

However, here I want to question whether it is only old things that deserve our respect. The narrative of an object may only have a recent, relatively short history, compared to the geological timeframe or archeological past. Perhaps the object was produced only last month before I purchased it. Does this mean that it does not merit a similar respect, or it must wait for a long time before it becomes worthy of respect? What about the future and hopefully long-term narrative I will create by living with this object through growing old together, experiencing different stages of aging process, sometimes the object supporting me and some other times I care for it through maintenance and repair work? Although it may be more natural for us to treat old objects with care and respect, I believe that it is particularly important today to include the object's narrative to include its future, as we are responsible for creating the right kind of narrative for the material world for the sake of the future generation.

Care activity for the material world should thus be directed toward futurity, in addition to here and now, the point stressed by Christopher Groves in his notion of "intergenerational justice." Care, according to him, operates in "a web of virtual futures and embodied pasts encrusted with present actuality," and it is "a relationship in which time and especially futurity are its vital core."[68] Of course, the specifics of what counts as care for the material world directed toward futurity are context-dependent, and I doubt there can be a one-size-fits-all formulae or rule. However, care ethics regarding the material world includes consideration of futurity, and I shall argue in the next section that our aesthetic engagement is one important means of facilitating it.

5 Aesthetics of Care Activities for the Material World

I argued in Chapter 1 that care ethics is primarily oriented toward a first-person account, rather than a third-party perspective with an emphasis on making a judgment that characterizes ethics dominated by duty, justice, and rights. This is a matter of orientation and emphasis, of course. So, it is possible to judge someone else's action from the care ethic perspective, while it is also possible to advocate cultivating a sense of duty and practice upholding justice and respecting rights. However, it seems to me that care ethics' main concern is for each of us to practice and develop a care relationship with the appropriate other. It does not remain just a theory but a call to action for practice. Although specifically referring to the Japanese view on ethics, the following observation made by Carter applies to care ethics:

> Correct ethical action most often grows out of concrete, physical training or repetition, and is best described as a cluster of attitudes about who one is in the world and how to properly and effectively interact with others. Ethics is not a theoretical, intellectual "meta" search, but a way of walking (or being) in the world.[69]

I pointed out that this action-oriented characterization also applies to aesthetic experience by emphasizing its active dimensions such as willful surrender to the object, responsive engagement, and activation of imagination. This characterization of aesthetic experience is meant both as its analysis and a call for cultivating sensibility that facilitates such an experience. Here I shall go further in exploring the aesthetics of actually doing things for/with artifacts that are motivated by care for them.

Just as I cannot claim to care for my friend if I never lift a finger even if it is as minimal and simple as giving her a word of encouragement, developing a care relationship with objects and cultivating an ethical way of being in the world surrounded with artifacts requires tangible manifestations. We have already seen examples of handling a pottery piece, garden materials, and flowers. The way in which these objects are handled is characterized as being gentle and tender.

However, such handling of objects is the minimum requirement for a care relationship with objects. Recall Simon James's discussion of virtue-centric ethics of gentleness shown toward inanimate objects. He contrasts such handling with inflicting wanton damage to them. Hoły-Łuczaj also emphasizes, in her discussion of the moral considerability of artifacts, that "the key to morally proper behavior in this framework entails the elimination of actions that lead to destroying things."[70] Note that both emphasize "refraining from" damaging objects. However, *not* harming them can stem from indifference or neglect. Imagine a person who does not do anything to break or destroy an object but does not do anything in way of care activities, such as cleaning and repairing. If disengagement from the object by not breaking it is a part of virtuous relationship with it, active engagement with the object through acts of care and maintenance should also be a part. That is, care for objects includes not only refraining from damaging them but also proactively *doing* things to maintain them in good order.

The distinction between negative duty and positive duty is helpful here. The former primarily consists of refraining from violating others' rights, such as killing, assaulting, stealing, raping, cheating, and the like. In a way, these duties mark the standard below which we should never fall. However, a person who does not fall below this minimum standard but neither does anything at all in way of helping others can hardly be characterized as a moral person. Such a hurdle is too low to clear for a moral character. Care ethics advocates our moral relationship with others by honoring their positive rights, although this is not how care ethics would phrase it, as the point of their theory is to get us away from thinking of ethics in terms of rights. Nevertheless, if we apply care ethics to our relationship with artifacts, we should be guided not only by the requirements of negative duty but also by positive duty. What then constitutes care for the objects in the positive, active sense?

We know from our daily dealings with artifacts that they need care and maintenance: washing, cleaning, dusting, polishing, painting, freshening, sprucing up, touching up, tuning up, repairing, and so on. Most of us engage in these activities quite regularly. These maintenance activities for objects constitute the ubiquitous way in which we engage in care for the material world. Speaking primarily of built environment, Lance Hosey observes that "acts of maintenance . . . can create meaningful bonds, which is why we call this 'caring' for something."[71]

Maintenance workers, cleaning crews, and professional repairers all perform maintenance work on material objects. Although their activities can be motivated by care relationship with the objects, contractual obligations are the primary motivator of their activities in general. Recall Noddings's observation that "we do not say with any conviction that a person cares if that person acts routinely according to some fixed rule."[72] Professional maintenance workers *tend to* fall into this category, although I should not generalize because, as Dewey points out, "the intelligent mechanic engaged in his job, interested in doing well and finding satisfaction in his handiwork, caring for his materials and tools with genuine affection, is artistically engaged."[73] So, the kind of maintenance and repair work I am interested in is performed primarily by amateurs (with no contractual obligation) who work on the object with which they have developed or will develop an intimate relationship and in whose longevity they invest. Among various maintenance works we undertake, let me focus on repair because I find this activity to be most pregnant with different ways in which we engage with the material world, including aesthetic engagement. I limit my subsequent discussion on repair to those acts that fix perceivable damage, such as cracks and rips, and that have aesthetic implications, thereby excluding those repair works that fix problems that are not perceivable (at least to nonprofessionals), such as plumbing, car engines, and computers.

6 Aesthetics of Repair(ing)

6.1 Values of Repair(ing)

Although it is not that long ago, it now feels like an ancient history that, while growing up in Japan, I used to fix the run on stockings because cheap pantyhoses were not available then. I also remember a handyman coming around the neighborhood regularly to fix holes in the pots and pans, as well as broken umbrellas. However, the practice of repair has ceased to be a way of life for many of us living in the affluent societies that are overflowing with manufactured goods. One reason is the overabundance of relatively inexpensive consumer goods which encourages us to treat various objects as disposables because replacement is easy to come by. In actuality, however, the cheapness of many goods today is deceptive because the contemporary economic system hides the "true cost" of production by "externalizing" the cost to the environment, human health and safety, characterized variously as spillovers, side effects, intangibles, diseconomics, disamenities, or side conditions.[74]

Another reason for the demise of repair is the difficulty, often impossibility, of fixing broken objects. This is particularly true of hi-tech objects. Their repair requires expert knowledge and special equipment, and the cost of repair often exceeds the price of a new purchase. The lack of incentive to repair today in favor of throwing away a broken object and purchasing a new product, combined with the near impossibility of repair, gives rise to excessive consumerism that is responsible for environmental devastation as well as human rights violations of factory workers and garbage pickers in developing nations. These concerns have led to the passage of the right-to-repair legislations in some states in the United States and elsewhere. They also have given rise to grassroots initiatives to promote repair. For example, a Dutch group, platform 21, issued the Repair Manifesto in 2009, soon followed by another Repair Manifesto issued by iFixit, a California company. The same year saw the opening of the first Repair Café in Amsterdam that since then has spread to 1,500 venues globally where experts share their knowledge and skills with people to help them repair broken objects.[75]

The recent emergence of repair activism is a response to rampant consumerism and fast fashion that have given rise to a throwaway lifestyle, orchestrated by the industry strategy of planned obsolescence. First proposed to stimulate the economy during the age of the New Deal in the United States, industry practice has systematically been producing goods that are "made to break," as well as difficult to disassemble for repair and cleaning.[76] In an influential 1932 essay, "Ending the Depression through Planned Obsolescence," Bernard London, a real estate broker, argued for increasing industry production by encouraging replacing "old articles with new *for reasons of fashion and up-to-dateness*."[77] According to him, "furniture and clothing and other commodities should have a span of life. . . . When used for their allotted time, they should be retired, and replaced by fresh merchandise." Although his statement predates the notion of fast fashion, it is noteworthy that his suggestion of planned obsolescence regards not only functionality but also aesthetics, which is referred to today as aesthetic or perceived obsolescence, the primary motivation of fast fashion. We the consumers are not encouraged to let objects develop their own history through accumulation of patina, accidental damage, or our interaction with them through use, maintenance, and repair.

Repair wouldn't be necessary, Elizabeth Spelman observes, "if things never broke, never frayed, never splintered or fell to pieces." Such a world would be "filled with unchanging unbreakable eternal objects," a material version of Platonic Forms.[78] With the rapid advancement in material science, it is conceivable that manufactured objects can soon self-clean, self-heal, and remain unchanged. In fact, Daniela Rosner who "always loved cracks" entertained this possibility when a reporter asked her to comment on such a scientific advancement taking place in UK.[79] Thus, this possibility is more than a science fiction, and it is certainly welcome for things like airplanes and bridges. We may also appreciate the freedom from tedious, and often time-consuming and labor-intensive, chores of cleaning and fixing things. But the primary concern with them is safety and we as nonprofessionals cannot work on their maintenance and repair.

What about objects from our everyday life that *we* can maintain and repair without much specialized knowledge or skill? In the hypothetical world under consideration, we certainly gain freedom from much of our chores around the house, as we will never have to clean or fix anything. But does this make the world a better place? Don't we lose something by not having to cultivate a care relationship with the world through providing maintenance of care, or even by having no reason to handle objects gently and with care, because even if it breaks due to our careless or rough handling, it will put itself back together? It will be comparable to letting my children grow by themselves without my parental care because they are preprogrammed to mature on their own accord. Just as parents themselves grow through caring for their children, we also grow with our entanglement with objects that need our care. We develop an enduring relationship as they proceed with their changes through our active interaction by maintenance, care, and repair.

By not developing such a relationship, we also suffer aesthetic losses. According to Dewey, "there are two sorts of possible worlds in which esthetic experience would not occur," and one of them is a world with no change: "a world that is finished, ended, would have no traits of suspense and crisis, and would offer no opportunity for resolution. Where everything is already complete, there is no fulfillment."[80] Because, for Dewey, aesthetic experience is generated from the interaction between humans as live creatures and their environment, which gives the rhythmic process of undergoing and doing, there will be no traction if the world does not change and stays in its perfect condition.

Let me explore specific ways such losses happen in this (currently) hypothetical scenario. First, our aesthetic palette will become severely curtailed by the unchanging appearance of the objects, as everything will stay brand new. In his vast historical survey of the attitudes toward the appearance of aging in the Western tradition, David Lowenthal observes that "the balance of evidence . . . shows general dislike of age and decay. We prefer youth, not only in living creatures but in our surroundings, including our own creation." While he is fully aware that "distaste for the marks of age is far from universal," he admits that the appreciation for the aged appearance "is the exception."[81]

With respect to artifacts, in particular manufactured objects of industrial production, brand new, smooth, and shiny surfaces are preferred to those with stains, scratches, dents, cracks, frays, faded colors, peeling paint, accidental damages, and the like, except for some objects like jeans and carpentry tools that are considered to improve as they are broken in. This is due to what Steven Jackson calls a "productionist bias" or "production-centered ethos" created by today's industrial system, which identifies the "original" state of a manufactured object as the end of the production process when the product is in "mint" condition. It dictates the design process to create a finished product that is considered perfect and unalterable.[82] This productionist bias reflects commodification of products and consumers' obsession with newness promoted by industrial capitalism, which nudges them to replace old-looking objects with newer, defect-free products.

I should note that this productionist bias is challenged by designers and design theorists. For example, Stuart Walker points out that "most products demand *passive acceptance* by the user; there is little or nothing to be added or contributed by the user. Even the repair of a simple scratch or break is not invited and it would be difficult to achieve a satisfactory result."[83] Instead, he and others propose design that is rough, good enough, or unfinished, so that we the users engage with them through what one commentator refers to as the "craft of use."[84] Somewhat paradoxically, facilitating longevity of an object is possible only by accepting its ephemerality. This requires embracing and making a creative use of the signs of ephemerality by incorporating allowance for the signs of change from the beginning.

There are plenty of alternatives or challenges to this obsession with the new and the perfect. The most prominent aesthetic movements are the eighteenth-century British picturesque and the long-held Japanese *wabi* aesthetics. The former gave rise not only to the picturesque gardens but also, perhaps more important today, to the cult of ruins which still captivates popular imagination. Japanese *wabi* aesthetics, although initially established as an aesthetic to accompany the art of tea ceremony in the sixteenth century, continues to be influential today not just in Japan but worldwide. In addition, these signs of imperfection also provide inspirations for contemporary art, ranging from pottery and metalwork to glass and textiles.[85] There is no denying that the aged appearance with cracks, dents, scratches, faded colors, missing parts, musty smells, and the historical associations accompanying them enrich our aesthetic lives and that the hypothetical world of unchanging objects severely limits the scope of the aesthetic palette. This enrichment of aesthetic palette is reflected in the different ways of repairing objects.

6.2 Invisible Repair

According to the conventional mode of repair, the sign of repair should be made as inconspicuous as possible so that the object can be restored to its "finished" or "mint" condition, following the aforementioned productionist bias. Accordingly, maintenance work, including repair, is directed toward maintaining this original state of the object. The most common type of repair thus privileges the unblemished and undamaged appearance: invisible repair. At the 2018–19 exhibit *Repair and Design Futures* at the Rhode Island School of Design Museum, many objects, predominantly fabric, were covered by a glass top with a marking indicating where the mending occurred.[86] Even then, I had to scrutinize closely to find the repaired parts, and the resulting experience was similar to the amusement and amazement of finding natural creatures' camouflage. In addition, I could not help but admire the considerable skills involved in such meticulous and exquisite results.

In our daily lives, too, we normally try to make the signs of repair as inconspicuous and, better still, invisible as possible. We use the same-colored thread and fabric to patch up a rip and a yarn to darn socks.[87] When putting broken pottery pieces back together, we apply a transparent glue. The paint used for touching up the scratches on a car needs to match the rest of the body. There is an implicit aesthetic judgment that the original appearance of an object is superior to its later changed appearance, which is almost always characterized negatively as damage, dilapidation, defect, or degradation. Such a fall from grace needs to be made as invisible as possible, and the repaired object must hide any visible indication that the object was damaged and was repaired.

However, this privileging the invisibility of signs of repair enhances the notion behind productionist bias that the material objects are static rather than ever-changing active matters.

As Cameron Tonkinwise points out, the assumption is that material objects are "inert products" that are "unchangingly perfect," ignoring their "in-time-ness of being," and "matter-in-motion."[88] As an alternative to the productionist bias, Jackson proposes what he calls the "broken world thinking," which foregrounds "erosion, breakdown, and decay, rather than novelty, growth, and progress, as our starting points."[89] Instead of relegating these processes of breaking down, restoring, and repairing to background, broken world thinking illuminates "the remarkable resilience, creativity, and sheer magnitude of the work represented in the ongoing maintenance and reproduction of established order," and encourages developing "a deep wonder and appreciation for the ongoing activities by which stability . . . is maintained."[90] Creativity, originality, and imagination are features not only of ex-nihilo conception of design and production but they also characterize the tasks involved in care, maintenance, and repair, when working with the objects' specific condition at the time.[91]

In this regard, it is helpful to make a comparison of industrial production to gardening. David Cooper calls attention to the "time- and energy-consuming" nature of gardening activity not in the sense of a begrudged chore but in the sense "the specific demands and development of the 'materials'—the need, say, of certain plants to be pruned at a certain time of the year—constrain and shape the gardener's life."[92] As living entities, plants grow and constantly change. Gardening therefore is an ongoing engagement because it is never "finished," but rather "one whose maintenance, enhancement, and transformation are long-term commitment."[93] Although artifacts are unlike plants because they don't grow or change according to their own nature, I suggest that the so-called finished product in its frozen state, as it were, which is typically said of an artifact, is a misnomer because one of the fundamental facts of material existence is that it never stays the same. Some changes are more evident and faster than others, but nothing escapes this law of nature.

As Ezio Manzini points out from the designer's point of view, the view that recognizes the world to be fluid rather than stable so that we cannot expect artifacts to stay put once created "tells us about the importance of attention and of listening to things in the long term, about care for their upkeep. In short, it tells us the importance of caring."[94] It is noteworthy that Manzini suggests that designers should be guided with a metaphor of objects as plants in a garden, and they see themselves as planting "a garden of objects." For the gardeners who care for plants, their "value cannot be measured in banally economic terms" or the benefit of gaining flowers and fruits; their tending is motivated by "love of the plants."[95] Similarly, artifacts "have lives of their own" and "perform services and require care." Although his target audience is other designers, the analogy of artifacts with garden plants effectively describes the care attitude we as consumers adopt and care activities we should perform.

6.3 Challenges of Visible Repair

Today's repair activists, whether professionals, amateurs, or artists, challenge the assumptions behind invisible repair by advocating visible repair. As previously mentioned, the conventional form of repair, invisible repair, is based upon the assumption that the best state of an object is when it is in mint condition, usually at the end of the production process. Any transformations after that through aging, wear and tear, or accidental breakage are considered to compromise its aesthetics, and the repair aims at restoring the object to its former glory. But, as Jackson's productionist bias indicates, invisible repair denies the nature of the material world that is inevitably subject to vicissitude. No material objects stay "finished" or "frozen." Once we regard such changes positively as development or growth, the signs of the so-called damage or defect suggest a different state of the object in its continuing existence, rather than a fall from grace. Today's activists and artists pursuing repair projects thus advocate visible repair that accentuates the signs of repair rather than hiding them.

Probably the best-known example of visible repair is proudly displayed patches and stitches on clothing, sometimes literally worn on the sleeves.[96] Some contemporary art projects also feature visible repair. Let me list several: Daniel Eatock's *Visible Vehicle Repairs* (2017~), which results in two-colored cars; Rachel Sussman's *Sidewalk Kintsukuroi* (2016~), which appropriates the Japanese *kintsugi* method in repairing sidewalk cracks by filling them with gold-colored paint; Jan Vormann's *Dispatchwork* (2007~), in which, across different parts of the world and often together with the area residents, he repairs the crumbling edifice of brick structures with colorful Lego pieces; Charlotte Bailey's repaired broken vases, which she has wrapped with fabric of the same pattern, and has sewed the pieces with gold threads (2016); Tomomi Kamoshita's patchwork chopstick rests and mismatched earrings, which piece together ceramic shards (2014 ~); Yee Sookyung's *Translated Vases* (2002 ~), which piece together shards from multiple vases using the *kintsugi* method; Elisa Sheehan's *Kintsugi Eggshells*, an ongoing project presenting eggshells "repaired" with the *kintsugi* method, described by the artist herself as "a visual representation of imperfection as a true value and where flaws are celebrated and viewed as beautiful"; and Tatiane Freitas' *My Old New Series* (2010 ~), broken wooden furniture "fixed" with parts made with acrylic resin.[97]

As is evident from this list, many artists are inspired by the Japanese repair practice called *kintsugi* (金継 gold joinery) or *kintsukuroi* (金繕い repair by gold). *Kintsugi* originated as a mending method for tea bowls used in the tea ceremony. According to a legend, Shōgun Ashikaga Yoshimasa (足利義政 1436–90) had a prized celadon porcelain tea bowl from China which became cracked. He sent it back to China for repair. It came back repaired with metal staples, which did not satisfy his aesthetic taste, so he ordered a craftsman to come up with a more attractive repair. The craftsman repaired the bowl with the *kintsugi* method. This repair method was subsequently popularized with the sixteenth-century establishment of the *wabi* tea ceremony, as indicated by the tea master Sen no Rikyū (千利休)'s observation: "We might naturally find it awkward to use . . . a cracked tea bowl of present-day porcelain. On the other hand, however, we are accustomed to make use of or even very ready to use, despite defects, the antique tea-caddy imported from China for instance, sparing no pain of having it mended with lacquer."[98] As this passage indicates, despite the impression given by the term "gold joinery" or "repair by gold," lacquer is used as an adhesive and gold, sometimes silver or tin, flakes are applied as an ornamental touch.

Although cracks may be the best-known example, there are different kinds of "damage" repaired by this method: incomplete cracks called *nyū* (にゅう) that do not compromise functionality;

chips called *kake* (欠け); peeling away of the material surface called *hotsure* (ほつれ); and a complete breakage called *ware* (割れ). While most cases of *kintsugi* put broken pieces of an object back together, sometimes a piece from a different object is used for filling, the technique called *yobitsugi* (呼継ぎ) or *yosetsugi* (寄せ継ぎ), meaning "repairing by calling forth" or "joint call." This is the most extreme form of *kintsugi*, sometimes effectively used in art projects.[99]

Kintsugi suggests several important aesthetic implications that are applicable beyond its culture- and history-specific origin. First, it regards various forms of so-called damage as having their own integrity for what they are and providing an opportunity for exercising imagination and creativity.[100] In keeping with Zen Buddhism, the philosophy underlying the tea ceremony, which advocates respecting and appreciating the Buddha nature of everything whatsoever, *wabi* aesthetics celebrates, rather than laments, the so-called damage or imperfection. It is noteworthy that the new pattern created by those damages is considered to evoke a landscape, *keshiki* (景色), and it becomes further articulated through visible repair. For example, one of the best-known tea bowls repaired with *kintsugi* by a noted craftsman Hon'ami Kōetsu (本阿弥光悦 1558–1637) is named *Seppō* (雪峯), a snow-clad mountain peak.[101]

The aesthetic paradigm of visible repair thus shuns uniformity and accentuates the individuality of a particular object and its singular history by presenting a tangible record of repair, as well as the care and affection for the object. The owner, the user, or the repairer cared enough about the object to take the time and effort to give it a renewed life. For the spectator, the visible mark of repair stimulates the imagination to speculate on its unique (hi)story and its prior condition, the cause of breakage, and its future life, while at the same time encouraging the appreciation of the skill and care involved in the repair.

6.4 *Aesthetics of Repairing*

Thus, the hypothetical world with unchanging objects entertained by Spelman diminishes the aesthetic palette considerably by losing the so-called imperfect, defective, or broken appearances of material objects and the signs of repair that can add imaginative and creative spins on them. Such aesthetic loss also implies that we will be deprived of the opportunities to truly interact with the material world through care and maintenance, as our interaction will be limited to using them. However, by not engaging in care work for the material world, we suffer another aesthetic loss. Again, taking repair as example, we lose the opportunity for an aesthetic experience by directly engaging in the activity of repair*ing*.

The aesthetic attraction of engaging in this activity can be seen in the globally growing popularity of *kintsugi* among amateurs. As Fujiwara points out, today transparent epoxy can repair the breakage much faster and easier, but people specifically choose the labor-intensive and time-consuming *kintsugi* repair because it involves exercise of imagination and creativity, a full aesthetic engagement.[102]

The experience involved in "doing" things tends to fall outside of the traditional aesthetic radar that favors a spectator's viewpoint. There are at least three reasons for this. First, doing things almost always involves physical activities, thus involving bodily engagement, and the Western philosophical tradition has long neglected issues related to body. Second, doing things in everyday life often involves chores, such as cooking, cleaning, laundering, taking care of the yard, and the like, which also get excluded from the worthy subjects for philosophical examination. Recent developments in philosophy, particularly feminism and somaesthetics, as well as in art, help challenge this neglect of the body and daily chores, as some of my examples have shown. Third, the experience of "doing" is not recognized as part of aesthetics because it is not amenable to an evaluative aesthetic judgment. There is no clear "object" of experience which makes it possible to form an aesthetic judgment. For example, Jane Forsey points out that "cleaning, chopping, and repairing are clearly quotidian *but not clearly objects of any kind*."[103] We can dispute about whether a garden is pretty, but can we dispute about whether the pleasure I am having while gardening qualifies as an aesthetic experience? When David E. Cooper observes that "it is symptomatic of a primarily aesthetic approach largely to ignore the practice of gardening," I interpret him to be referring to the spectator-oriented approach of aesthetics and not suggesting that the activity of gardening is not a fit subject for aesthetics discourse in general.[104] The worry about including doing things in aesthetics is that it remains a private experience and cannot allow intersubjectivity. For Christopher Dowling, "mere first-person reports . . . are of little interest to others because others can never share them," hence lacking "aesthetic credentials."[105]

If we confine aesthetics to a judgmental discourse, these reasons for excluding doing things may make sense. However, I believe that the scope of aesthetics can be expanded from the spectator-oriented and judgment-directed ones. Otherwise, a large swath of our life experience is kept outside of aesthetics. In addition, doing things often involves taking a spectator-like observational and judgmental stance, just as the aesthetic engagement of a spectator involves active interaction with object through activating imagination. As Gernot Böhme proposes, a phenomenological account of aesthetics should have a place in aesthetics discourse: "the old aesthetics is essentially a judgmental aesthetics, that is, it is concerned not so much with experience, especially sensuous experience . . . as with judgments, discussion, conversation."[106] Furthermore, phenomenological accounts of doing things do not necessarily remain private, making intersubjective sharing impossible, as I will show by considering the first-person reports on mending activities.

Repair attends to the *specifics* of the object, material, and the nature of damage. The *kintsugi* method requires close observation to devise the intervention most appropriate for and respectful of the particular damage. For example, if a deep crack needs repair, it is recommended that the break be completed by splitting the object open. In order to determine whether the crack is deep enough, we put our ear against the object while squeezing the object to see whether a clicking sound is heard.

As for fabric mending, Katrina Rodabaugh characterizes her practice as "respond(ing) to each individual repair as the garment demands. It means that every patch, stitch, darn, or other combinations of mending techniques can be in response to that particular damage."[107] Another practitioner states that "every stitch requires listening and responding to what the fabric, and the hole, might need."[108] This way of mending is echoed by a denim repairer: "Rather than having a predetermined vision of the finished garment, we let the contours of the damage dictate the repair."[109] Spelman also reports that her acquaintance, a successful car repairer who enjoys his work, "comes up with nifty case-specific solutions to the constant stream of unique challenges" and draws an analogy to care ethics: "the ethics of care highlights the intimacy of the knowledge of the moral agent as problem solver: intimate both in the sense of having or seeing specific and nuanced and contextualized knowledge of the people involved and the situation they are in, and in the sense of acknowledging or creating a close relationship to the people involved."[110] In short, our repair work expresses our respect and care for the object with its specific condition.

Finally, mending fabric occurs where "this active space of at/tending—assessing, touching, thinking, and intuiting—entwines into an embodied knowledge, a soft technique, during which the ameliorative thread is sewn this way and that."[111] This intimate engagement with the other's specificity and the emotional investment in the process characterize a care relationship, different from a mechanical mode of repair that simply follows instructions in a manual. It is also an *aesthetic* engagement because its process is imbued with respecting the singularity of the object in question and creating a satisfactory solution through collaboration with the object's current condition, all performed with an affection for the object, its owner, or user. Insofar as the activity of mending requires an embodied knowledge, skills, and working according to the material's dictate, the process can be considered an apt example of the reciprocal, cumulative, and continuous relationship of "doing" and "undergoing" proposed by John Dewey when characterizing an aesthetic experience.[112] In addition to providing a possible occasion for "an" experience, such active and care-full engagement with the object cannot but nurture one's affection for the object, rendering it not only an object of aesthetic appreciation but also a cherished object destined for longevity.[113]

Contrary to the objection that doing things remains a private experience and lacks intersubjectivity, when hearing or reading those menders' accounts of their activities, it is possible to join their experience vicariously through imagination. Their accounts resonate with us, and we join an imaginary community of menders across the globe and history and enjoy a kind of camaraderie. With such an imaginative engagement, the activity gains a dimension that goes beyond a simple chore to be performed in a solitary confinement, but rather experienced as taking part in a time-honored and intimate activity that has been shared by so many. Even those who have never experienced mending activities are not excluded from joining this community, because the door is open for them to gain relevant experiences but, perhaps more importantly, they are invited to participate by activating imagination.

Sometimes such an imaginative experience can be very powerful. When I encountered a clumsily mended buttonhole on a victim's uniform of Auschwitz at a 2019 exhibit at the Jewish Heritage Museum in New York City, the experience was visceral, and it took me a while to sort through the gush of emotions I experienced. Although it is beyond my imagination to fathom the circumstances under which this mender repaired the frayed buttonhole, and I am experiencing the object as a spectator, the common humanity derived from the activity I can share connected me to this anonymous mender. Not only did I feel a sense of camaraderie but also was I moved by the mender's desperate effort to retain the last shred of dignity and normalcy. This imaginative sharing of experience is what we often go through by the experience of art. Intersubjectivity of doing things is thus possible, although it is neither a means to nor results from any judgment-making.

6.5 Two Caveats Regarding Repair

So far, I have argued for the aesthetic benefits associated with repair. However, I need to offer a couple of caveats. First, recall that care ethics does not advocate universal caring. I pointed out in Chapter 2 that it is neither possible nor desirable for a person to devote herself to developing a care relationship with as many people as possible. The person will be sure to burn out, diluting the possibility of genuine acts of care because it is simply not possible to care for everyone in one's life all the time by attending to each person's individual needs.

Similarly, it is neither possible nor desirable to engage in care activities for objects *indiscriminately*. Judicious selection is called for to avoid needless clutter, or, worse, hoarding. Similarly, the aesthetic value of repair may depend upon a balance between repaired and undamaged objects. If our everyday environment is surrounded by too many repaired objects, particularly with visible repair, its aesthetic potency gets diluted. Imagine what it will be like if every crumbled built structure is repaired by Lego, or *kintsugi*-inspired repair appears on every cracked pavement. Certainly, in light of the serious environmental problems, we should strive to facilitate the longevity of what we have through caring for them by maintenance and repair. But an object may reach a point where it makes more sense to either discard it or turn it into something else through recycling or repurposing. As warned by Spelman, "a voracious appetite for fixing can lead to poor judgment about what is and is not desirable or even possible to repair. Pride in our repairing abilities may push us into believing that whatever has been broken can be and ought to be fixed."[114] We need practical wisdom, or what a cultural geographer Caitlin DeSilvey calls "curated decay," rather than indiscriminate repair of everything.[115] Even Ezio Manzini whose view inspired the Eternally Yours project that aims to promote the psychological lifetime and cultural durability of artifacts points out that "one cannot possibly feel attached to each and every product."[116] The care relationship with artifacts should be promoted as a default mode of interaction with them, to be adjusted by further deliberation of whether a care activity on a specific object is desirable. At the same time, commitment to developing a care relationship with material objects will encourage us to be judicious and mindful when adding new things to our lives to make sure that they are worthy of being my partner to which I invest time, effort, and affection.

In addition, some broken objects with a special historical significance should not be repaired but rather preserved as is. For example, repair may compromise the historical authenticity of the object. In addition, some, but perhaps not all, ruined structures that result from a war or an evil human deed should be preserved in their ruined state as historical witnesses and cautionary reminders of "never again" for future generations.[117] Similarly, Shannon Lee Dawdy argues against completely eradicating the traces of destruction caused by Hurricane Katrina in New Orleans and replacing them with a sanitized version of how things used to be, or, worse, their Disneyfication for consumption by tourists. She instead argues for a judicious preservation of patina, which she defines as "a medium of aesthetic value *perceived* to have accumulated through time that represents the social palimpsest" and supports "a process of both accumulation and decay that must be kept in a cared-for balance."[118]

Second, the recent popularity of visible repair and repair cafés may be culturally and economically situated in affluent societies with material abundance that can afford to take pleasure and amusement in the signs of repair. What about those who are living in circumstances marked by poverty and scarcity and are forced to make do with what little they have? After all, the stunning beauty of quilts in the American South reflects the poor living condition of the makers. The same is true for the Japanese fisherman's kimonos mended with *boro*, tattered rags.[119] These repeatedly mended clothes resulted from the extreme scarcity of resources in the northern part of the Japanese mainland. In fact, *wabi* aesthetics, tea ceremony, and *kintsugi* supported by the wealthy and powerful were criticized by a nineteenth-century Japanese Confucian scholar: "Today's tea men take filthy and damaged old bowls, whose ages they cannot know, repair them with lacquer and other materials, and then use them. It is an unspeakably disgusting custom," because "whatever tea dilettantes do is a copy of the poor and humble. It may be that the rich and noble have a reason to find pleasure in copying the poor and humble. But why should those who are, from the outset, poor and humble find pleasure in further copying the poor and humble?"[120]

In a similar vein, contemporary advocates of visible repair warn against "the exploitative chic-ing of the shabby," "the idealization of repair," and "the romanticization of strategies of survival," so as not to be complicit with capitalism and colonialism.[121] Fetishization and commercialization of visible repair can endanger this practice by contributing to another fashion trend within a capitalist framework that can easily be replaced by another trend. This is the same concern with today's so-called ruin porn and poverty tourism in cities like Detroit and New Orleans as well as impoverished nations, where physical manifestations of social ills and suffering become an object of the gaze primarily by (more affluent) nonresidents.[122]

6.6 Repairing Human Psyche through Material Repair

I want to end my exploration of repair as a care activity for the material world with its extension into repairing damaged human psyches, another form of care activity. Material repair is sometimes taken as a metaphorical expression of repairing a fractured psyche and fragility turned into resilience in the field of psychology. Scott Barry Kaufman, for example, features a *kintsugi*-repaired pottery in his article, "Post-Traumatic Growth: Finding Meaning and Creativity in Adversity" subtitled "Resilience and strength can often be attained through unexpected routes."[123] Reflecting on her practice of mending fabric, Lisa Morgan offers a similar observation:

> Tending to the wound in the garment facilitates a tending of ourselves, and through mending a hole there is the sense of stitching oneself almost whole, a reflecting on what has gone before and a bringing together and uniting of what remains. The scar may never disappear, but it indicates in detail how it was healed. The darn becomes the celebration of a story.[124]

There are art projects that feature repairing activities in response to various traumas. Nishiko, a Japanese artist practicing in the Netherlands, has been working on the *Repairing Earthquake Project* since the earthquake and tsunami hit the northeastern coast of Japan in March of 2011. In addition to documenting its aftermath through eyewitness accounts and photographing various objects, her project includes collecting fragments and debris from this catastrophe and putting them back together. The repaired item encased in a box specifically created for it is either returned to the owner, if found, or placed with a foster family for safekeeping. The objects and processes are presented through photography, videos, installations, performances, publications, and blogs. The broken pieces symbolize the scars left by this natural disaster and the act of repair a process of healing.[125]

Earthquakes, frequent occurrences in Japan, provide an inspiration for another *kintsugi* project. Kunio Nakamura, a Japanese *kintsugi* artist, volunteers his time and expertise to put broken pottery pieces back together for the residents of the Kumamoto prefecture that was hit by a massive earthquake in 2016.[126] He also expresses his hope for a peaceful world by combining plate pieces from two nations caught in a problematic relationship, such as South Korea and North Korea. This art project called *Kintsugi Pieces in Harmony* presents the possibility and hope for a harmonious coexistence of feuding nations by symbolically attaching two disparate pieces.[127]

While these repair projects are carried out by the artists who present broken pieces put back together as new pieces to the owners, there are other art projects that involve people's participation. Yoko Ono's *Mend Piece* project (1966/2015) invites museum visitors to put together broken china cups and saucers gathered on a table with glue, tape, and string. The resultant objects are displayed on shelves. By encouraging literal participation, this project gives meditative time and space to engage in the literal activity of mending which leads to the contemplation on the healing of fractures and damages afflicting one's psyche as well as community and the world. Her words on the installation's wall reads: "Mend with wisdom/ mend with love./ It will mend the earth/ at the same time."[128]

Lee Mingwei's *The Mending Project* (2009–18) invites museum/ gallery visitors to bring textile items to be mended. As the artist or a volunteer mends the item, the owner engages in a conversation about the story and memory associated with the item, but the conversation reportedly often extends into the status of the broken world, whether politically, environmentally, or socially, and its remedy. The mending done is visible repair. As stated in one museum catalogue, "For the artist, it is important that the reparation of the piece isn't hidden; on the contrary the idea is to acknowledge the history of the clothing through the mending; as something to celebrate."[129]

What is common to these art projects is that repair is visible. The objects are not restored to their pre-broken appearance. Whether by repairing with *kintsugi* method, putting broken pieces together by tying them into a bundle as in some examples of Ono's project, or mending fabric with visible repair as in Lee's project, the idea embraced by these projects is that healing and repairing the scars, damages, and fractures start with acknowledging and embracing them as a springboard toward a new creation.[130] They mark a stage in the object's ongoing life and the caring relationship with it accepts its history and *works with* it. Care for a wounded psyche and a damaged world requires working with such wounds and damages, rather than obliterating those signs. It is to acknowledge and accept the impermanence and imperfection of this world and engage with them proactively.

* * *

This chapter was devoted to demonstrating the significance of developing a care relationship with the material world despite its inanimate and nonsentient status. I argued that cultivating such a relationship is important for practicing ethically grounded mode of being in the world rather than based upon the potential moral considerability of the material world, although the result may be the same. We interact with the materials objects by honoring our interdependent relationship with them. This care toward the material world is expressed not only by refraining from damaging it but, more importantly, by actively engaging in care activities through maintenance and repair work. The maintenance work, however, should honor the material objects' inevitable vicissitudes through aging process and marks of our active engagement including wear and tear, as well as damage. Objects of daily use should be cherished as our faithful companions with which we share history and commitment to each other.

Developing a caring relationship with the material world is particularly pressing today. The longevity of material objects is severely compromised by the consumer culture that encourages us to decry any changes to their brand-new condition as deterioration and treat such "imperfect" objects as disposables. It is not only that this situation causes problems of overproduction, which leads to a host of damages to the environment and human rights. More importantly, it diminishes the opportunity for us to develop an intimate relationship with the materials objects of daily use by sharing our lives together and nurturing their longevity. It is through aesthetic experience of active engagement that we can develop such care relationship with the material world and reclaim and celebrate our interdependence with the world around us.

Conclusion

Care ethics is commonly understood as concerned with how to interact ethically with other people, nature, and possibly artifacts, whereas the notion of aesthetic experience addresses how to enrich our aesthetic lives. As such, they appear to operate in the different spheres of our management of daily lives. However, we embarked on this book's journey by exploring the structural similarities between care ethics and aesthetic experience. It should be clear by now that the commonality between them is not a matter of mere coincidence. I hope to have shown that care ethics requires aesthetic sensibility and expression, which need to be cultivated and practiced. At the same time, aesthetic experience is grounded in the ethical practice of care as we relate to people and the world around us. There is an intimate, and indeed inseparable, relationship between the ethical and aesthetic modes of being in the world. In our interactions with the other, whether it be other people or objects, a successful experience results from focusing on their individual singularity and working collaboratively with open-minded receptivity and imaginative engagement. Thus, whether we are trying to live an ethical life motivated by care for others or enriching our aesthetic life, these two spheres of concern converge as the authentic mode of existence based upon interdependence and relationality. Both concerns regard how we should negotiate the social landscape and the world around us with which we are deeply entangled. I suggested that care should be the default mode of interacting with the world around us, though it should be accompanied by practical wisdom to determine whether or not and how to develop a caring relationship with a specific person or an object.

Care is also a crucial value that should guide macro-level projects, such as constructing a humane and civilized society, designing and creating built environments and artifacts that reflect care for the dwellers and users, reorienting medical practice from cure focused to care driven, and improving the state of the world to fulfill humanity's responsibility to future generations in light of climate change. Implementing various policies, systems, and practices toward these ends requires a concerted effort from professionals from various sectors: political institutions, design professions, medical organizations, environmental agencies, and many others.

However, what is often neglected when appealing to these professionals to improve the world's status quo to reflect more consideration of care is the fact that all of us are also active agents empowered to contribute to better world-making. Unless we are one of the aforementioned professionals, we tend to view ourselves as the recipients of the effort made by them. However, unless we ourselves act with care toward other people and the objects around us, the efforts made by those professionals will come to naught. Imagine a society in which everyone's well-being is ensured insofar as it has in place an extensive social welfare program, economic security, equal educational opportunity and access to healthcare, political participation, and environment and artifacts designed with care. At the same time, imagine further that, in this society, people's interactions with others and the world around them do not reflect care but indifference, neglect, or even hostility instead. That is, people in this imaginary world never listen to each other, engage in a meaningful dialogue, care about the others' well-being, handle artifacts with care and affection, or extend their horizon by trying to understand and develop an appreciation of those objects that do not appeal to them immediately.[1] Would we want to live in such a society? I think the answer is clear.

All of us are implicated in practicing and promoting caring relationships with other people and the world around us. Despite acting on a micro-level, we can all participate in making the world a caring place. While emphasizing the individual responsibility in this regard may sound moralistic, preachy, and heavy-handed, engaging in such practice as an aesthetic endeavor should render the project a joyful and fulfilling process. Deep engagement with other people and the world around us cannot help but invoke an aesthetic engagement with an open-minded appreciation of their individual singularity.

In my previous work on everyday aesthetics, I emphasized our power and responsibility in the better world-making project by calling attention to the seemingly trivial and innocuous aesthetic preferences and judgments that we make in our daily lives. They often result in purchasing decisions, management of our environment, and support for certain causes. Furthermore, whether or not we are aware, these actions lead to serious social, political, and environmental consequences. Thus, I argued for the importance of developing what may be called aesthetic literacy and vigilance. What I have explored in this book is a further role we can play in better world-making by cultivating and practicing care relationships with the people and the world around us that are invariably facilitated by aesthetic sensibility and engagement. We may never achieve a state with perfectly caring relationships with everyone and everything around us. However, when developing land ethics, Aldo Leopold remarked: "We shall never achieve harmony with land any more than we shall achieve absolute justice or liberty for people. In these higher aspirations the important thing is not to achieve, but to strive."[2] Cultivating and practicing the care relationship with others should provide aspiration for living a good and virtuous life and contribute to the good life of others.

As mentioned before, a society in which every member is cared for requires a concerted and coordinated effort by various professionals devising policies, systems, and organizations. However, equally and absolutely necessary is a network of caring interpersonal relationships that can only be enacted at the individual level. By interacting with the other as You rather than It, we elevate not only the quality of life of those who are directly affected but also our caring interactions with the artifactual and natural worlds. This is the best gift we can hand down to future generations.

Notes

Introduction

1 Iris Murdoch, *The Sovereignty of Good* (London: Routledge, 1970), 68–9.

2 Ibid., 63.

3 Ibid.

4 Ibid., 64.

5 Ibid., 40.

6 R. W. Hepburn and Iris Murdoch, "Symposium: Vision and Choice in Morality," *Proceedings of the Aristotelian Society, Supplementary Volume* 30 (1956): 14–58.

7 Ronald W. Hepburn, "Values of Art and Values of Community," in *On Community*, ed. Leroy S. Rouner (Notre Dame: University of Notre Dame Press, 1991), 46. I present Hepburn's aesthetic theory as an educational journey in "Aesthetic Experience as an Educational Journey," in *Aesthetics, Nature and Religion: Ronald W. Hepburn and His Legacy*, ed. Endre Szécsényi (Aberdeen: Aberdeen University Press, 2020), 215–33.

8 Arnold Berleant, *Sensibility and Sense: The Aesthetic Transformation of the Human World* (Exeter: Imprint Academic, 2010), 88.

9 Ibid., 9.

10 David E. Cooper, "Beautiful People, Beautiful Things," *British Journal of Aesthetics* 48, no. 3 (2008): 259.

11 Ibid., 260.

12 Josephine Donovan, *The Aesthetics of Care: On the Literary Treatment of Animals* (London: Bloomsbury Academic, 2016), 215.

13 Ibid., this and the next passage from 11.

14 Marcia Eaton, *Merit, Aesthetic and Ethical* (Oxford: Oxford University Press, 2001), preface v.

15 Ibid., 62 and the next passage from 94.

16 A good summary of those debates can be found in the Introduction of María Puig de la Bellacasa's *Matters of Care: Speculative Ethics In More than Human Worlds* (Minneapolis: University of Minnesota Press, 2017).

17 See Ivan Morris's *The World of the Shining Prince: Court Life in Ancient Japan* (New York: Kodansha International, 1995).

18 For the aesthetics of falling cherry blossoms and its utilization by the military, see Emiko Ohnuki-Tierney's *Kamikaze, Cherry Blossoms, and Nationalisms: The Militarization of Aesthetics in Japanese History* (Chicago: The University of Chicago Press, 2002).

19 I explore Japanese aesthetics' neglect of social and political implications in "Ethically-Grounded Nature of Japanese Aesthetic Sensibility," in *Oxford Handbook of Ethics and Art*, ed. James Harold (Oxford: Oxford University Press, forthcoming in 2022).

Chapter 1

1 I will address the first part of this issue in Chapter 3.

2 For fuller accounts regarding art, see Noël Carroll, "Art and the Moral Realm," in *The Blackwell Guide to Aesthetics*, ed. Peter Kivy (Malden: Blackwell, 2004), 126–51; Richard Eldridge, "Aesthetics and Ethics," in *The Oxford Handbook of Aesthetics*, ed. Jerrold Levinson (Oxford: Oxford University Press, 2005), 722–73; Berys Gaut, "Morality and Art," in *Companion to Aesthetics*, ed. Stephen Davies, et al. (Malden: Blackwell, 2009), 428–31. For environmental issues, see *Nature, Aesthetics, and Environmentalism*, ed. Allen Carlson and Sheila Lintott (New York: Columbia University Press, 2008) and the special issue of *The Journal of Aesthetics and Art Criticism: The Good, the Beautiful, the Green: Environmentalism and Aesthetics* 76, no. 4 (Fall 2018). For issues in everyday aesthetics, see my *Aesthetics of the Familiar: Everyday Life and World-Making* (Oxford: Oxford University Press, 2017), Chapters 6 and 7.

3 Makoto Ueda, *Literary and Art Theories in Japan* (Cleveland: Press of Case Western Reserve University, 1967), 226.

4 Tom Roberts, "Aesthetic Virtues: Traits and Faculties," *Philosophical Studies* 175 (2018): 429.

5   Peter Goldie, "Towards a Virtue Theory of Art," *British Journal of Aesthetics* 47, no. 4 (October 2007): 376.

6   Ibid., 377.

7   David M. Woodruff, "A Virtue Theory of Aesthetics," *Journal of Aesthetic Education* 35, no. 3 (Fall 2001): 34.

8   Goldie, "Towards," 383.

9   Matthew Kieran, "The Vice of Snobbery: Aesthetic Knowledge, Justification and Virtue in Art Appreciation," *The Philosophical Quarterly* 60, no. 239 (April 2010): 243–63.

10 Goldie, "Towards," 383.

11 Peter Goldie, "Virtues of Art and Human Well-Being," *Proceedings of the Aristotelian Society, Supplementary Volume* 82 (2008): 190. The next passage is also from the same page.

12 Goldie, "Towards," 385.

13 Roberts, "Aesthetic Virtues," 440, emphasis added.

14 Ibid., 441, emphasis added.

15 Ibid., 441, emphasis added; 443, emphasis added.

16 Kieran, "The Vice," 259, emphasis added; 255, emphasis added.

17 Goldie, "Virtues," 190.

18 Goldie, "Towards," 386–7.

19 Woodruff, "A Virtue Theory," 31.

20 Roberts, "Aesthetic Virtues," 445.

21 See Barbara Weber's "Childhood, Philosophy and Play: Friedrich Schiller and the Interface between Reason, Passion and Sensation," *Journal of Philosophy of Education* 45, no. 2 (2011): 235–50.

22 The second edition of Noddings's *Caring* is subtitled *A Relational Approach to Ethics and Moral Education* (2013), and it indicates that she thought it more appropriate to characterize her ethical view as a more gender-neutral notion of "relational" that is gaining increasing attention, rather than limiting it as a strictly feminist approach. There is also a danger of essentializing the feminine. I discuss the issues related to the notion of relationality in Chapter 2.

23 For a good summary of these debates and controversies, see María Puig de la Bellacasa's *Matters of Care*, Introduction.

24 Nel Noddings, *Caring: A Relational Approach to Ethics and Moral Education* (Oakland: University of California Press, 2013), 8.

25 Ibid., 10.

26 Caitlin DeSilvey, *Curated Decay: Heritage Beyond Saving* (Minneapolis: University of Minnesota Press, 2016), 180.

27 Christopher Groves, *Care, Uncertainty and Intergenerational Ethics* (New York: Palgrave Macmillan, 2014), 128.

28 Noddings, *Caring*, 13. This is often the case with routine maintenance or repair done to objects by professionals such as plumbers and IT technicians. See Groves, *Care*, 107, and Chapter 4, Section 5.

29 Noddings, *Caring*, xiv.

30 Ibid., 10.

31 Ibid., 9.

32 Daniel Engster, "Rethinking Care Theory: The Practice of Caring and the Obligation to Care," *Hypatia* 20, no. 3 (2005): 55, original italics. Also see Groves, *Care*, 106.

33 Iris Murdoch, *Metaphysics as a Guide to Morals* (London: Penguin Books, 1992), 52.

34 Donovan, *The Aesthetics of Care*, 11. Also see Groves, *Care*, 107.

35 Groves, *Care*, 121 and the next passage 120.

36 Arnold Berleant, "Objects into Persons: The Way to Social Aesthetics," *Espes* 6, no. 2 (2017): 9–18.

37 Cited by Jenefer Robinson and Stephanie Ross, "Women, Morality, and Fiction," in *Aesthetics in Feminist Perspective*, ed. Hilde Hein and Carolyn Korsmeyer (Bloomington: Indiana University Press, 1993), 108.

38 Lawrence A. Blum, "Gilligan and Kohlberg: Implications for Moral Theory," *Ethics* 98 (1988): 476–7.

39 Noddings, *Caring*, 24.

40 Aristotle, "Nicomachean Ethics," in *Introduction to Aristotle*, ed. Richard McKeon and trans. Richard Ross (Chicago: The University of Chicago Press, 1973), 471 (1142a). See Andrew Sayer, *Why Things Matter to People: Social Science, Values and Ethical Life* (Cambridge: Cambridge University Press, 2011), 82.

41 Daniel Putman, "Relational Ethics and Virtue Theory," *Metaphilosophy* 22, no. 3 (1991): 234.

42 Ezio Manzini, *Politics of the Everyday*, trans. Rachel Anne Coad (London: Bloomsbury Visual Arts, 2019), 25.

43 Margus Vihalem, "Everyday Aesthetics and Jacques Rancière: Reconfiguring the Common Field of Aesthetics and Politics," *Journal of Aesthetics & Culture* 10, no. 1 (2018): 8.

44 Felicia Cohn, "Existential Medicine: Martin Buber and Physician-Patient Relationships," *The Journal of Continuing Education in the Health Professions* 21 (2001): 174.

45 I will be using "You" following the Kaufmann translation of Buber's work to which I am referring, although the title is *I and Thou.* Kaufmann indicates his dissatisfaction with the use of "Thou" but explains how it came about in his acknowledgment page of *I and Thou,* trans. Walter Kaufmann (New York: Charles Scribner's Sons, 1970).

46 Ibid., 80–1. The passages in the next sentence are from 81, and in the last sentence from 80.

47 Ibid., 59, for this and the next passage.

48 Cohn, "Existential Medicine," 180, emphasis added.

49 Ibid., 178. This point is brought home to me by my spouse who is an optometrist. Although he uses various machines to gauge a patient's vision, which crunch the number for a new prescription for glasses or contact lens, he has to adjust the prescription according to various facts about the patient, such as the occupation (a computer programmer or a construction worker?) or how much the new prescription differs from the current prescription (to spare the patient of a radical readjustment).

50 Buber, *I and Thou,* 59, and the next passage 39.

51 Donovan, *The Aesthetics of Care,* 73, for this and the next passages.

52 Hepburn, "Values of Art and Values of Community," 42, emphasis added.

53 Ibid., 46, emphasis added. Several scholars point out that for Hepburn this experience of the particular, if it regards a natural object, is an entry into the experience of the ineffable unity of us and the world. See David E. Cooper's "Aesthetic Experience, Metaphysics and Subjectivity: Ronald W. Hepburn and 'Nature-Mysticism,'" 90–101, and Emily Brady's "Nature, Aesthetics and Humility," 161–75, both in *Aesthetics, Nature and Religion: Ronald W. Hepburn and His Legacy,* ed. Endre Szécsényi (Aberdeen: Aberdeen University Press, 2020).

54 Kendall L. Walton, "Categories of Art," *Philosophical Review* 78 (1970): 334–67.

55 Hepburn, "Values of Art and Values of Community," 42.

56 Soetsu Yanagi, *The Beauty of Everyday Things,* trans. Michael Brase (New York: Penguin Classics, 2018); all the phrases so far are from 279.

57 Ibid.

58 Ibid., 273, 154.

59 What belongs to an art object is often debated as a problem of "framing." That is, to take an example from the literal frame, it is not clear whether everything we see within a painting's frame is a part of the painting as a work of art, such as the signature, a shadow reflected on the painted surface, cracks seen on the painted surface, and so on. At the same time, what is outside of the frame may be an important aspect of a work of art, such as in the case of installation art. For the purpose of the discussion here, however, I will not pursue this complication.

60 Harry Broudy, *Enlightened Cherishing: An Essay on Aesthetic Education* (Urbana: University of Illinois Press, 1994), 29–30.

61 Ibid., 31.

62 Ronald W. Hepburn, "Life and Life-Enhancement as Key Concepts in Aesthetics," in *The Reach of the Aesthetic: Collected Essays on Art and Nature* (Hants: Ashgate, 2001), 72.

63 Ronald W. Hepburn, "Truth, Subjectivity and the Aesthetic," in *The Reach of the Aesthetic* (Hants: Ashgate, 2001), 18.

64 Ronald W. Hepburn, "Nature Humanised: Nature Respected," *Environmental Values* 7 (1998): 270.

65 The reference to Virgin Mary is from Ronald W. Hepburn, "Trivial and Serious in Aesthetic Appreciation of Nature," in *The Reach of the Aesthetics*, 11, and basket of laundry from "Contemporary Aesthetics and the Neglect of Natural Beauty," in *"Wonder" and Other Essays: Eight Studies in Aesthetics and Neighboring Fields* (Edinburgh: Edinburgh University Press, 1984), 29.

66 Emily Brady, "Imagination and the Aesthetic Appreciation of Nature," in *The Aesthetics of Natural Environments*, ed. Allen Carlson and Arnold Berleant (Peterborough: Broadview Press, 2004), 166.

67 Arnold Berleant, *Re-thinking Aesthetics: Rogue Essays on Aesthetics and the Arts* (Aldershot: Ashgate, 2004), 45.

68 Ibid.

69 See also Groves's discussion of Gilligan's criticism of justice-centric ethics based upon the notion of disinterestedness in *Care*, 105.

70 Immanuel Kant, *Critique of Judgment*, trans. J. H. Bernard (New York: Hafner Press, 1974), 58 (sec. 13).

71 David E. Cooper, "Edification and the Experience of Beauty," in *International Yearbook of Aesthetics: Diversity and Universality* *in Aesthetics*, ed. Wang Keping, vol. 14 (2010), 74. Cooper also identifies this open-minded stance toward the other as the wisdom taught by Daoism and Buddhism (70–5).

72 Murdoch, *The Sovereignty of Good*, 82, emphasis original.

73 Ibid., 85.

74 Ibid., 64, emphasis original.

75 John Dewey, *Art as Experience* (New York: Capricorn Books, 1958), 325. Note the same metaphor of "veil" is used by both Dewey and Murdoch.

76 Ibid., 333.

77 Joseph Kupfer, *Experience as Art: Aesthetics in Everyday Life* (Albany: SUNY Press, 1983), 71.

78 Ibid., 73 and 77.

79 Elaine Scarry, *On Beauty and Being Just* (Princeton: Princeton University Press, 1999), 109–15.

80 Ibid., 112.

81 Ibid., 90.

82 The best primary text is Dōgen's major work, *Shōbōgenzō* (正法眼蔵 *The Storehouse of True Knowledge*). The most important chapters are translated and compiled by Thomas Cleary in *Shōbōgenzō: Zen Essays by Dōgen* (Honolulu: University of Hawaii Press, 1986).

83 The notion of "making oneself slender" so that one enters into the object was advocated by Matsuo Bashō in the art of making haiku. See Hattori Dohō's record of Bashō's teaching in "The Red Booklet," trans. Toshihiko and Toyo Izutsu, in *The Theory of Beauty in the Classical Aesthetics of Japan* (The Hague: Martinus Nijhoff Publishers, 1981), 159–67.

84 Robert Carter, *The Japanese Art and Self-Discipline* (Albany: SUNY Press, 2008), 2. I explore this aesthetic approach to nature in "Appreciating Nature on its Own Terms," *Environmental Ethics* 20 (1998): 135–49.

85 Yanagi, *The Beauty*, 282, 283. It is noteworthy that the same idea of "reining in the tongue" is discussed by Annie Dillard in her essay, "Seeing," the same term used by Yanagi in his comparison to "knowing." (See Section 3 of this chapter.) Dillard states that true seeing can happen when one succeeds in "a discipline requiring a lifetime of dedicated struggle" to "gag the commentator, to hush the noise of useless interior babble that keeps me from seeing," so that one can "unpeach the peaches."

Annie Dillard, "Seeing" originally in *Pilgrim at Tinker Creek* (1974), included in *Environmental Ethics: Divergence and Convergence*, ed. Richard G. Botzler and Susan J. Armstrong (Boston: McGraw-Hill, 1998), 121, 119.

86 Ibid., 281.

87 Ibid., 283.

88 Eaton, *Merits, Aesthetic and Ethical*, 215, emphasis in the original.

89 Milton Mayeroff, *On Caring* (New York: HarperCollins, 1971), 53–4.

90 Engster, "Rethinking Care Theory," 52.

91 Neil Pembroke, "Human Dimension in Medical Care: Insights from Buber and Marcel," *Southern Medical Journal* 103, no. 12 (2010): 1210.

92 The original text Pembroke cites is Martin Buber, "Elements of the Interhuman," trans. Roald Gregor Smith, *Psychiatry* 20, no. 2 (1957): 110, 112, 110.

93 Pembroke, "Human Dimension," 1211. Another area in which imagination becomes a critical tool for care regards intergenerational ethics regarding future generation. For this discussion, see Groves's *Care* and Sanna Lehtinen's "Building as Objects of Care in the Urban Environment," in *Aesthetics in Dialogue: Applying Philosophy of Art in a Global World*, ed. Zoltán Somhegyi and Max Ryynänen (Berlin: Peter Lang, 2020), 223–36.

94 Noddings, *Caring*, 9.

95 Ibid., 22.

96 Ibid.

97 Ibid., 26.

98 Friedrich Nietzsche, *The Will to Power*, trans. Walter Kaufmann and R. J. Hollingdale, ed. Walter Kaufmann (New York: Vintage Books, 1968), 429, emphasis added; Friedrich Nietzsche, *On the Genealogy of Morals* in *Basic Writings of Nietzsche*, trans. and ed. Walter Kaufmann (New York: The Modern Library, 1968), 539; Friedrich Nietzsche, *The Gay Science*, trans. Walter Kaufmann (New York: Vintage Books, 1974), 241.

99 Gernot Böhme, "Atmosphere as the Fundamental Concept of a New Aesthetics," trans. David Roberts, *Thesis Eleven* 36 (1993): 114.

100 Dewey, *Art as Experience*, 53, emphasis added.

101 Ibid., 52.

102 Paul Ziff, "Reasons in Art Criticism," in *Philosophy and Education*, ed. Israel Scheffler (Boston: Allyn and Bacon, 1958), 219–36.

103 Berleant, *Sensibility and Sense*, 119. Also see his critique of disinterestedness in *The Aesthetics of Environment* (Philadelphia: Temple University Press, 1992), 157–8.

104 Berleant, "Objects into Persons," 11.

105 Arnold Berleant, *Living in the Landscape: Toward an Aesthetics of Environment* (Lawrence: University Press of Kansas, 1997), 164.

106 Emily Brady, "Adam Smith's 'Sympathetic Imagination' and the Aesthetic Appreciation of Environment," *The Journal of Scottish Philosophy* 9, no. 1 (2011): 104.

107 Ibid.

108 For a good discussion of Dewey's notion of the temporal dimension of aesthetic experience, see Section 2 of Kalle Puolakka's "The Aesthetics of Conversation: Dewey and Davidson," *Contemporary Aesthetics* 15 (2017), https://digitalcommons.risd.edu/liberalarts_contempaesthetics/vol15/iss1/20/, accessed August 13, 2020. I will incorporate Puolakka's discussion on the aesthetics of conversation in Chapter 3.

109 Noddings, *Caring*, 22. In another place, she states: "As we discuss our relationships to animals, plants, things, and ideas, we shall observe a shading-off from the ethical into the sensitive and aesthetic" (149).

Chapter 2

1 Noddings, *Caring*, 4.

2 Cited by Rosemarie Tong, *Feminine and Feminist Ethics* (Belmont: Wadsworth Publishing Company, 1993), 115.

3 Mayeroff, *On Caring*, 95.

4 Marin Heidegger, *Being and Time*, trans. Joan Stambaugh (Albany: SUNY Press, 1996), 180.

5 Ibid., 179.

6 Ibid., 180, for these phrases and the next passage.

7 In Chapter 3, I will discuss these invisible care activities that support presumably more important work, and, in Chapter 4, some contemporary artists' works that highlight care activities.

8 Engster, "Rethinking Care Theory," 60.

9 Ibid., 61.

10 Groves, *Care*, 120.

11 Carla Cipolla and Ezio Manzini, "Relational Services," *Knowledge, Technology & Policy* 22 (2009): 46.

12 Ibid., 47.

13 Ibid., 48.

14 Ibid., 49.

15 Ibid., 49–50.

16 Buber, *I and Thou*, 85.

17 Pamela Fisher and Dawn Freshwater, "Towards Compassionate Care through Aesthetic Rationality," *Scandinavian Journal of Caring Sciences* 28 (2014): 768.

18 Cohn, "Existential Medicine," 171.

19 Fisher and Freshwater, "Toward Compassionate Care," 771, emphasis added.

20 Ibid., citing Roslyn Wallach Bologh. They continue that the "focus was not on the abstract but on the person at hand, seen as an embodied, feeling and thinking agent. While emotionally charged relationships may be draining, there is a growing body of sociologically informed literature suggesting that denying emotional engagement in caring environments leads to yet greater devitalization."

21 Ibid., 773.

22 Ibid., 772.

23 Noddings, *Caring*, xiii. Rosemarie Tong interprets Noddings to be developing a framework for ethics based upon relationality larger than the "feminist" framework; see Tong, *Feminine*, 114–15.

24 Nicolas Bourriaud, *Relational Aesthetics*, trans. Simon Pleasance and Fronza Woods (Dijon: les presses du reel, 2002).

25 Ibid., 113.

26 Claire Bishop, "Antagonism and Relational Aesthetics," *October* 110 (Fall 2004): 62.

27 Bourriaud, *Relational Aesthetics*, 28.

28 Ibid., 26, and the next passage 22.

29 For these points, see Beata Hock's entry on "Relational Aesthetics," in *Encyclopedia of Aesthetics*, ed. Michael Kelly, Vol. 5 (Oxford: Oxford University Press, 2014), 350–4.

30 Hepburn, "Contemporary Aesthetics and the Neglect of Natural Beauty," 13.

31 Berleant, "Objects into Persons," 10.

32 Arnold Berleant, *Aesthetics beyond the Arts: New and Recent Essays* (Farnham: Ashgate, 2012), 85.

33 Berleant, "Objects into Persons," 11.

34 Ibid.

35 Böhme, "Atmosphere as the Fundamental Concept of a New Aesthetics," 122.

36 Gernot Böhme, "Atmosphere as an Aesthetic Concept," *Daidalos* 68 (1998): 112.

37 Carter, *The Japanese Arts and Self-Discipline*, 5.

38 Yū Inutsuka, "Sensation, Betweenness, Rhythms: Watsuji's Environmental Philosophy and Ethics in Conversation with Heidegger," in *Japanese Environmental Philosophy*, ed. J. Baird Callicott and John McRae (New York: Oxford University Press, 2017), 103.

39 Yanagi, *The Beauty*, 155.

40 Lorenzo Marinucci, "Mood, *Ki*, Humors: Elements and Atmospheres between Europe and Japan," *Studi di estetica* 48, no. 4 (2019): 181. I thank Don Keefer for referring me to this article.

41 Paracelsus, *Paracelsus Selected Writings*, trans. Norbert Guterman, ed. Jolande Jacobi (London: Routledge & Kegan Paul, 1951), 132.

42 Ibid., 133. So as not to render the notion of relationality between self and the world a historical or an anthropological curiosity, we should note Heidegger's acknowledgment of affinity with East Asian philosophy. Reinhard May compiles many records of conversations Heidegger held with visitors that indicate he found in Daoism and Zen Buddhism a kindred spirit. For example, regarding the Buddhist notion of nothingness, Heidegger stated that "that is what I have been saying my whole life long." After reading a book on Zen Buddhism by D. T. Suzuki, Heidegger is said to have stated: "If I understand this man correctly, this is what I have been trying to say in all my writings." Both passages are from p. 3 of Reinhard May, *Heidegger's Hidden Sources: East Asian Influence on His Work*, trans. Graham Parkes (New York: Routledge, 1996). Yanagi also includes a similar saying by Heidegger: "If I had come into contact with the works of Daisetsu Suzuki on Zen at an earlier date, I could have reached my present conclusions much sooner" (Yanagi, *The Beauty*, 144).

43 Buber, "Elements of the Interhuman," 105–13. It should be noted that Buber was responsible for introducing *Zhuangzi* (*Chuang Tzu*) to German readers by editing and publishing a selection in 1910, which was familiar to Heidegger who refers to some passages in his work. See May, *Heidegger's Hidden Sources*, 4.

44 Ibid., 106. I will address the aesthetics involved in conversation in the next chapter.

45 Ibid., 111.

46 Anthony Ashley Cooper, Third Earl of Shaftesbury, "The Moralist," in *Philosophies of Art and Beauty: Selected Readings in Aesthetics from Plato to Heidegger*, ed. Albert Hofstadter and Richard Kuhns (New York: The Modern Library, 1964), the references to the tree and the land from 247, the ocean from 246.

47 Kant, *Critique of Judgment*, 39 (sec. 2).

48 Ibid., 39 and 41, section 4.

49 Arnold Berleant, *Re-thinking Aesthetics: Rogue Essays on Aesthetics and the Arts* (Aldershot: Ashgate, 2004), 47.

50 Ibid., 48.

51 Ibid.

52 Donovan, *The Aesthetics of Care*, 17.

53 Yaakov Jerome Garb cited by Josephine Donovan, "Everyday Use and Moments of Being: Toward a Nondominative Aesthetic," in *Aesthetics in Feminist Perspective*, ed. Hilde Hein and Carolyn Korsmeyer (Bloomington: Indiana University Press, 1993), 54.

54 Carol Gilligan, "Moral Orientation and Moral Development," in *Ethics: Classical Western Texts in Feminism and Multicultural Perspectives*, ed. James P. Sterba (New York: Oxford University Press, 2000), 556.

55 Michele M. Moody-Adams, "Gender and the Complexity of Moral Voices," in *Feminist Ethics*, ed. Claudia Card (Lawrence: University Press of Kansas, 1991), 203.

56 See Tong, *Feminine*, 101.

57 Noddings, *Caring*, xviii.

58 Buber, "Elements of the Interhuman," 110.

59 Putman, "Relational Ethics and Virtue Theory," 236, for this and the next passages.

60 Scarry, *On Beauty and Being Just*, 90, 90, 92.

61 Hepburn, "Values of Art and Values of Community," 48.

62 Kupfer, *Experience as Art*, 68.

63 Murdoch, *The Sovereignty of Good*, 84.

64 Broudy, *Enlightened Cherishing*, 37.

65 Friedrich Schiller, *On the Aesthetic Education of Man*, trans. Reginald Snell (New York: Frederick Ungar Publishing, 1977), 135.

66 For the value of subtlety, see Alex King's "The Virtue of Subtlety and the Vice of a Heavy Hand," *British Journal of Aesthetics* 57, no. 2 (April 2017): 119–37.

67 For this view, see the essays included in the section on "Nature and Positive Aesthetics," in *Nature, Aesthetics, and Environmentalism: From Beauty to Duty*, ed. Allen Carlson and Sheila Lintott (New York: Columbia University Press, 2007).

68 Aldo Leopold, *A Sand County Almanac* (New York: Ballantine Books, 1977), 280–95.

69 Ibid., 102, 268, 180.

70 Ibid., 76 and 73 for "underdog bias," 102 for values, 76 for brush, 193 for weeds and bush, and 180 for Kansas plains.

71 Glenn Parsons and Allen Carlson, *Functional Beauty* (Oxford: Oxford University Press, 2008), 153.

72 Jane Forsey, *The Aesthetics of Design* (Oxford: Oxford University Press, 2013), 190.

73 Here, the context in which we experience these objects may make a difference. If lethal weapons, such as Japanese swords, are exhibited in a museum setting, rendered functionless in this case, we can attend to their sensuous features and admire their lethal power through imagination, thereby appreciating their functional beauty. In the context of them actually being used for killing people, I think the judgment will differ.

74 Berleant, *Aesthetics beyond the Arts*, 198–9. Also see 110.

75 Katya Mandoki, *Everyday Aesthetics: Prosaics, the Play of Culture and Social Identities* (Aldershot: Ashgate, 2007), 38. The next passage is from the same page.

76 Broudy, *Enlightened Cherishing*, 45, for this and the next passages. I will address the aesthetics of conversation in the next chapter.

77 Ibid., 6, emphasis added.

78 Buber, *I and Thou*, 85.

79 Lotte Darsø, *Artful Creation: Learning-Tales of Arts-in-Business* (Frederiksberg, Denmark: samfundslitteratur, 2004), 14, for this and the next passages.

80 R. Winder and N. Baker cited by David Silverman, "Routine Pleasures: The Aesthetics of the Mundane," in *The Aesthetics of Organization*, ed. Stephen Linstead and Heather Höpfl (London: SAGE Publications, 2000), 137.

81 Darsø, *Artful Creation*, 120.

82 Dewey, *Art as Experience*, 3.

83 Dewey characterizes the mundane, the ordinary, and humdrum as "anesthetic" (Ibid., 40). However, I maintain that such rather boring aspects of our lives do have their own texture, though perhaps not enjoyable or pleasurable in the same way. See 23–31 of my *Aesthetics of the Familiar: Everyday Life and World-Making* (Oxford: Oxford University Press, 2017).

84 Nodding, *Caring*, 18.

85 Engster, "Rethinking Care Theory," 66.

86 Sayer, *Why Things Matter to People*, 83.

87 Plato, "Apology," in *The Trial and Death of Socrates*, trans. G. M. A. Grube (Indianapolis: Hackett Publishing, 1975), 32.

88 Ibid., 33. Of course, from today's point of view, we can challenge him here by pointing out that caring for one's soul is inseparable from caring for one's body.

89 Dōgen Zenji, *Shōbōgenzō: The Eye and Treasury of the True Law*, trans. Kōsen Nishiyama and John Stevens, Vol. 2 (Tokyo: Nakayama Shobō, 1977), 87, fascicle on *Senjō* (Rules for the lavatory).

90 Dōgen Zenji, *Shōbōgenzō: The Eye and Treasury of the True Law*, trans. Kōsen Nishiyama, et al., Vol. 4. (Tokyo: Nakayama Shobō, 1983), 3, and 4, fascicle on *Senmen* (Washing the face).

91 Heidegger, *Being and Time*, 185.

92 For this point, see Richard White, "Foucault on the Care of the Self as an Ethical Project and a Spiritual Goal," *Human Studies* 37, no. 4 (Winter 2014): 498.

93 Ibid., 499.

94 For this point, see Carter's *Japanese Arts* that includes his interviews with contemporary masters in various arts, and Ueda's *Literary and Art Theories in Japan* that presents and analyzes writings by old masters in various arts.

95 Michael Foucault, *The Foucault Reader*, ed. Paul Rabinow (New York: Pantheon Books, 1984), 350, for this and the next passages.

96 Ibid., 352.

97 Nietzsche, *The Gay Science*, 232, emphasis added.

98 Friedrich Nietzsche, *Beyond Good and Evil* in *Basic Writings of Nietzsche*, trans. and ed. Walter Kaufmann (New York: The Modern Library, 1968), 344.

99 Nietzsche, *The Gay Science*, 233.

100 Graham Parkes, *Composing the Soul: Reaches of Nietzsche's Psychology* (Chicago: The University of Chicago Press, 1994), 169.

101 The reference to a statue every part of which is painted with gorgeous colors appears on 86–7, and a cloak decorated with all kinds of ornaments on 206–7 in *Plato's Republic*, trans. G. M. A. Grube (Indianapolis: Hackett Publishing Company, 1974).

Chapter 3

1 Berleant, "Objects into Persons," 9–18.

2 Berleant, *Living in the Landscape*, 39.

3 Berleant, "Objects into Persons," 12.

4 Berleant, *Sensibility and Sense*, 95.

5 Berleant, "Objects into Persons," 14.

6 Puolakka, "The Aesthetics of Conversation."

7 Ibid., Sec. 2.

8 Kenya Hara, *White*, trans. Jooyeon Rhee (Baden: Lars Müller Publishers, 2010), Prologue. Hara's discussion of emptiness is also found in *Mujirushi Ryōhin no Dezain* (*Mujirushi Ryōhin's Design*) (Tokyo: Nikkei BP sha, 2015), 50, 67–9, and the chapter on "Simple and Empty—Genealogy of Aesthetic Sensibility," in *Nihon no Dezain—Biishiki ga Tsukuru Mirai* (*Japanese Design—Future Created by Aesthetic Sensibility*) (Tokyo: Iwanami Shoten, 2012).

9 Georg Simmel, *Simmel on Culture*, ed. and trans. David Frisby and Mike Featherstone (London: SAGE Publications, 2000), 121.

10 Ibid., this passage from 124 and the next passage from 127.

11 Sayer, *Why Things Matter to People*, 124.

12 Bishop, "Antagonism and Relational Aesthetics," 67.

13 James Thompson, "Towards an Aesthetics of Care," in *Performing Care: New Perspectives on Socially Engaged Performance*, ed. Amanda Stuart Fisher and James Thompson (Manchester: Manchester University Press, 2020), 43.

14 Ibid., 45.

15 Ibid., 46, emphasis in the original.

16 Ibid., 47.

17 Noddings, *Caring*, 9.

18 Nancy Sherman, "Of Manners and Morals," *British Journal of Educational Studies* 53, no. 3 (2005): 285.

19 Eaton, *Merits, Aesthetic and Ethical*, 92.

20 David E. Cooper, "Buddhism, Beauty and Virtue," in *Artistic Visions and the Promise of Beauty*, ed. Kathleen M. Higgins, et al. (Cham: Springer International Publishing, 2017), 132.

21 The issue may be a bit more complicated and nuanced than the way I presented. This body movement of throwing paper towels should be further put into context of the thrower's overall character. The "same" movement performed by Trump and, say, Obama may be interpreted differently if we consider the whole "gestalt" of each person. See the following discussion on the gestalt of a person.

22 Sometimes it is codified in the language use, as in Japanese informal speech, that distinguishes words and expressions expected to be used by males and those by females. The recent remark by the then head of the 2020 Tokyo Olympic Games Organizing Committee, Yoshirō Mori, that is critical of female members' participation taking up too much time in meetings implies that modesty and reticence are virtues expected of female members. Needless to say, his remark was met by a flurry of criticisms of gender stereotyping and expectation, forcing him to resign from his post. In addition to linguistic expectations, there is also different body movements and composures that are gender specific in Japan, such as sitting on a floor cross-legged being allowed for males but not for (respectable) females. For a discussion of "oppressive aesthetic demands" that disproportionately affect women, see Alfred Archer and Lauren Ware's "Beyond the Call of Beauty: Everyday Aesthetic Demands Under Patriarchy," *Monist* 101 (2018): 114–27.

23 Ossi Naukkarinen, "Everyday Aesthetic Practices, Ethics and Tact," *Aisthesis* 7, no. 1 (2014): 32 and 31.

24 Eaton, *Merits, Aesthetic and Ethical*, 92, emphasis added.

25 Marcia Muelder Eaton, *Aesthetics and the Good Life* (Rutherford: Fairleigh Dickinson University Press, 1989), 175.

26 Putman, "Relational Ethics and Virtue Theory," 235.

27 Buber, "Elements of the Interhuman," 107, for this and the next passages.

28 The concern here reminds us of the virtue theory of aesthetic cited in Chapter 1. As I indicated, its focus is the creation and activity of art, but the same consideration of requiring virtuous motive can apply to our action here.

29 Eric Mullis, "Thinking through an Embodied Confucian Aesthetics of Persons," in *Artistic Visions and the Promise of Beauty*, ed. Kathleen M. Higgins, et al. (Cham: Springer International Publishing, 2017), 144.

30 Nicholas F. Gier, "The Dancing *Ru*: A Confucian Aesthetics of Virtue," *Philosophy East & West* 51, no. 2 (2001): 288, emphasis added.

31 Mullis, "Thinking," 142 for this passage and 143 for the next passage.

32 Kristin Surak, *Making Tea, Making Japan: Cultural Nationalism in Practice* (Stanford: Stanford University Press, 2013), 52; Eiko Ikegami, *Bonds of Civility: Aesthetic Networks and the Political Origins of Japanese Culture* (Cambridge: Cambridge University Press, 2005), 227.

33 Liza Crihfield Dalby, "The Art of the Geisha," *Natural History* 92, no. 2 (1983): 51, for this and the next passages.

34 Carter, *The Japanese Arts and Self-Discipline*, 5 for this passage and 2 for the next passage.

35 Alexander Pope, "An Epistle to Lord Burlington," in *The Genius of the Pace: The English Landscape Garden 1620–1820*, ed. John Dixon Hunt and Peter Willis (Cambridge, MA: The MIT Press, 1990), 213. This avoidance of symmetrical design also reminds one of William Hogarth's notion of a serpentine line as the line of beauty.

36 For visual images of Japanese gardens and contemporary streetscapes, see 152–63 and 172–7 of my *Aesthetics of the Familiar: Everyday Life and World-Making* (Oxford: Oxford University Press, 2017).

37 These items are culled from the sixteenth-century tea master Sen no Rikyū's teachings recorded by his disciple, Nanbō Sōkei, in *Nanbōroku* (*Record of Nanbō*). *Nanbōroku o Yomu* (*Reading Nanbōroku*), ed. Isao Kumakura (Kyoto: Tankōsha, 1989).

38 Carter, *The Japanese Arts and Self-Discipline*, 93.

39 For many other examples, see http://462photoblog.net/?page_id =19, accessed March 10, 2021.

40 Because of my interest in manhole covers, over the years my friends and colleagues have sent me what they found in their everyday landscape as well as during their travel, including Serbia

and Denmark. I thank Peter Cheyne, Susan Feagin, Carolyn Korsmeyer, and Russ Quacchia for adding to my collection!

41 Graham Parkes, "Savoring Taste," in *New Essays in Japanese Aesthetics*, ed. A. Minh Nguyen (Lanham: Lexington Books, 2018), 111.

42 Carter, *The Japanese Arts and Self-Discipline*, 90.

43 Ibid., 86.

44 Ibid., 90.

45 I thank one of the participants in the graduate seminar at Uppsala University who asked a question regarding this example by criticizing the annoyingly harsh sound apparently common in Sweden.

46 Akiko Busch, *The Uncommon Life of Common Objects: Essays on Design and the Everyday* (New York: Metropolis Books, 2004), 84.

47 Nigel Taylor, "Ethical Arguments about the Aesthetics of Architecture," in *Ethics and the Built Environment*, ed. Warwick Fox (London: Routledge, 2000), 201–2. The next passage is from 205.

48 Warwick Fox, "Architecture Ethics," in *A Companion to the Philosophy of Technology*, ed. Jan Kyrre Berg Olsen, et al. (Chichester: Wiley-Blackwell, 2009), this and the next passage from 388.

49 Warwick Fox, *A Theory of General Ethics: Human Relationships, Nature, and the Built Environment* (Cambridge, MA: The MIT Press, 2006).

50 Ezio Manzini, "Prometheus of the Everyday: The Ecology of the Artificial and the Designer's Responsibility," in *Discovering Design: Explorations in Design Studies*, ed. Richard Buchanan and Victor Margolin (Chicago: The University of Chicago Press, 1995), 220, 219.

51 Julia Jacobs, "Prominent Architects Group Prohibits Design of Death Chambers," *The New York Times*, December 11, 2020. https://www.nytimes.com/2020/12/11/arts/design/american-institute-of-architects-execution.html?campaign_id=2&emc=edit_th_20201213&instance_id=24999&nl=todaysheadlines&regi_id=40614031&segment_id=46781&user_id=67fb6c4431a7ea59156285c346a5aac9, accessed December 13, 2020. These kinds of objects pose a challenge to whether we can even make sense of functional beauty in terms of the specific design serving the intended function well, as I discussed in Chapter 2, Section 3. Here my point regards the ethical responsibility for architects not to support an inhumane treatment of humans, rather than the relevance of such an unethical end to the object's aesthetic value.

52 Taylor, "Ethical Arguments," 201–2.

53 However, I pointed out in Chapter 1 that we don't really have access to the presence or absence of a virtuous attitude and motivation behind the artist's creative act.

54 Juhani Pallasmaa, "Toward an Architecture of Humility," *Harvard Design Magazine* (1999): 22–5. The terms cited occur throughout this article.

55 David E. Cooper, "Human Landscapes, Virtue, and Beauty," presented at a conference on *Ethics and Aesthetics of Architecture and the Environment*, Newcastle University, July 11–13, 2012, retrieved from academia.edu. p. 3.

56 Ibid.

57 David E. Cooper, "Beautiful People, Beautiful Things," *British Journal of Aesthetics* 48, no. 3 (2008): 258.

58 Peter-Paul Verbeek, *What Things Do: Philosophical Reflections on Technology, Agency, and Design* (University Park: Pennsylvania State University Press, 2005), 215 for this passage and 216 for the next passage.

59 Ibid., 207–8.

60 The example of speed bumps and the notion of actant are from Bruno Latour, "Where Are the Missing Masses? The Sociology of a Few Mundane Artifacts," in *Shaping Technology/Building Society: Studies in Sociotechnical Change*, ed. Wiebe E. Bijker and John Law (Cambridge, MA: MIT Press, 1992): 225–58. The example of the fence and the notion of commendable closure are from Robert Rosenberger, *Callous Objects: Designs against the Homeless* (Minneapolis: University of Minnesota Press, 2017) and "On Hostile Design: Theoretical and Empirical Prospects," *Urban Studies* 1, no. 11 (2019): 1–11. The example of the urinal and the notion of libertarian paternalism is from Richard H. Thayer and Cass R. Sunstein, *Nudge: Improving Decisions about Health, Wealth, and Happiness* (New York: Penguin Books, 2008).

61 See Langdon Winner's discussion in *The Whale and the Reactor: A Search for Limits in an Age of High Technology* (Chicago: The University of Chicago Press, 1989), 22–4.

62 I cite these terms from Robert Rosenberger's works referenced in note 60. He prefers the term "unhoused" to "homeless" because of the common negative connotation associated with the latter. See p. 2 of his *Callous Objects*. The term "obstinate objects" is used by Roman Mars and Kurt Kohlstedt in *The 99% Invisible City: A Field Guide to the Hidden World of Everyday Design* (Boston: Houghton

Mifflin Harcourt, 2020). Although the visual images I am including are all from the United States, such hostile architecture is not limited to the United States or Western hemisphere. For example, see a recent discussion of Japanese examples in Philip Brasor's "How Hostile Design Keeps Japan's Homeless at Arm's Length," *The Japan Times*, December 12, 2020. https://www.japantimes .co.jp/news/2020/12/12/national/media-national/homeless-bench -designs/ accessed December 13, 2020.

63 Rosenberger, *Callous Objects*, 53.

64 Katsuoki Horikawa and Tomoaki Hosaka, "Mother: Bus Driver 'Refused' to Let Me Board with Twin Buggy," *The Asahi Shinbun*, November 12, 2019.

65 Rosenberger, *Callous Objects*, 58.

66 Shen-yi Liao and Bryce Huebner, "Oppressive Things," *Philosophy and Phenomenological Research* 103 (2021): 94. I thank Anne Eaton for calling attention to this article.

67 Ibid., 98.

68 I thank one of the participants in the colloquium at the University of Illinois in Chicago who raised this point.

69 There are interventions by artists that subvert the exclusionary intent of those objects. See Rosenberger, *Callous Objects*, 60–4. More examples of hostile architecture and some artistic interventions can also be seen in "Unpleasant Design & Hostile Urban Architecture" (July 5, 2016) at https://99percentinvisible.org /episode/unpleasant-design-hostile-urban-architecture/, accessed October 14, 2021. Another example of artistic intervention is Sarah Tooley's installation project in the Washington D.C. involving the area residents, "Public Dialogues in Public Places," which installed brightly colored park benches with the residents' statements about what they use the benches for, as a protest against the removal of benches by the city to prevent homeless people from sleeping on them. The interesting twists and turns created by this project is narrated in "Community Response to Defensive Architecture" posted by Hidden Hostility DC (no date) at https:// www.hiddenhostilitydc.com/responses, accessed October 14, 2021.

70 Busch, *The Uncommon Life*, 87, emphasis added.

71 Joan Iverson Nassauer, "Care and Stewardship: From Home to Planet," *Landscape and Urban Planning* 100 (2011): 322.

72 See Nassauer's "Messy Ecosystems, Orderly Frames," *Landscape Journal* 14, no. 2 (1995): 161–70 and "Cultural Sustainability: Aligning Aesthetics and Ecology," in *Placing Nature: Culture and*

Landscape Ecology, ed. Joan Iverson Nassauer (Washington: Island Press, 1997): 65–83.

73 Nassauer, "Care and Stewardship," 321.

74 Ibid., 322.

75 Ibid., 323.

76 Thompson, "Towards an Aesthetics of Care," 38.

77 James Thompson, "Performing the 'Aesthetics of Care,'" in *Performing Care: New Perspectives on Socially Engaged Performance*, ed. Amanda Stuart Fisher and James Thompson (Manchester: Manchester University Press, 2020), 218, 219.

78 Ibid.

Chapter 4

1 Berleant, "Objects into Persons," 15, emphasis added.

2 Buber, *I and Thou*, 172.

3 Ibid., 173, for this and the next passages.

4 See some examples of bridges and tunnels in Starre Vartan's "How Wildlife Bridges over Highways Make Animals—and People—Safer," *National Geographic*, April 16, 2019, at https://www.nationalgeographic.com/animals/2019/04/wildlife-overpasses-underpasses-make-animals-people-safer/#close. Other examples can be seen in https://www.nationalgeographic.org/article/wildlife-crossings/; https://www.theguardian.com/environment/2019/aug/21/los-angeles-wildlife-bridge-mountain-lions; and https://www.smithsonianmag.com/smart-news/animals-are-using-utahs-largest-wildlife-overpass-earlier-expected-180976420/, all accessed December 1, 2020.

5 Elizabeth Lynch, "Equal Opportunity Housing," in *The New Earthwork: Art Action Agency*, ed. Twylene Moyer and Glenn Harper (Hamilton: ISC Press, 2011), 161. For Lynn Hull's trans-species art, see an interview with Robert Preece and visual images, 157–60.

6 Buffalo Bird Woman, "From *Buffalo Bird Woman's Garden*," in *Cooking, Eating, Thinking: Transformative Philosophies of Food*, ed. Deane W. Curtin and Lisa M. Heldke (Bloomington: Indiana University Press, 1992), 275.

7 David E. Cooper, *A Philosophy of Gardens* (Oxford: Oxford University Press, 2006), 74.

8 Carter, *The Japanese Arts and Self-Discipline*, 59. Carter anticipates such a practice will be considered "weird" or "flaky" particularly from "Western cultural climates."

9 Buber, *I and Thou*, 173.

10 Magdalena Hoły-Łuczaj gives a useful discussion of the different views on the moral status of nature and its members in her "Artifacts and the Limitations of Moral Considerability," *Environmental Ethics* (Spring 2019): 69–87. Simon P. James discusses how environmental holism can be made compatible with the intrinsic value of individual things by reference to Buddhism, Heidegger, and deep ecology in "Holism in Buddhism, Heidegger, and Deep Ecology," *Environmental Ethics* 22, no. 4 (Winter 2000): 359–75.

11 Hoły-Łuczaj, "Artifacts." Following Hoły-Łuczaj, by artifacts I refer to physical/material objects, such as a desk and a cup, throughout this book. That is, like her, I do not include in my discussion nonphysical artifacts such as a computer program or an urban traffic system.

12 Steven Vogel, "Thinking Like a Mall," in *Environmental Aesthetics: Crossing Divides and Breaking Ground*, ed. Martin Drenthen and Jozef Keulartz (New York: Fordham University Press, 2014), 180.

13 Andrew Light and Holmes Rolston III, "Introduction: Ethics and Environmental Ethics," in *Environmental Ethics: An Anthology*, ed. Andrew Light and Holmes Rolston III (Malden: Blackwell, 2003), 6.

14 Vogel, "Thinking Like a Mall," 181.

15 Ibid., 187.

16 Anne Eaton, "Artifacts and Their Functions," in *Oxford Handbook of History and Material Culture*, ed. Ivan Gaskell and Sarah Anne Carter (Oxford: Oxford University Press, 2020), 48.

17 "'Memorial' Held for Discarded *Hanko* Seals as Digitization Takes Root," *The Japan Times*, October 19, 2020.

18 Yanagi, *The Beauty*, 35.

19 Ibid., 36 for these passages and 37 for the next passage.

20 Pat Schneider, "The Patience of Ordinary Things," in *Another River: New and Collected Poems* (Amherst: Amherst Writers and Artists Press, 2005), 111, reprinted with permission by the Estate of Pat Schneider. I thank Lisa Heldke for introducing me to this poem.

21 Martin Heidegger, "The Thing," in *Poetry, Language, Thought*, trans. Albert Hofstadter (New York: Harper & Row, 1971), 169.

22 Ibid., 172.

23 Ibid., 182.

24 Hoły-Łuczaj, "Artifacts," 74.

25 Cooper, *A Philosophy of Gardens*, 87.

26 Murdoch, *The Sovereignty of Good*, 36.

27 Another way of putting it is to borrow the legal concept of "innocent until proven guilty" and hold that care relationship should be assumed until or unless it is shown that the object of care is not worthy of receiving care. At the very least, this may offer a possible strategy as we encounter thorny cases of how we should deal with those objects and beings with undetermined moral status such as AI and extraterrestrial beings.

28 Simon P. James, "For the Sake of a Stone? Inanimate Things and the Demands of Morality," *Inquiry* 54, no. 4 (August 2011): 384–97.

29 Ibid., 392.

30 Stan Godlovitch discusses the moral wrongness of destroying inanimate natural objects, such as ice, even when there is no possible and future harm to sentient beings. His reason for its wrongness is different from James's reason in that he believes the proper human attitude toward nature, sentient or nonsentient, has to be acentric. It is unclear whether his view extends to artifacts. "Ice Breakers: Environmentalism and Natural Aesthetics," *Journal of Applied Philosophy* 11, no. 1 (1994): 15–30. The issue here also calls into question whether "delicacy" or "gentleness" must be expressed toward artifacts which are created specifically for evil purposes, such as a weapon of mass destruction or a torture device, an issue I mentioned in Chapter 2, Section 3.

31 James, "For the Sake of a Stone?" 393.

32 Ibid., 392.

33 Carter, *The Japanese Arts and Self-Discipline*, 61, emphasis added.

34 Ibid., 70, emphasis added.

35 Cited by Carter, Ibid., 63 and 66.

36 For the paradox involved in the art of *ikebana,* see Ryosuke Ohashi's entry on "Kire and Iki" in *Encyclopedia of Aesthetics*, ed. Michael Kelly (New York: Oxford University Press, 2014), Vol. 4, 13.

37 Carter, *The Japanese Arts and Self-Discipline*, 102, emphasis added.

38 Ibid., 108–9.

39 Ibid., 124.

40 Heidegger, *Being and Time*, 96.

41　I should note that at least when I was growing up, the cleaning of school buildings was performed by the students. I believe this fostered a sense of collective responsibility for caring for their environment because they are the ones who end up having to clean the mess. It also enhanced the mutual respect for one another among students.

42　Steven Jackson, "Rethinking Repair," in *Media Technologies: Essays on Communication, Materiality, and Society*, ed. Tarleton Gillespie, et al. (Cambridge, MA: The MIT Press, 2014), 229.

43　Another case in point is the same invisibility of the act of cleanup after the January 6, 2021, riot that destroyed parts of the US Capitol Building. How much labor was needed to clean up the mess and repair the damage was never highlighted in TV or newspaper reporting.

44　Sandra Laugier, "War on Care," *Series: Corona-Times* (November 5, 2020) at https://ethicsofcare.org/war-on-care/, accessed September 21, 2021.

45　*Mierle Laderman Ukeles: Maintenance Art*, ed. Patricia C. Phillips (New York: Queens Museum, 2016), 210. See this book for the visual images of Ukeles's *oeuvre*, including her *Manifesto*.

46　"Never Done" is the title of an essay by Lucy R. Lippard included in Ibid., 15–20.

47　Cited by Lippard, "Never Done," 17.

48　Tom Finkelpearl's statement included in "Mierle Laderman Ukeles in Conversation with Tom Finkelpearl and Shannon Jackson," in *Mierle Laderman Ukeles: Seven Work Ballets*, ed. Kari Conte (Amsterdam: Kunstverein Publishing, 2016), 219. One may question whether such a reaction by the audience creates a case of a gazer objectifying the worker. I believe that the willing participation and the pride of the workers render this case one of celebration rather than exacerbating the dehumanization of workers. I owe this question to Don Keefer.

49　Ramiro Gomez, "On Tenth Avenue," in *Manual: A Journal about Art and its Making* (Providence: Museum of Art, Rhode Island School of Design) 11 (Fall 2018), 35.

50　A good analysis of Burtynski's *Shipbreaking* can be found in Jackson, "Rethinking." As with other photographs of devastating landscapes by Burtynski, a series of photographs in *Shipbreaking* are stunningly beautiful, raising questions about the possible problem of aestheticizing devastations. At the same time, *Shipbreaking* can be interpreted as a celebration of the ingenuity, resilience, and industriousness of Bangladeshi people who dismantle this huge mammoth.

51 *Koolhaas Houselife* (directed and produced by Ila Bêka and Louise Lemoine, 2013). In an interview following the film, Koolhaas admits that he shares with other designers and makers obsession with keeping their creation in perfect condition.

52 Jacques Rancière, *The Politics of Aesthetics*, trans. Gabriel Rockhill (London: Continuum, 2004), 13.

53 See Thompson, "Performing the 'Aesthetics of Care,'" 219.

One of the memorable students' projects for my class on ecological responsibility in art and design at the Rhode Island School of Design was the redesigning of receptacles for recyclable items. The students observed not only people's actions of throwing cans and papers into those receptacles but they accompanied the night cleaning crews as they emptied them. They found that those containers were designed for the convenience of the people throwing recyclable items in, but not for the cleaning crews who had to empty them. Their alternative design addressed this problem of emptying the containers.

54 Jayne Lloyd, "Taking Care of the Laundry in Care Homes," in *Performing Care: New Perspectives on Socially Engaged Performance*, ed. Amanda Stuart Fisher and James Thompson (Manchester: Manchester University Press, 2020), 209.

55 Ibid., 206.

56 Igor Kopytoff, "The Cultural Biography of Things: Commoditization as Process," in *The Social Life of Things: Commodities in Cultural Perspective*, ed. Arjun Appadurai (Cambridge: Cambridge University Press, 2013), 64–91.

57 Shannon Lee Dawdy, *Patina: A Profane Archaeology* (Chicago: The University of Chicago Press, 2016), 140.

58 I borrow this term from Lindsay French, who titled one of her anthropology courses at the Rhode Island School of Design "(Hi)Stories of Repair."

59 George Santayana, *The Sense of Beauty: Being the Outline of Aesthetic Theory* (New York: Dover Publications, 1955), 121.

60 Ibid., 120.

61 Verbeek, *What Things Do*, 220.

62 Ibid., 225, emphasis added.

63 Naoto Fukasawa and Jasper Morrison, *Super Normal: Sensations of the Ordinary* (Baden: Lars Müller Publishers, 2008), 104.

64 Ibid., 110 for *shutaku* and 106 for *wabi-sabi*.

65 Ibid., 111, emphasis added.

66 Simon P. James, "Why Old Things Matter," *Journal of Moral Philosophy* 12 (2015): 313.

67 Ibid., 327.

68 Groves, *Care*, 130.

69 Carter, *The Japanese Arts and Self-Discipline*, 5.

70 Hoły-Łuczaj, "Artifacts," 83.

71 Lance Hosey, *The Shape of Green: Aesthetics, Ecology, and Design* (Washington: Island Press, 2012), 106.

72 Noddings, *Caring*, 13.

73 Dewey, *Art as Experience*, 5.

74 The problem of externalizing true cost is discussed by Paul Hawken in *Ecology of Commerce: A Declaration of Sustainability* (New York: HarperBusiness, 1994). The 2015 film, *The True Cost*, dir. Andrew Morgan (Bullfrog Films), is helpful in exposing the true cost of today's global economy.

75 See http://www.platform21.nl/page/4315/en, https://www.ifixit.com/Manifesto, and https://repaircafe.org/en/, all accessed June 7, 2020.

76 For the history of planned obsolescence in the United States, see Giles Slade's *Made to Break: Technology and Obsolescence in America* (Cambridge: Harvard University Press, 2007) and Daniel M. Abramson's *Obsolescence: An Architectural History* (Chicago: The University of Chicago Press, 2016). I believe that many of us have experienced the frustration of trying to clean a lighting fixture, teapot, a fancy dress, and the like.

77 Bernard London, "Ending the Depression Through Planned Obsolescence," (1932) retrieved from https://upload.wikimedia.org/wikipedia/commons/2/27/London_(1932)_Ending_the_depression_through_planned_obsolescence.pdf on June 7, 2020, p. 2 (emphasis added), and the following passage from p. 5. As a real estate developer, London must have been familiar with the notion of architectural obsolescence as an economic strategy to justify tax advantage based upon the buildings' depreciation over time. Tax deductibility for building depreciation was incorporated in the US federal income tax code, introduced in 1909. Daniel Abramson discusses how various writings at the time made "obsolescence appear to be an inevitable and incontrovertible law of development and change—something that just happens to buildings—rather than the result of specific business practices and historical actors." Abramson, *Obsolescence*, 34. I thank Ivan Gaskell for pointing out this historical context for London's writing and the reference to Abramson's book.

78 Elizabeth V. Spelman, *Repair: The Impulse to Restore in a Fragile World* (Boston: Beacon Press, 2002), 5.

79 Daniela K. Rosner, "A Beautiful Oops," *Continent* 6, no. 1 (2017): 77.

80 Dewey, *Art as Experience*, 16, 17. The other world where aesthetic experience does not occur, according to him, is a world of constant flux.

81 David Lowenthal, *The Past is a Foreign Country* (Cambridge: Cambridge University Press, 1990), all the passages from 127.

82 Jackson, "Rethinking," 221–39. This productionist bias is also reflected in the way in which many artifacts are designed that do not take into consideration easy disassembly for cleaning and repair, as mentioned before. In a similar way, Jon Stewart's activism regarding the care for veterans of wars makes clear that the governments (at least of the United States) focus on funding for the war effort but not its aftermath, such as the care for veterans and reclaiming the environment devastated by wars. See "Jon Stewart Advocates for Congressional Aid for Sick Veterans Exposed to Military Burn Pits" at https://www.pbs.org/newshour/nation/watch-jon-stewart-advocates-for-congressional-aid-for-sick-veterans-exposed-to-military-burn-pits accessed December 1, 2020.

83 Stuart Walker, *Sustainable by Design: Explorations in Theory and Practice* (London: Earthscan, 2006), 118, emphasis added.

84 See many examples in Kate Fletcher's *Craft of Use: Post-Growth Fashion* (London: Routledge, 2016).

85 To take only one example, consider the *Stain* project by Bethan Laura Wood that features teacups' interiors that gradually reveal elegant patterns that have been pretreated to stain faster. For visual images, see http://www.bethanlaurawood.com/work/stain/, accessed June 7, 2020. For other examples, see Kiff Slemmons, "On Imperfection," *Metalsmith* 28, no. 1 (2008): 26–9; Allen S. Weiss, "The Toilet Bowl and the Tea Bowl," *ArtUS* 27 (2009): 80–5; Allen S. Weiss, "Cracks," *ArtUS* 29 (2010): 62–7; Lois Martin, "Patina of Cloth," *Surface Design Journal* 28, no. 4 (Summer 2004): 16–21.

86 See https://risdmuseum.org/exhibitions-events/exhibitions/repair-and-design-futures, accessed June 7, 2020.

87 For discussion and examples of invisible fabric mending, see Alison Gwilt, "Producing Sustainable Fashion," in *Shaping Sustainable Fashion: Changing the Way We Make and Use Clothes*, ed. Alison Gwilt and Timo Rissanen (London: Earthscan, 2011), 59–73.

88 Cameron Tonkinwise, "Is Design Finished? Dematerialisation and Changing Things," in *The Design Philosophy Reader*, ed. Anne-Marie Willis (London: Bloomsbury, 2019), 156 for "in-time-ness" and the rest 157.

89 Jackson, "Rethinking," 221. Tatsushi Fujiwara, a Japanese agricultural historian, points out that soil formation is largely due to decay rather than production but the former rarely garners due recognition. While erosion, breakdown, and decay all have a negative connotation, these processes *are* actually the world's movers and shakers. Without these processes carried out by largely invisible actors, such as bacteria and insects in the natural world, and the various maintenance workers, cleaning crew, and repairers in the human world, more visible and presumably more productive and creative works cannot take place. With industrial production, if it weren't for the work of taking things apart for recycling and reusing, the earth would be buried in garbage. *Bunkai no Tetsugaku: Huhai to Hakkō o meguru Shikō* (*Philosophy of Decomposition: Thoughts on Decay and Fermentation*) (Tokyo: Seidosha, 2019), 46 and 48. Jackson makes the same point by referencing Burtynski's series of photographs, Shipbreaking, as mentioned before (see note 50).

90 Jackson, "Rethinking," 222.

91 For further exploration of this point, see Steven J. Jackson and Laewoo Kang, "Breakdown, Obsolescence and Reuse: HCI and the Art of Repair," *CHI 214: Proceedings of the SIGCHI Conference on Human Factors in Computing Systems*, April 2014: 449–58.

92 Cooper, *A Philosophy of Gardens*, 75.

93 Ibid., 72.

94 Manzini, *Politics of the Everyday*, 8.

95 Manzini, "Prometheus of the Everyday," 239 for these and next passages.

96 See Gwilt and Rissanen, *Shaping*, and Katrina Rodabaugh, *Mending Matters* (New York: Abrams, 2018) for innovative examples of visible repair.

97 See examples at https://eatock.com/books/visible-vehicle-repairs/, http://www.rachelsussman.com/portfolio#/sidewalk-kintsukuroi, https://www.janvormann.com/testbild/dispatchwork/, https://mymodernmet.com/charlotte-bailey-kintsugi-patchwork-porcelain/, https://hangingbyathreadembroidery.wordpress.com/ https://rittau.jimdofree.com/ https://www.yeesookyung.com/translated-vase- https://elisasheehan.com/collections/eggshells https://tatianefreitas.com/My-Old-New-Series https://mymodernmet.com

/kintsugi-kintsukuroi/2/ all accessed on June 7, 2020. I thank Sanna Lehtinen for the Vormann reference.

98 Sōkei Nanbō, "A Record of Nanbō," in *The Theory of Beauty in the Classical Aesthetics of Japan*, ed. and trans. Toshihiko and Toyo Izutsu (The Hague: Martinus Nijhoff Publishers, 1981), 146.

99 The information about *kintsugi* in this and subsequent paragraphs is culled from the following sources: Irahara Mitsumi and Nakamura Makoto, *Zero kara no Kintsugi Nyūmon: Utsuwa o Yomigaeraseru, Urushi no Tsukoroi* (*Introduction to Kintsugi from Zero: Restoring Containers by Mending with Lacquer*) (Tokyo: Seibundō Shinkōsha, 2017); Nakamura Kunio, *Kintsugi Techō: Hajimete no Tsukuroi* (*Kintsugi Notebook: First Repair*) (Tokyo: Genkōsha, 2017); Ozawa Noriyo, *Kintsugi no Susume: Mono o Taisetsuni suru Kokoro* (*Recommendation on Kintsugi: The Mindset to Cherish Things*) (Tokyo: Seibundō Shinkōsha, 2014).

100 Erna Husukić and Emina Zejnilović support preserving some war-torn ruins in Sarajevo for this reason. See "The Environmental Aesthetics of Sarajevo: A City Shaped by Memory," *Urbani Izziv* 28, no. 1 (2017): 96–106. The same argument is given on the same matter by Lebbeus Woods, *War and Architecture*, trans. Aleksandra Wagner (New York: Princeton Architectural Press, 1993).

101 See the image at https://www.ebara.co.jp/foundation/hatakeyama/information/collection.html, accessed October 22, 2021. The piece is the third one from the top.

102 Fujiwara, *Bunkai no Tetsugaku*, 289–90.

103 Forsey, *The Aesthetics of Design*, 237, emphasis added.

104 Cooper, *A Philosophy of Gardens*, 68. Also see 63.

105 Christopher Dowling, "The Aesthetics of Daily Life," *British Journal of Aesthetics* 50 (2010): 238.

106 Böhme, "Atmosphere as the Fundamental Concept of a New Aesthetics."

107 Rodabaugh, *Mending Matters*, 141–2.

108 Lisa Z. Morgan, "Kate Kittredge's Stockings," *Manual: A Journal about Art and its Making* (Providence: Museum of Art, Rhode Island School of Design) 11 (Fall 2018): 70.

109 Matt Rho cited by Rodabaugh, *Mending Matters*, 119.

110 Spelman, *Repair*, 47.

111 Morgan, "Kate Kittredge's Stockings," 70.

NOTES

NOTES

112 "An experience has pattern and structure, because it is not just doing and undergoing in alternation, but consists of them in relationship." Dewey, *Art as Experience*, 44. I thank Ivan Gaskell for calling attention to this passage.

113 Fujiwara observes: "Clothes, houses, bicycles, and cars are all repaired, used, and repaired again when broken again. They are cleaned, washed, polished, and maintained. After repeating these activities, we develop attachment to these objects and want to keep them with us as long as possible. Attachment does not mean not hurting. Rather, it is to appreciate thoroughly the scars and frays as much as possible and as long as functionality is not lost." *Bunkai no Tetsugaku*, 285, my translation. I also explore the seeming paradox of facilitating the longevity of consumer goods through accepting and appreciating their transience in "Consumer Aesthetics and Environmental Ethics: Problems and Possibilities," *The Journal of Aesthetics and Art Criticism* 76, no. 4 (Fall 2018): 429–39.

114 Spelman, *Repair*, 6.

115 DeSilvey, *Curated Decay*.

116 Cited by Verbeek, *What Things Do*, 224.

117 See my "Reflections on the Atomic Bomb Ruin in Hiroshima," in *Philosophical Perspectives on Ruins, Monuments, and Memorials*, ed. Jeanette Bicknell, et al. (New York: Routledge, 2020), 201–14. It should be noted, however, that preservation itself needs care work to maintain the ruined structure. This is the case with the Hiroshima Atomic Bomb Dome structure.

118 Dawdy, *Patina*, 5 and 16.

119 For *boro*, see Timo Rissanen, "Designing Endurance," in *Shaping Sustainable Fashion*, ed. Gwilt and Rissanen, 130, and Sasha Rabin Wallinger's "Mottainai: The Fabric of Life, Lessons in Frugality from Traditional Japan," *Textile: The Journal of Cloth and Culture* 10, no. 3 (November 2012): 336–45. For quilts, see *The Quilts of Gee's Bend*, William Arnett, et al. (Atlanta: Tinwood Books, 2002) and *Gee's Bend: Women and Their Quilts*, ed. John Beardsley, et al. (Atlanta: Tinwood Books, 2002).

120 Dazai Shundai, *Dokugo* (1816), cited by Hiroshi Minami, *Psychology of the Japanese People*, trans. Albert R. Ikoma (Toronto: University of Toronto Press, 1971), 90.

121 "The exploitative chic-ing" is from Rosner, "Beautiful Oops," 78–9. The other two phrases are from Shannon Mattern, "Maintenance and Care," *Places Journal* (November 2018), Section on "Cracks:

Fixing Objects," https://placesjournal.org/article/maintenance-and
-care/, accessed July 10, 2020.

122 See Renee M. Conroy, "Rust Belt Ruins," in *Philosophical
Perspectives*, ed. Bicknell, et al., 121–32, as well as Kate
Wells, "Detroit Was Always Made of Wheels: Confronting Ruin
Porn in Its Hometown" and Christopher T. Gullen, "Gods and
Monsters: A Solastalgic Examination of Detroit's Ruins and
Representation," both in *Ruin Porn and the Obsession with
Decay*, ed. Siobhan Lyons (Cham: Palgrave Macmillan, 2018),
13–29 and 31–44.

123 The article can be found in *Scientific American* [blog], April 20,
2020, at https://blogs.scientificamerican.com/beautiful-minds/post
-traumatic-growth-finding-meaning-and-creativity-in-adversity/.

124 Morgan, "Kate Kittredge's Stockings," 70.

125 The description and visual images of this project can be found
in a booklet, *Repairing Earthquake Project* (Den Haag: Stroom
Den Haag, 2019) and at https://www.stroom.nl/activiteiten/
tentoonstelling.php?t_id=408800, accessed November 1, 2019. I
thank Joanna van der Zanden for this example.

126 It is described in https://mymodernmet.com/kunio-nakamura
-kintsugi-pottery-repair/, accessed July 10, 2020. Fujiwara
observes how people's sympathy and compassion toward the
victims of the earthquake have also become directed toward
broken wares. *Bunkai no Tetsugaku*, 293.

127 You can see this project at https://www.youtube.com/watch?v
=i8m_AeTGcmk, accessed November 1, 2019.

128 See the description of her project at https://www.amfedarts.org/
yoko-ono-mend-piece/; https://renniemuseum.org/exhibitions/yoko
-ono-mend-piece/; and https://www.artbasel.com/catalog/artwork
/69701/Yoko-Ono-Mend-Piece-Galerie-Lelong-version, all accessed
October 16, 2021.

129 "The Mending Project" at Bonniers Konsthall at https://
bonnierskonsthall.se/en/the-mending-project/. Also see https://
www.gardnermuseum.org/experience/exhibition/common-threads/
mending-project and https://www.mori.art.museum/english/contents
/lee_mingwei/highlight/index.html, all accessed October 16, 2021.

130 This recalls Nietzsche's idea of self-creation through accepting
and incorporating one's weaknesses into an overall unified whole,
discussed in Chapter 2.

Conclusion

1 I admit that this thought experiment is counterintuitive because the caring societal setup and artifactual world *tend to* promote more humane and civilized social interactions. However, I think the point of this hypothetical example should be clear.

2 Leopold, *A Sand County Almanac*, 210.

Bibliography

99% Invisible. "Unpleasant Design & Hostile Urban Architecture." July 5, 2016. https://99percentinvisible.org/episode/unpleasant-design -hostile-urban-architecture/ (Accessed October 14, 2021).

Abramson, Daniel M. *Obsolescence: An Architectural History*. Chicago: The University of Chicago Press, 2016.

American Federation of Arts. "Yoko Ono: Mend Piece." https://www .amfedarts.org/yoko-ono-mend-piece/ (Accessed October 16, 2021).

Archer, Alfred, and Lauren Ware. "Beyond the Call of Beauty: Everyday Aesthetic Demands Under Patriarchy." *Monist* 101 (2018): 114–27.

Aristotle. "Nicomachean Ethics." In *Introduction to Aristotle*, edited by Richard McKeon and translated by Richard Ross, 337–581. Chicago: The University of Chicago Press, 1973.

Arnet, William, et al. *The Quilts of Gee's Bend*. Atlanta: Tinwood Books, 2002.

Art|Basel. "Mend Piece (Galerie Lelong version), 1966–2018." 2018. https://www.artbasel.com/catalog/artwork/69701/Yoko-Ono-Mend -Piece-Galerie-Lelong-version (Accessed October 16, 2021).

Bailey, Charlotte. "Kintsugi Vases." *Hanging by a Thread*, June 2, 2016. https://hangingbyathreadembroidery.wordpress.com/ (Accessed June 7, 2020).

Beardsley, John, William Arnett, Alvia Wardlaw, and Jane Livingston. *Gee's Bend: Women and Their Quilts*. Atlanta: Tinwood Books, 2002.

Bêka, Ila, and Louise, Lemoine, directors and producers. *Koolhaas Houselife*. 2013.

Berleant, Arnold. *The Aesthetics of Environment*. Philadelphia: Temple University Press, 1992.

Berleant, Arnold. *Living in the Landscape: Toward an Aesthetics of Environment*. Lawrence: University Press of Kansas, 1997.

Berleant, Arnold. *Re-thinking Aesthetics: Rogue Essays on Aesthetics and the Arts*. Aldershot: Ashgate, 2004.

Berleant, Arnold. *Aesthetics and Environment: Variations on a Theme*. Aldershot: Ashgate, 2005.

Berleant, Arnold. *Sensibility and Sense: The Aesthetic Transformation of the Human World*. Exeter: Imprint Academic, 2010.

Berleant, Arnold. *Aesthetics beyond the Arts: New and Recent Essays.* Farnham: Ashgate, 2012.

Berleant, Arnold. "Objects into Persons: The Way to Social Aesthetics." *Espes* 6, no. 2 (2017): 9–18.

Bishop, Claire. "Antagonism and Relational Aesthetics." *October* 110 (2004): 51–79.

Blum, Lawrence A. "Gilligan and Kohlberg: Implications for Moral Theory." *Ethics* 98, no. 3 (1988): 472–91.

Böhme, Gernot. "Atmosphere as the Fundamental Concept of a New Aesthetics." Translated by David Roberts. *Thesis Eleven* 36 (1993): 113–26.

Böhme, Gernot. "Atmosphere as an Aesthetic Concept." *Daidalos* 68 (1998): 112–15.

Bourriaud, Nicolas. *Relational Aesthetics.* Translated by Simon Pleasance and Fronza Woods. Dijon: les presses du reel, 2002.

Brady, Emily. "Adam Smith's 'Sympathetic Imagination' and the Aesthetic Appreciation of Environment." *The Journal of Scottish Philosophy* 9, no. 1 (2011): 95–109.

Brady, Emily. "Imagination and the Aesthetic Appreciation of Nature." In *The Aesthetics of Natural Environments*, edited by Allen Carlson and Arnold Berleant, 156–69. Peterborough: Broadview Press, 2004.

Brady, Emily. "Nature, Aesthetics and Humility." In *Aesthetics, Nature and Religion: Ronald W. Hepburn and his Legacy*, edited by Endre Szécsényi, 161–75. Aberdeen: Aberdeen University Press, 2020.

Brasor, Philip. "How Hostile Design Keeps Japan's Homeless at Arm's Length." *The Japan Times*, December 12, 2020. https://www.japantimes.co.jp/news/2020/12/12/national/media-national/homeless-bench-designs/ (Accessed December 13, 2020).

Broudy, Harry S. *Enlightened Cherishing: An Essay on Aesthetic Education.* Urbana: University of Illinois Press, 1994.

Brown, Andrew. *Art & Ecology Now.* New York: Thames & Hudson, 2014.

Buber, Martin. *I and Thou.* Translated by Walter Kaufmann. New York: Charles Scribner's Sons, 1970.

Buber, Martin. "Elements of The Interhuman." Translated by Roald Gregor Smith. *Psychiatry* 20, no. 2 (1957): 105–13.

Buffalo Bird Woman. "From *Buffalo Bird Woman's Garden*." In *Cooking, Eating, Thinking: Transformative Philosophies of Food*, edited by Deane W. Curtin and Lisa M. Heldke, 270–9. Bloomington: Indiana University Press, 1992.

Busch, Akiko. *The Uncommon Life of Common Objects: Essays on Design and the Everyday.* New York: Metropolis Books, 2004.

Carlson, Allen, and Sheila Lintott, eds. *Nature, Aesthetics, and Environmentalism.* New York: Columbia University Press, 2008.

Carroll, Noël. "Art and the Moral Realm." In *The Blackwell Guide to Aesthetics*, edited by Peter Kivy, 126–51. Malden: Blackwell, 2004.

Carter, Robert E. *The Japanese Arts and Self-Discipline*. Albany: SUNY Press, 2008.

Cipolla, Carla, and Ezio Manzini. "Relational Services." *Knowledge, Technology & Policy* 22 (2009): 45–50.

Cohn, Felicia. "Existential Medicine: Martin Buber and Physician-Patient Relationships." *The Journal of Continuing Education in the Health Professions* 21, no. 3 (2001): 170–81.

Conroy, Renee M. "Rust Belt Ruins." In *Philosophical Perspectives on Ruins, Monuments, and Memorials*, edited by Jeanette Bicknell, et al., 121–32. New York: Routledge, 2020.

Cooper, David E. *A Philosophy of Gardens*. Oxford: Oxford University Press. 2006.

Cooper, David E. "Beautiful People, Beautiful Things." *British Journal of Aesthetics* 48, no. 3 (2008): 247–60.

Cooper, David E. "Edification and the Experience of Beauty." In *International Yearbook of Aesthetics: Diversity and Universality in Aesthetics*, edited by Wang Keping, Vol. 14, 61–79. Beijing: Beijing International Studies University, 2010.

Cooper, David E. "Human Landscapes, Virtue, and Beauty." 2012. acdemia.edu.

Cooper, David E. "Buddhism, Beauty and Virtue." In *Artistic Visions and the Promise of Beauty*, edited by Kathleen, M. Higgins, et al., 125–37. Cham: Springer International Publishing, 2017.

Cooper, David E. "Aesthetic Experience, Metaphysics and Subjectivity: Ronald W. Hepburn and 'Nature-Mysticism.'" In *Aesthetics, Nature and Religion: Ronald W. Hepburn and his Legacy*, edited by Endre Szécsényi, 90–101. Aberdeen: Aberdeen University Press, 2020.

Dalby, Liza Crihfield. "The Art of the Geisha." *Natural History* 92, no. 2 (1983): 47–54.

Darsø, Lotte. *Artful Creation: Learning-Tales of Arts-in-Business*. Frederiksberg, Denmark: samfundslitteratur, 2004.

Dawdy, Shannon Lee. *Patina: A Profane Archaeology*. Chicago: The University of Chicago Press, 2016.

DeSilvey, Caitlin. *Curated Decay: Heritage Beyond Saving*. Minneapolis: University of Minnesota Press, 2017.

Dewey, John. *Art as Experience*. New York: Capricorn Press, 1958.

Dillard, Annie. "Seeing" originally in *Pilgrim at Tinker Creek* (1974). In *Environmental Ethics: Divergence and Convergence*, edited by Richard G. Botzler and Susan J. Armstrong, 114–21. Boston: McGraw-Hill, 1998.

Dōgen. *Shōbōgenzō: Zen Essays by Dōgen*. Edited and translated by Thomas Cleary. Honolulu: University of Hawaii Press, 1986.

Dōgen, Zenji. *Shōbōgenzō: The Eye and Treasury of the True Law*, Vol. 2. Translated by Kōsen Nishiyama and John Stevens. Tokyo: Nakayama Shobō, 1977.

Dōgen, Zenji. *Shōbōgenzō: The Eye and Treasury of the True Law*, Vol. 4. Translated by Kōsen Nishiyama, et al. Tokyo: Nakayama Shobō, 1983.

Donovan, Josephine. *The Aesthetics of Care: On the Literary Treatment of Animals*. London: Bloomsbury Academic, 2016.

Eatock, Daniel. "Visible Vehicle Repairs." 2017. https://eatock.com/books/visible-vehicle-repairs/ (Accessed June 7, 2020).

Eaton, Anne. "Artifacts and Their Functions." In *Oxford Handbook of History and Material Culture*, edited by Ivan Gaskell and Sarah Anne Carter, 35–53. Oxford: Oxford University Press, 2020.

Eaton, Marcia Muelder. *Aesthetics and the Good Life*. Rutherford: Fairleigh Dickinson University Press, 1989.

Eaton, Marcia Muelder. *Merit, Aesthetic and Ethical*. Oxford: Oxford University Press, 2001.

Ekuan, Kenji. *The Aesthetics of the Japanese Lunchbox*. Translated by Don Kenny. Cambridge, MA: The MIT Press, 2000.

Eldridge, Richard. "Aesthetics and Ethics." In *The Oxford Handbook of Aesthetics*, edited by Jerrold Levinson, 722–32. Oxford: Oxford University Press, 2005.

Engster, Daniel. "Rethinking Care Theory: The Practice of Caring and the Obligation to Care." *Hypatia* 20, no. 3 (2005): 50–74.

Finkelpearl, Tom. "Mierle Laderman Ukeles in Conversation with Tom Finkelpearl and Shannon Jackson." In *Mierle Laderman Ukeles: Seven Work Ballets*, edited by Kari Conte, 219–27. Amsterdam: Kunstverein Publishing, 2015.

Fisher, Pamela, and Dawn Freshwater. "Towards Compassionate Care through Aesthetic Rationality." *Scandinavian Journal of Caring Sciences* 28 (2014): 767–74.

Fletcher, Kate. *Craft of Use: Post-Growth Fashion*. London: Routledge, 2016.

Forsey, Jane. *The Aesthetics of Design*. Oxford: Oxford University Press, 2013.

Foucault, Michel. *The Foucault Reader*. Edited by Paul Rabinow. New York: Pantheon Books, 1984.

Fox, Warwick. *A Theory of General Ethics: Human Relationships, Nature, and the Built Environment*. Cambridge, MA: The MIT Press, 2006.

Fox, Warwick. "Architecture Ethics." In *A Companion to the Philosophy of Technology*, edited by Jan Kyrre Berg Olsen, et al., 387–91. Chichester: Wiley-Blackwell, 2009.

Freitas, Tatiane. "Artist's Website." https://tatianefreitas.com/My-Old-New-Series (Accessed June 7, 2020).

Fujiwara, Tatsushi. *Bunkai no Tetsugaku: Huhai to Hakkō o Meguru Shikō* (*Philosophy of Decomposition: Thoughts on Decay and Fermentation*). Tokyo: Seidosha, 2019.

Fukasawa, Naoto, and Jasper Morrison. *Super Normal*. Translated by Mardi Miyake. Baden: Lars Müller Publishers, 2008.

Gaut, Berys. "Morality and Art." In *Companion to Aesthetics*, edited by Stephen Davies, et al., 428–31. Malden: Blackwell, 2009.

Gier, Nicholas F. "The Dancing *Ru*: A Confucian Aesthetics of Virtue." *Philosophy East & West* 51, no. 2 (2001): 280–305.

Gilligan, Carol. "Moral Orientation and Moral Development." In *Ethics: Classical Western Texts in Feminism and Multicultural Perspectives*, edited by James P. Sterba, 552–63. New York: Oxford University Press, 2000.

Godlovitch, Stan. "Ice Breakers: Environmentalism and Natural Aesthetics." *Journal of Applied Philosophy* 11, no. 1 (1994): 15–30.

Goldie, Peter. "Towards a Virtue Theory of Art." *British Journal of Aesthetics* 47, no. 4 (2007): 372–87.

Goldie, Peter. "Virtues of Art and Human Well-Being." *Proceedings of the Aristotelian Society, Supplementary Volume* 82 (2008): 179–95.

Gomez, Ramiro. "On Tenth Avenue." *Manual: A Journal about Art and Its Making* 11 (2018): 35–7.

Groves, Christopher. *Care, Uncertainty and Intergenerational Ethics*. New York: Palgrave Macmillan, 2014.

Gullen, Christopher T. "Gods and Monsters: A Solastalgic Examination of Detroit's Ruins and Representation." In *Ruin Porn and the Obsession with Decay*, edited by Siobhan Lyons, 31–44. Cham: Palgrave Macmillan, 2018.

Gwilt, Alison. "Producing Sustainable Fashion." In *Shaping Sustainable Fashion: Changing the Way We Make and Use Clothes*, edited by Alison Gwilt and Timo Rissanen, 59–73. London: Earthscan, 2011.

Hara, Kenya. *White*. Translated by Jooyeon Rhee. Baden: Lars Müller Publishers, 2010.

Hara, Kenya. *Nihon no Dezain: Biishiki ga Tsukuru Mirai* (*Japanese Design: Future Created by the Sense of Beauty*). Tokyo: Iwanami Shoten, 2012.

Hara, Kenya. *Mujirushi Ryōhin no Dezain* (*Mujirushi Ryōhin's Design*). Tokyo: Nikkei BP sha, 2015.

Hattori, Dohō. "The Red Booklet." Translated by Toshihiko and Toyo Izutsu. In *The Theory of Beauty in the Classical Aesthetics of Japan*, edited by Toshihiko and Toyo Izutsu, 159–67. The Hague: Martinus Nijhoff Publishers, 1981.

Hawken, Paul. *Ecology of Commerce: A Declaration of Sustainability*. New York: HarperBusiness, 1994.

Heidegger, Martin. "The Thing." In *Poetry, Language, Thought*, translated by Albert Hofstadter, 165–86. New York: Harper & Row, 1971.

Heidegger, Martin. *Being and Time*. Translated by Joan Stambaugh.
    Albany: SUNY Press, 1996.
Hendry, Joy. *Wrapping Culture: Politeness, Presentation, and Power in
    Japan and Other Societies*. Oxford: Clarendon Press, 1993.
Hepburn, Ronald W. and Iris Murdoch. "Symposium: Vision and Choice
    in Morality." *Proceedings of the Aristotelian Society, Supplementary
    Volume* 30 (1956): 14–58.
Hepburn, Ronald W. "Contemporary Aesthetics and the Neglect of
    Natural Beauty." In *'Wonder' and Other Essays: Eight Studies in
    Aesthetics and Neighboring Fields*, 9–35. Edinburgh: Edinburgh
    University Press, 1984.
Hepburn, Ronald W. "Values of Art and Values of Community." In
    On Community, edited by Leroy S. Rouner, 27–55. Notre Dame:
    University of Notre Dame Press, 1991.
Hepburn, Ronald W. "Nature Humanised: Nature Respected."
    Environmental Values 7 (1998): 267–79.
Hepburn, Ronald W. "Data and Theory in Aesthetics: Philosophical
    Understanding and Misunderstanding." In *The Reach of the
    Aesthetic: Collected Essays on Art and Nature*, 130–47. Hants:
    Ashgate, 2001.
Hepburn, Ronald W. "Life and Life-Enhancement as Key Concepts in
    Aesthetics." In *The Reach of the Aesthetic: Collected Essays on Art
    and Nature*, 63–76. Hants: Ashgate, 2001.
Hepburn, Ronald W. "Trivial and Serious in Aesthetic Appreciation of
    Nature." In *The Reach of the Aesthetic: Collected Essays on Art and
    Nature*, 1–15. Hants: Ashgate, 2001.
Hepburn, Ronald W. "Truth, Subjectivity and the Aesthetic." In *The
    Reach of the Aesthetic: Collected Essays on Art and Nature*, 16–37.
    Hants: Ashgate, 2001.
Hidden Hostility DC. "Community Response to Defensive Architecture."
    https://www.hiddenhostilitydc.com/responses (Accessed October
    14, 2021).
Hock, Beata. "Relational Aesthetics." In *Encyclopedia of Aesthetics*,
    edited by Michael Kelly, Vol. 5, 350–4. Oxford: Oxford University
    Press, 2014.
Hoły-Łuczaj, Magdalena. "Artifacts and the Limitations of Moral
    Considerability." *Environmental Ethics* 41, no. 1 (2019): 69–87.
Horikawa, Katsuoki, and Tomoaki Hosaka. "Mother: Bus Driver
    'Refused' to Let Me Board with Twin Buggy." *The Asahi Shinbun*,
    November 12, 2019.
Hosey, Lance. *The Shape of Green: Aesthetics, Ecology, and Design*.
    Washington: Island Press, 2012.
Husukić, Erna and Emina Zejnilović. "The Environmental Aesthetics of
    Sarajevo: A City Shaped by Memory." *Urbani Izziv* 28, no. 1 (2017):
    96–106.

iFixit. "Repair Manifesto." 2010. https://www.ifixit.com/Manifesto (Accessed June 7, 2020).

Ikegami, Eiko. *Bonds of Civility: Aesthetic Networks and the Political Origins of Japanese Culture*. Cambridge: Cambridge University Press, 2005.

Inutsuka, Yū. "Sensation, Betweenness, Rhythms: Watsuji's Environmental Philosophy and Ethics in Conversation with Heidegger." In *Japanese Environmental Philosophy*, edited by J. Baird Callicott and John McRae, 97–104. New York: Oxford University Press, 2017.

Irahara, Mitsumi, and Makoto Nakamura. *Zero kara no Kintsugi Nyūmon: Utsuwa o Yomigaeraseru, Urushi no Tsukoroi* (*Introduction to Kintsugi from Zero: Restoring Containers by Mending with Lacquer*). Tokyo: Seibundō Shinkōsha, 2017.

Jackson, Steven J., and Laewoo Kang. "Breakdown, Obsolescence and Reuse: HCI and the Art of Repair." *CHI 214: Proceedings of the SIGCHI Conference on Human Factors in Computing Systems*, April 2014: 449–58.

Jackson, Steven J. "Rethinking Repair." In *Media Technologies: Essays on Communication, Materiality, and Society*, edited by Tarleton Gillespie, et al., 221–39. Cambridge, MA: The MIT Press, 2014.

Jacobs, Julia. "Prominent Architects Group Prohibits Design of Death Chambers." *The New York Times*, December 11, 2020. https://www .nytimes.com/2020/12/11/arts/design/american-institute-of-architects -execution.html?campaign_id=2&emc=edit_th_20201213&instance _id=24999&nl=todaysheadlines&regi_id=40614031&segment_id =46781&user_id=67fb6c4431a7ea59156285c346a5aac9 (Accessed December 13, 2020).

James, Simon P. "Holism in Buddhism, Heidegger, and Deep Ecology." *Environmental Ethics* 22, no. 4 (Winter 2000): 359–75.

James, Simon P. "For the Sake of a Stone? Inanimate Things and the Demands of Morality." *Inquiry* 54, no. 4 (August 2011): 384–97.

James, Simon P. "Why Old Things Matter." *Journal of Moral Philosophy* 12 (2015): 313–29.

Kamoshita, Tomomi. "Artist's Website." https://rittau.jimdofree.com/ (Accessed June 7, 2020).

Kant, Immanuel. *Critique of Judgment*. Translated by J. H. Bernard. New York: Hafner Press, 1974.

Kaufman, Scott Barry. "Post-Traumatic Growth: Finding Meaning and Creativity in Adversity." *Scientific American*, April 20, 2020. https:// blogs.scientificamerican.com/beautiful-minds/post-traumatic-growth -finding-meaning-and-creativity-in-adversity/ (Accessed June 1, 2020).

Kieran, Matthew. "The Vice of Snobbery: Aesthetic Knowledge, Justification and Virtue in Art Appreciation." *The Philosophical Quarterly* 60, no. 239 (2010): 243–63.

King, Alex. "The Virtue of Subtlety and the Vice of a Heavy Hand." *British Journal of Aesthetics* 57, no. 2 (2017): 119–37.

"Kintsugi Pieces in Harmony." *YouTube*, April 12, 2017. https://www .youtube.com/watch?v=i8m_AeTGcmk (Accessed November 1, 2019).

Kopytoff, Igor. "The Cultural Biography of Things: Commoditization as Process." In *The Social Life of Things: Commodities in Cultural Perspective*, edited by Arjun Appadurai, 64–91. Cambridge: Cambridge University Press, 2013.

Kupfer, Joseph. *Experience as Art: Aesthetics in Everyday Life*. Albany: SUNY Press, 1983.

Latour, Bruno. "Where Are the Missing Masses? The Sociology of a Few Mundane Artifacts." In *Shaping Technology/Building Society: Studies in Sociotechnical Change*, edited by Wiebe E. Bijker and John Law, 225–58. Cambridge: MIT Press, 1992.

Laugier, Sandra. "War on Care." *Series: Corona -Times*, November 5, 2020. https://ethicsofcare.org/war-on-care/ (Accessed September 21, 2021).

Lehtinen, Sanna. "Building as Objects of Care in the Urban Environment." In *Aesthetics in Dialogue: Applying Philosophy of Art in a Global World*, edited by Zoltán Somhegyi and Max Ryynänen, 223–36. Berlin: Peter Lang, 2020.

Leopold, Aldo. *A Sand County Almanac*. New York: Ballantine Books, 1977.

Liao, Shen-yi and Bryce Huebner. "Oppressive Things." *Philosophy and Phenomenological Research* 103 (2021): 92–113.

Light, Andrew, and Holmes Rolston III. "Introduction: Ethics and Environmental Ethics." In *Environmental Ethics: An Anthology*, edited by Andrew Light and Holmes Rolston III, 1–11. Malden: Blackwell, 2003.

Lippard, Lucy R. "Never Done: Women's Work by Mierle Laderman Ukeles." In *Mierle Laderman Ukeles: Maintenance Art*, edited by Patricia C. Phillips, 14–20. New York: Queens Museum, 2016.

Lloyd, Jayne. "Taking Care of the Laundry in Care Homes." In *Performing Care: New Perspectives on Socially Engaged Performance*, edited by Amanda Stuart Fisher and James Thompson, 204–29. Manchester: Manchester University Press, 2020.

London, Bernard. "Ending the Depression Through Planned Obsolescence." 1932. https://upload.wikimedia.org/wikipedia/ commons/2/27/London_(1932)_Ending_the_depression_through _planned_obsolescence.pdf (Accessed June 7, 2020).

Lowenthal, David. *The Past Is a Foreign Country*. Cambridge: Cambridge University Press, 1990.

Lynch, Elizabeth. "Equal Opportunity Housing." In *The New Earthwork: Art Action Agency*, edited by Twylene Moyer and Glenn Harper, 161–4. Hamilton: ISC Press, 2011.

Machemer, Theresa. "Animals Are Using Utah's Largest Wildlife Overpass Earlier Than Expected." *Smithsonian Magazine*, November 20, 2020. https://www.smithsonianmag.com/smart-news/animals-are-using-utahs-largest-wildlife-overpass-earlier-expected-180976420/ (Accessed December 1, 2020).

Mandoki, Katya. *Everyday Aesthetics: Prosaics, the Play of Culture and Social Identities*. Aldershot: Ashgate, 2007.

Manzini, Ezio. "Prometheus of the Everyday: The Ecology of the Artificial and the Designer's Responsibility." In *Discovering Design: Explorations in Design Studies*, edited by Richard Buchanan and Victor Margolin, 219–43. Chicago: The University of Chicago Press, 1995.

Manzini, Ezio. *Politics of the Everyday*. Translated by Rachel Anne Coad. London: Bloomsbury Visual Arts, 2019.

Marinucci, Lorenzo. "Mood, *Ki*, Humors: Elements and Atmospheres between Europe and Japan." *Studi di estetica* 48, no. 4 (2019): 169–92.

Mars, Roman, and Kurt Kohlstedt. *The 99% Invisible City: A Field Guide to the Hidden World of Everyday Design*. Boston: Houghton Mifflin Harcourt, 2020.

Martin, Lois. "Patina of Cloth." *Surface Design Journal* 28, no. 4 (2004): 16–21.

Mattern, Shannon. "Maintenance and Care." *Places Journal*, November 2018. https://placesjournal.org/article/maintenance-and-care/ (Accessed July 10, 2020).

May, Reinhard. *Heidegger's Hidden Sources: East Asian Influence on His Work*. Translated by Graham Parkes. New York: Routledge, 1996.

Mayeroff, Milton. *On Caring*. New York: HarperCollins, 1971.

"'Memorial' Held for Discarded *Hanko* Seals as Digitization Takes Root." *The Japan Times*. October 19, 2020.

Minami, Hiroshi. *Psychology of the Japanese People*. Translated by Albert R. Ikoma. Toronto: University of Toronto Press, 1971.

Mitchell, Kristine. "Craftsman Voluntarily Repairs Any Family Heirloom Ceramics Damaged By Earthquakes in Japan." *My Modern Met*, April 23, 2016. https://mymodernmet.com/kunio-nakamura-kintsugi-pottery-repair/ (Accessed July 10, 2020).

Moody-Adams, Michele M. "Gender and the Complexity of Moral Voices." In *Feminist Ethics*, edited by Claudia Card, 195–212. Lawrence: University Press of Kansas, 1991.

Morgan, Andrew, director. *The True Cost*. Bullfrog Films, 2015.

Morgan, Lisa Z. "Kate Kittredge's Stockings." *Manual: A Journal about Art and its Making* 11 (2018): 70–1.

Morris, Ivan. *The World of the Shining Prince: Court Life in Ancient Japan*. New York: Kodansha International, 1995.

Moyer, Twylene, and Glenn Harper, eds. *The New Earthwork: Art Action Agency*. Hamilton: ISC Press, 2011.

Mullis, Eric. "Thinking Through an Embodied Confucian Aesthetics of Persons." In *Artistic Visions and the Promise of Beauty*, edited by Kathleen M. Higgins, et al. 139–49. Cham: Springer International Publishing, 2017.

Murdoch, Iris. *The Sovereignty of Good*. London: Routledge, 1970.

Murdoch, Iris. *Metaphysics as a Guide to Morals*. London: Penguin Books, 1992.

Nakamura, Kunio. *Kintsugi Techō: Hajimete no Tsukuroi (Kintsugi Notebook: First Repair)*. Tokyo: Genkōsha, 2017.

Nanbō, Sōkei. "Nanbōroku (Record of Nanbō)." In *Nanbōroku o Yomu (Reading Nanbōroku)*, edited by Isao Kumakura, 9–371. Kyoto: Tankōsha, 1989.

Nassauer, Joan Iverson. "Messy Ecosystems, Orderly Frames." *Landscape Journal* 14, no. 2 (1995): 161–70.

Nassauer, Joan Iverson. "Cultural Sustainability: Aligning Aesthetics and Ecology." In *Placing Nature: Culture and Landscape Ecology*, edited by Joan Iverson Nassauer, 65–83. Washington: Island Press, 1997.

Nassauer, Joan Iverson. "Care and Stewardship: From Home to Planet." *Landscape and Urban Planning* 100 (2011): 321–23.

National Geographic Society. "Wildlife Crossings." July 16, 2019. https://www.nationalgeographic.org/article/wildlife-crossings/ (Accessed December 1, 2020).

Naukkarinen, Ossi. "Everyday Aesthetic Practices, Ethics and Tact." *Aisthesis* 7, no. 1 (2014): 23–44.

Nietzsche, Friedrich. *Beyond Good and Evil*. In *Basic Writings of Nietzsche*, translated and edited by Walter Kaufmann,179–435. New York: The Modern Library, 1968.

Nietzsche, Friedrich. *On the Genealogy of Morals*. In *Basic Writings of Nietzsche*, translated and edited by Walter Kaufmann, 449–599. New York: The Modern Library, 1968.

Nietzsche, Friedrich. *The Will to Power*. Translated by Walter Kaufmann and R. J. Hollingdale, edited by Walter Kaufmann. New York: Vintage Books, 1968.

Nietzsche, Friedrich. *The Gay Science*. Translated by Walter Kaufmann. New York: Vintage Books, 1974.

"Nishiko: Repairing Earthquake Project." https://www.stroom.nl/activiteiten/tentoonstelling.php?t_id=408800 (Accessed November 1, 2019).

Noddings, Nel. *Caring: A Relational Approach to Ethics and Moral Education*, 2nd ed. Oakland: University of California Press, 2013.

Ohashi, Ryosuke. "Kire and Iki." In *Encyclopedia of Aesthetics*, edited by Michael Kelly, 12–15 of Vol. 4. New York: Oxford University Press, 2014.

Ohnuki-Tierney, Emiko. *Kamikaze, Cherry Blossoms, and Nationalisms: The Militarization of Aesthetics in Japanese History*. Chicago: The University of Chicago Press, 2002.

Ozawa, Noriyo. *Kintsugi no Susume: Mono o Taisetsuni suru Kokoro* (*Recommendation on Kintsugi: The Mindset to Cherish Things*). Tokyo: Seibundō Shinkōsha, 2014.

Pallasmaa, Juhani. "Toward an Architecture of Humility." *Harvard Design Magazine* 7 (1999): 22–5.

Paracelsus. *Selected Writings.* Translated by Norbert Guterman and edited by Jolande Jacobi. Princeton: Princeton University Press, 1988.

Parkes, Graham. *Composing the Soul: Reaches of Nietzsche's Psychology.* Chicago: The University of Chicago Press, 1994.

Parkes, Graham. "Savoring Taste." In *New Essays in Japanese Aesthetics*, edited by A. Minh Nguyen, 109–19. Lanham: Lexington Books, 2018.

Parsons, Glenn, and Allen Carlson. *Functional Beauty.* Oxford: Oxford University Press, 2008.

PBS News. "Jon Stewart Advocates for Congressional Aid for Sick Veterans Exposed to Military Burn Pits." September 15, 2020. https://www.pbs.org/newshour/nation/watch-jon-stewart-advocates-for-congressional-aid-for-sick-veterans-exposed-to-military-burn-pits (Accessed December 1, 2020).

Pellegrini, Leah. "Broken Vases Are Restored by Sewing Them Back Together with Gold Thread." *My Modern Met*, May 5, 2016. https://mymodernmet.com/charlotte-bailey-kintsugi-patchwork-porcelain/ (Accessed June 7, 2020).

Pembroke, Neil. "Human Dimension in Medical Care: Insights from Buber and Marcel." *Southern Medical Journal* 103, no. 12 (2010): 1210–13.

Phillips, Patricia C., ed. *Mierle Laderman Ukeles: Maintenance Art.* New York: Queens Museum, 2016.

Plato. "Apology." In *The Trial and Death of Socrates.* Translated by G. M. A. Grube, 21–42. Indianapolis: Hackett Publishing, 1975.

Platform21. "Repair Manifesto." 2009. https://www.platform21.nl/page/4360/en.html (Accessed June 7, 2020).

Pope, Alexander. "An Epistle to Lord Burlington (1731)." In *The Genius of the Place: The English Landscape Garden 1620–1820*, edited by John Dixon Hunt and Peter Willis, 211–14. Cambridge, MA: The MIT Press, 1990.

Puig de la Bellacasa, María. *Matters of Care: Speculative Ethics in More Than Human Worlds.* Minneapolis: University of Minnesota Press, 2017.

Puolakka, Kalle. "The Aesthetics of Conversation: Dewey and Davidson." *Contemporary Aesthetics* 15 (2017). https://digitalcommons.risd.edu/liberalarts_contempaesthetics/vol15/iss1/20/ (Accessed August 13, 2020).

Putman, Daniel. "Relational Ethics and Virtue Theory." *Metaphilosophy* 22, no. 3 (1991): 231–38.

Rancière, Jacques. *The Politics of Aesthetics*. Translated by Gabriel
    Rockhill. London: Continuum, 2004.
Rennie Museum. "Yoko Ono: Mend Piece." https://renniemuseum.org/
    exhibitions/yoko-ono-mend-piece/ (Accessed October 16, 2021).
Repairing Earthquake Project. Den Haag: Stroom Den Haag, 2019.
Richman-Abdou, Kelly. "Kintsugi: The Centuries-Old Art of Repairing
    Broken Pottery with Gold." *My Modern Met*, September 5, 2019.
    https://mymodernmet.com/kintsugi-kintsukuroi/2/ (Accessed June 7,
    2020).
Rissanen, Timo. "Designing Endurance." In *Shaping Sustainable
    Fashion: Changing the Way We Make and Use Clothes*, edited by
    Alison Gwilt and Timo Rissanen, 127–38. London: Earthscan, 2011.
Roberts, Tom. "Aesthetic Virtues: Traits and Faculties." *Philosophical
    Studies* 175 (2018): 429–47.
Robinson, Jenefer, and Stephanie Ross. "Women, Morality, and Fiction."
    In *Aesthetics in Feminist Perspective*, edited by Hilde Hein and Carolyn
    Korsmeyer, 105–18. Bloomington: Indiana University Press, 1993.
Rodabaugh, Katrina. *Mending Matters*. New York: Abrams, 2018.
Rosenberger, Robert. *Callous Objects: Designs against the Homeless*.
    Minneapolis: University of Minnesota Press, 2017.
Rosenberger, Robert. "On Hostile Design: Theoretical and Empirical
    Prospects." *Urban Studies* 1, no. 11 (2019): 1–11.
Rosner, Daniela K. "A Beautiful Oops." *Continent* 6, no.1 (2017): 77–80.
Saito, Yuriko. "Japanese Gardens: The Art of Improving Nature."
    Chanoyu Quarterly 83 (1996): 40–61.
Saito, Yuriko. "Appreciating Nature on its Own Terms." *Environmental
    Ethics* 20, no. 2 (1998): 135–49.
Saito, Yuriko. "The Moral Dimensions of Japanese Aesthetics." *The
    Journal of Aesthetics and Art Criticism* 65, no.1 (2007): 85–97.
Saito, Yuriko. *Aesthetics of the Familiar: Everyday Life and World-
    Making*. Oxford: Oxford University Press, 2017.
Saito, Yuriko. "Consumer Aesthetics and Environmental Ethics:
    Problems and Possibilities." *The Journal of Aesthetics and Art
    Criticism* 76, no. 4 (2018): 429–39.
Saito, Yuriko. "Aesthetic Experience as an Educational Journey." In
    Aesthetics, Nature and Religion: Ronald W. Hepburn and his Legacy,
    edited by Endre Szécsényi, 215–33. Aberdeen: Aberdeen University
    Press, 2020.
Saito, Yuriko. "Reflections on the Atomic Bomb Ruin in Hiroshima." In
    Philosophical Perspectives on Ruins, Monuments, and Memorials,
    edited by Jeanette Bicknell, et al., 201–14. New York: Routledge,
    2020.
Saito, Yuriko. "Ethically-Grounded Nature of Japanese Aesthetic
    Sensibility." In *Oxford Handbook of Ethics and Art*, edited by James
    Harold. Oxford: Oxford University Press, forthcoming.

Santayana, George. *The Sense of Beauty: Being the Outline of Aesthetic Theory*. New York: Dover Publications, 1955.

Sayer, Andrew. *Why Things Matter to People: Social Science, Values and Ethical Life*. Cambridge: Cambridge University Press, 2011.

Scarry, Elaine. *On Beauty and Being Just*. Princeton: Princeton University Press, 1999.

Schiller, Friedrich. *On the Aesthetic Education of Man*. Translated by Reginald Snell. New York: Frederick Ungar Publishing, 1977.

Schneider, Pat. "The Patience of Ordinary Things." In *Another River: New and Collected Poems*, 111. Amherst: Amherst Writers and Artists Press, 2005.

Shaftesbury, Anthony Ashley Cooper, Third Earl of. *Characteristics*. In *Philosophies of Art and Beauty: Selected Readings in Aesthetics from Plato to Heidegger*, edited by Albert Hofstadter and Richard Kuhns, 241–76. New York: The Modern Library, 1964.

Shapshay, Sandra, and Levi Tenen, eds. *The Journal of Aesthetics and Art Criticism: The Good, the Beautiful, the Green: Environmentalism and Aesthetics* 76, no. 4 (2018).

Sheehan, Elisa. "Artist's Website." https://elisasheehan.com/collections/eggshells (Accessed June 7, 2020).

Sherman, Nancy. "Of Manners and Morals." *British Journal of Educational Studies* 53, no. 3 (2005): 272–89.

Silverman, David. "Routine Pleasures: The Aesthetics of the Mundane." In *The Aesthetics of Organization*, edited by Stephen Linstead and Heather Höpfl, 130–53. London: SAGE Publications, 2000.

Simmel, Georg. *Simmel on Culture*. Translated and edited by David Frisby and Mike Featherstone. London: SAGE Publications, 2000.

Slade, Giles. *Made to Break: Technology and Obsolescence in America*. Cambridge: Harvard University Press, 2006.

Slemmons, Kiff. "On Imperfection." *Metalsmith* 28, no. 1 (2008): 26–9.

Spelman, Elizabeth V. *Repair: The Impulse to Restore in a Fragile World*. Boston: Beacon Press, 2002.

Surak, Kristin. *Making Tea, Making Japan: Cultural Nationalism in Practice*. Stanford: Stanford University Press, 2013.

Sussman, Rachel. "Sidewalk Kintsukuroi. 2016 ~ Ongoing." http://www.rachelsussman.com/sidewalk-kintsukuroi (Accessed June 7, 2020).

Taylor, Nigel. "Ethical Arguments about the Aesthetics of Architecture." In *Ethics and the Built Environment*, edited by Warwick Fox, 193–206. London: Routledge, 2000.

Thaler, Richard H., and Cass R. Sunstein. *Nudge: Improving Decisions About Health, Wealth, and Happiness*. New York: Penguin Books, 2009.

The Guardian. "Los Angeles to Build World's Largest Wildlife Bridge Across 10-Lane Freeway." August 21, 2019. https://www.theguardian

.com/environment/2019/aug/21/los-angeles-wildlife-bridge-mountain
-lions (Accessed December 1, 2020).

Thompson, James. "Performing the 'Aesthetics of Care.'" In *Performing Care: New Perspectives on Socially Engaged Performance*, edited by Amanda Stuart Fisher and James Thompson, 215–29. Manchester: Manchester University Press, 2020.

Thompson, James. "Towards an Aesthetics of Care." In *Performing Care: New Perspectives on Socially Engaged Performance*, edited by Amanda Stuart Fisher and James Thompson, 36–48. Manchester: Manchester University Press, 2020.

Tong, Rosemarie. *Feminine and Feminist Ethics*. Belmont: Wadsworth Publishing Company, 1993.

Tonkinwise, Cameron. "Is Design Finished? Dematerialisation and Changing Things." In *The Design Philosophy Reader*, edited by Anne-Marie Willis, 152–61. London: Bloomsbury, 2019.

Ueda, Makoto. *Literary and Art Theories in Japan*. Cleveland: Press of Case Western Reserve University, 1967.

Vartan, Starre. "How Wildlife Bridges over Highways Make Animals—and People—Safer." *National Geographic*, April 16, 2019. https://www.nationalgeographic.com/animals/2019/04/wildlife-overpasses-underpasses-make-animals-people-safer/#close (Accessed December 1, 2020).

Verbeek, Peter-Paul. *What Things Do: Philosophical Reflections on Technology, Agency, and Design*. University Park: The Pennsylvania State University, 2005.

Vihalem, Margus. "Everyday Aesthetics and Jacques Rancière: Reconfiguring the Common Field of Aesthetics and Politics." *Journal of Aesthetics & Culture* 10, no. 1 (2018): 1–11.

Vogel, Steven. "Thinking Like a Mall." In *Environmental Aesthetics: Crossing Divides and Breaking Ground*, edited by Martin Drenthen and Jozef Keulartz, 174–87. New York: Fordham University Press, 2014.

Vormann, Jan. "Dispatchwork. 2007 ~ Ongoing." https://www.janvormann.com/testbild/dispatchwork/ (Accessed June 7, 2020).

Walker, Stuart. *Sustainable by Design: Explorations in Theory and Practice*. London: Earthscan, 2006.

Wallinger, Sasha Rabin. "Mottainai: The Fabric of Life, Lessons in Frugality from Traditional Japan." *Textile: The Journal of Cloth and Culture* 10, no. 3 (2012): 336–45.

Walton, Kendall L. "Categories of Art." *Philosophical Review* 78 (1970): 334–67.

Weber, Barbara. "Childhood, Philosophy and Play: Friedrich Schiller and the Interface between Reason, Passion and Sensation." *Journal of Philosophy of Education* 45, no. 2 (2011): 235–50.

Weiss, Allen S. "The Toilet Bowl and the Tea Bowl." *ArtUS* 27 (2009): 80–5.

Weiss, Allen S. "Cracks." *ArtUS* 29 (2010): 62–7.

Wells, Kate. "Detroit Was Always Made of Wheels: Confronting Ruin Porn in Its Hometown." In *Ruin Porn and the Obsession with Decay*, edited by Siobhan Lyons, 13–29. Cham: Palgrave Macmillan, 2018.

White, Richard. "Foucault on the Care of the Self as an Ethical Project and a Spiritual Goal." *Human Studies* 37, no. 4 (2014): 489–504.

Winner, Langdon. *The Whale and the Reactor: A Search for Limits in an Age of High Technology*. Chicago: The University of Chicago Press, 1989.

Wood, Bethan Laura. "*Stain*." 2006. http://www.bethanlaurawood.com/work/stain/ (Accessed June 7, 2020).

Woodruff, David M. "A Virtue Theory of Aesthetics." *Journal of Aesthetic Education* 35, no. 3 (2001): 23–36.

Woods, Lebbeus. *War and Architecture*. Translated by Aleksandra Wagner. New York: Princeton Architectural Press, 1993.

Yanagi, Soetsu. *The Beauty of Everyday Things*. Translated by Michael Brase. New York: Penguin Classics, 2018.

Yeesookyung. "Artist's Website." https://www.yeesookyung.com/ (Accessed June 7, 2020).

Ziff, Paul. "Reasons in Art Criticism." In *Philosophy and Education*, edited by Israel Scheffler, 219–36. Boston: Allyn and Bacon, 1958.

Index